The
Science
of
Spice

The
Science
of
Spice

Understand
flavour connections
and revolutionize
your cooking

DR STUART FARRIMOND

CONTENTS

FOREWORD

Many cooks are intimidated by spices. All too often, a pot of spice is bought for a recipe then pushed into the gloomy depths of the back of a kitchen cupboard, where it remains untouched for many years. This should not be so, for spices are the life blood of countless dishes. Neglecting spices does a disservice to a cook's culinary talents. They not only enhance the natural flavours of a dish, but can bring new flavours and aromas to familiar foods, exciting all our senses. To cook without spices is like composing an orchestral opus without a string section; cooks who view spicing as a grind of black pepper or a spoon of curry powder need to embrace the richness that spices can offer.

This book is for cooks who want to experience new flavour combinations that will both excite and delight. Prescriptive recipes can frustrate the creative cook, but until recently, the only way to know which spices would blend together was by trial and error. Personal experience, tradition, and a sprinkle of intuition were the ingredients for making spice mixes. Not any more, because scientific discoveries have turned old-fashioned ideas on their head. Spices can be blended and added to dishes that had not previously been considered, and no-one should be shackled by recipes from chefs, internet "gurus", or family tradition. This book is the culmination of an ambitious, never-before-attempted project that aims to serve up some easy-to-follow, science-based principles that will hopefully transform the way you use spices in your cooking.

It is important that ancient wisdom is not cast aside, however. Centuries of cookery experience are the bedrock of every country's food heritage, and here you will explore the traditional range of spices used in key regions and countries around the world. A variety of top chefs who specialize in different regional cuisines have contributed some of their favourite spice mixes and recipes. Rather than starting from a blank canvas, you can use the spice blends as a foundation upon which new creations can be built. The recipes showcase some of these blends, and also suggest using innovative spice combinations to add a tantalizing twist to familiar dishes.

Whether you're an experienced cook or a complete beginner, I hope that you will be inspired and empowered to unleash your culinary talents. Add a sprinkle of flavour science or ladle in dollop-loads; let this guide open up a world of sensational new gastronomic delights. Never again will your spice jars languish in the dark!

Dr Stuart Farrimond

> *This book serves up easy-to-follow, science-based principles that will transform the way you use spices.*

SPICE | *science*

*Understand the science behind how spices work,
discover flavour compounds and flavour groups, and
learn how to create inspired spice blends.*

WHAT IS A SPICE?

Spices are plant parts that are more densely loaded with flavour than most other ingredients used in cooking. Whereas herbs always come from leafy parts, spices tend to derive from seeds, fruits, roots, stems, flowers, or bark, and are usually dried. That said, some strongly flavoured leaves, such as bay and curry leaf, can be considered spices because they are used more as a potent background flavouring than as a fresh addition.

Chemical stores

Spices have been valued throughout history, in religious ceremonies and medicine as much as in cooking. Science has shown us that these once-mystical plant parts are in fact the vessels of chemicals known as flavour (or aroma) compounds, generated to help plants survive and reproduce, performing roles such as repelling animals or protecting against bacteria. By happy coincidence, many of these compounds have aromas that are pleasant to humans.

> **"**
> *Spice flavours are chemicals produced by plants, often for defence.*
> **"**

STEMS

The stem of a plant distributes water and sugars to where they are needed. Few spices derive from stems: lemongrass is the stalk of a tropical grass and little-known mastic is the dried resin collected from lentisk trees; more famously, cinnamon and cassia are dried pieces of inner and outer bark, respectively, of *Cinnamomum* trees.

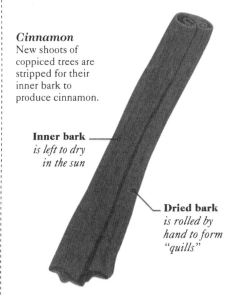

Cinnamon
New shoots of coppiced trees are stripped for their inner bark to produce cinnamon.

Inner bark *is left to dry in the sun*

Dried bark *is rolled by hand to form "quills"*

Communication
The spicy, woody aroma of cinnamon comes from a chemical compound called caryophyllene. When a plant is being eaten, its role is to act as an airborne signal that "primes" downwind plants to produce defensive chemicals.

ROOTS AND UNDERGROUND STORES

Roots are a plant's lifeline to water and nutrients, and rhizomes, corms, and bulbs are storage chambers with the ability to produce new shoots and roots. Liquorice comes from dried roots and asafoetida is derived from dried root sap. Turmeric, ginger, galangal, and garlic are all examples of underground stores.

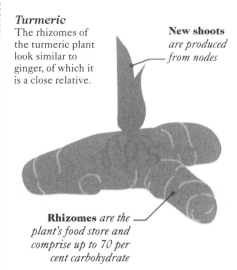

Turmeric
The rhizomes of the turmeric plant look similar to ginger, of which it is a close relative.

New shoots *are produced from nodes*

Rhizomes *are the plant's food store and comprise up to 70 per cent carbohydrate*

Animal deterrence
Turmeric's flavour profile includes a compound called cineole, which has a strong, penetrating, slightly medicinal flavour and has evolved to act as a bitter-tasting deterrence to animals who try eating the rhizomes.

Flavour stores

The vast majority of flavour compounds in spices are oil- rather than water-soluble and are stored within bubbles of oil. Spices are structured to keep these oils locked away, to be released only if the plant is damaged or attacked by infection. Once the bubbles rupture and the oil is exposed to air, the flavour compounds quickly evaporate into gases.

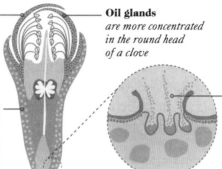

Round head *is made up of the dried, unopened petals of the bud*

Oil glands *are more concentrated in the round head of a clove*

"Stalk" *comprises the outer sepals of the flower bud, and also contains oil glands*

Cross section of a clove

Cloves are rich in highly flavoured oils, stored in oil glands just beneath the surface of both the rounded top of the bud and the "stalk".

Glands rupture *when the outer surface is damaged. In the kitchen this happens through bruising, grinding, and application of heat. Flavour compounds in the released oils evaporate as a fragrant gas.*

FRUITS

The seeds of flowering plants are contained in fruits. Many have evolved to be sugar-rich so that they make an appealing meal for animals, who thereby distribute the seeds over a wide area. Numerous spices are derived from fruits, including allspice, sumac, vanilla, and chillies. Several "seed" spices are technically fruits, including dill and ajwain.

Black pepper

Peppercorns are the small dried berries of one of around a thousand different flowering vine species in the plant family *Piperaceae*.

Berries *are carried in clusters on spikes*

Fully ripe *berries are pink-red in colour; black and green peppercorns are picked when underripe*

Insect repellence
The heat from pepper is produced by a chemical called piperine which, as well as irritating hot pain nerves on the tongue, is highly repellent to insects and has been harnessed by the chemical industry as an insecticide.

SEEDS

The majority of spices are seeds; think of cumin, cardamom, mustard, and fenugreek, or less obviously nutmeg, which is a seed kernel. It is little wonder that plants frequently concentrate their strongest-tasting defensive chemicals in seeds, since these are the precious packets of new life that will sprout into the next generation of plants.

Star anise

The seeds of this strikingly shaped spice are contained within a woody protective covering, called a carpel, where much of the flavour is in fact concentrated.

Seed pods *(fruits) are harvested when still unripe and allowed to dry*

Health protection
Star anise's dominant flavour comes from anethole, a substance that appears to have evolved to fight off infections and repel insects, and which incidentally has an appealing taste – 13 times sweeter than sugar – to the animal tongue.

FLOWERS

Many flowers are known for their attractive aromas, which have evolved to entice insects into paying a visit and pollinating the flower as they do so. Only a few have strong enough appealing flavours to be considered a spice, most famously saffron, whose red strands are pollen-receiving female sex parts (stigmas) of a crocus flower. Another notable flower spice, it may be surprising to discover, is clove.

Clove

The nail-shaped, dark brown clove is neither a seed nor a dried fruit, but the dried flower bud of an evergreen tree from Indonesia.

Fresh cloves *are picked when the buds have developed a pinkish tint*

Unpicked buds *open into flowers with frothy heads of stamens*

Pollinator attraction
Clove contains a high concentration of eugenol, a chemical with a warm, eucalyptus-like fragrance and sweet effect on the tongue. In the living plant, eugenol serves to attract pollinating insects and also repel infections and pests.

SPICES AND THEIR FLAVOUR COMPOUNDS

Flavour compounds are the tiny molecules that give each spice its unique flavour. When in the mouth, these molecules waft up the throat as a vapour into the nose, where they are experienced as if coming from the tongue. For the cook, learning about these flavour compounds is more than mere nerdy curiosity: it is the key to releasing true creativity in the use of spices in cooking.

SWEET WARMING PHENOLS

The warming, sweetly aromatic spices in this group owe their main flavour to compounds in the phenol family. Often strongly flavoured and potent, many share aniseed and eucalyptus flavours, and sometimes bitterness.

COMPOUND EXAMPLES
Eugenol in clove, anethole in fennel.

IN THE KITCHEN
Often strong-tasting and persistent, with the flavour only slowly reduced with cooking. Mostly dissolve and disperse in oil.

WARMING TERPENES

Terpenes are the broadest, most common type of flavour compounds. Spices in this group are dominated by warming terpenes, bringing warmth without strong sweetness. They tend to have woody, bitter, peppery, sometimes minty flavours.

COMPOUND EXAMPLES
Sabinene in nutmeg and mace, germacrene in annatto.

IN THE KITCHEN
Evaporate easily and are lost with prolonged cooking. Generally oil-soluble.

FRAGRANT TERPENES

Spices whose flavour is mostly due to this group of terpenes share pleasantly fresh, pine-like or floral flavour compounds, sometimes with woody notes. In nature, the aromas of these compounds spread far and wide when released.

COMPOUND EXAMPLES
Pinene in juniper, linalool in coriander.

IN THE KITCHEN
Fast-acting and short-lived, generally not tolerating long cooking times. Disperse almost exclusively in oil or alcohol, rather than water.

EARTHY TERPENES

With an earthy, dusty, even burnt flavour, these spices have an abundance of terpenes that convey woody spiciness. Serving in nature as poisons against pests, the compounds are not harmful to humans in small amounts.

COMPOUND EXAMPLES
Cuminaldehyde in cumin, cymene in nigella.

IN THE KITCHEN
Oil-soluble flavours are tenacious and lingering. Best combined with "lighter" fragrances.

PENETRATING TERPENES

Unlike other terpene flavour groups, spices in this group are dominated by powerful terpene compounds that hit the back of the nose and linger on the palate, with usually camphorous, eucalyptus-like, often medicinal flavours.

COMPOUND EXAMPLES
Fenchone in grains of Selim, cineole in cardamom.

IN THE KITCHEN
Potent and lingering, these spices need to be used in moderation or toasted to mask with other flavours.

CITRUS TERPENES

All these spices share compounds that we recognise as being like citrus fruit, giving them a tangy, refreshing, lemony flavour profile with some flowery and herbal aromas. They are found in many ripe fruits as well as spices.

COMPOUND EXAMPLES
Citronellal in lemon myrtle, citral in lemongrass.

IN THE KITCHEN
Fast-evaporating but found in high quantities in this group, so can withstand longer cooking times.

Flavour groups

Using features shared by compounds, I have organised spices into 12 flavour groups. Their characteristics are described in the chart below, and we have translated the groupings into a Periodic Table of Spices on pp14-15. Some elements of a spice's taste are not strictly flavour compounds because they cannot be sensed by the nose and so have no aroma or flavour. These substances (technically termed "tastants") act directly on the tongue, and include sugars and tart acids. Many are chemicals intended to deter predators – but which humans can enjoy – causing bitterness, numbness, coldness, or, in the case of pungent compounds, spicy heat.

SWEET-SOUR ACIDS

The fruit-based spices in this flavour group are dominated by sourness from acids, and are typically accompanied by the sweetness from plant sugars. Sometimes acids have an aroma, which can be like cheese or sweat.

COMPOUND EXAMPLES
Hexanoic and pentanoic acids in carob, citric acid in amchoor.

IN THE KITCHEN
Water-soluble and tolerant of long cooking. Suited to dishes containing sugar, which amplifies fruitiness and blunts strong sourness.

FRUITY ALDEHYDES

Aldehyde compounds are found in abundance in fruiting plants and are more subtle on the palate than other flavour compound groups. Spices in this group carry a distinct fruity, malty, or fresh green flavour, sometimes with fatty or sweaty nuances.

COMPOUND EXAMPLES
Nonanal in sumac, hexanal in barberry.

IN THE KITCHEN
Partly water-soluble, but disperse best in oil and alcohol. Aromas do not survive high heats or long cooking times. Cook briefly or use raw to savour their subtleties.

TOASTY PYRAZINES

These spices have been toasted as part of their processing or gain most of their flavour from being fried or toasted. Spices in this group carry nutty, roasted, caramel-like flavours, sometimes with smoky, meaty, fresh-bread-like nuances.

COMPOUND EXAMPLES
Each spice develops a unique combination of dozens of pyrazines.

IN THE KITCHEN
Create pyrazines by dry-toasting spices over 130°C (266°F). Flavours spread best in oil and enhance savoury dishes, in particular.

SULPHUROUS COMPOUNDS

Spices in this group tend to be dominated by oniony and meaty flavours, with cabbage- and horseradish-like nuances and a degree of pungency. In high concentrations, sulphur compounds can smell offensive and fetid.

COMPOUND EXAMPLES
Isothiocyanate in mustard, diallyl disulphide in garlic.

IN THE KITCHEN
Dispersing in fats, the meaty taste of these spices helps to bring depth of flavour to vegetable dishes.

PUNGENT COMPOUNDS

These sometimes alarmingly hot spices share compounds that are not flavours at all, but chemicals that create an illusion of burning by hijacking pain nerves that normally send warning signals to the brain above 42°C (108°F).

COMPOUND EXAMPLES
Capsaicin in chilli, piperine in black pepper.

IN THE KITCHEN
Pungent compounds have varying strengths and agency, so combine spices for more rounded heat. Cook with fats to fully disperse the heat.

UNIQUE COMPOUNDS

Some compounds are unique in the world of spices or do not fit in other groups. Spices dominated by such compounds can be earthy, mellow, penetrating, or herby, and usually partner with a wide range of other spices.

COMPOUND EXAMPLES
Picocrocin and safranal in saffron, tumerone in turmeric.

IN THE KITCHEN
These spices possess characteristics usually not found elsewhere and will bring unique aromas to a dish.

CINNAMON **Ci**	ANISE **An**	LIQUORICE **Lq**	VANILLA **Va**	DRIED LIME **Li**	LEMONGRASS **Le**
CASSIA **Ca**	STAR ANISE **St**	MAHLEB **Mb**	CUMIN **Cu**	LEMON MYRTLE **Lm**	TAMARIND **Ta**
CLOVE **Cl**	FENNEL **Fe**	MASTIC **Mc**	NIGELLA **Ni**	AMCHOOR **Am**	SUMAC **Su**
ALLSPICE **Al**	CARAWAY **Cw**	JUNIPER **Ju**	GRAINS OF SELIM **Sl**	ANARDANA **Ar**	CAROB **Cb**
NUTMEG **Nu**	DILL **Di**	ROSE **Ro**	BLACK CARDAMOM **Bl**	BAY **Ba**	BARBERRY **By**
MACE **Ma**	ANNATTO **Ao**	CORIANDER **Co**	CARDAMOM **Cm**	GALANGAL **Gg**	CACAO **Cc**

PERIODIC TABLE OF SPICES

Taking inspiration from the scientific world, I have devised this Periodic Table of Spices as a starting point for a new way of thinking about spices.

Each of the main spices featured in this book has been assigned to one of 12 flavour groups, according to the flavour compound that is most important to its taste profile.

Use the key below to identify the flavour group and turn back to pp12–13 for a full description of the characteristics defining each group.

Once you have familiarized yourself with the spice groupings, turn the page for step-by-step instructions on how to start using the Periodic Table of Spices to create your own pairings and unique blends.

KEY TO FLAVOUR GROUPS

Each group has been assigned a colour and the Spice Profiles on pp80–207 are ordered in their groups, with coloured borders matching the colours of the Periodic Table to help with navigation.

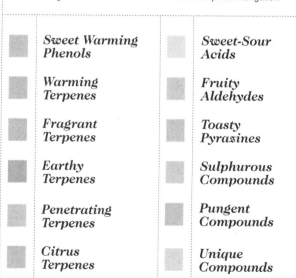

Sweet Warming Phenols	*Sweet-Sour Acids*
Warming Terpenes	*Fruity Aldehydes*
Fragrant Terpenes	*Toasty Pyrazines*
Earthy Terpenes	*Sulphurous Compounds*
Penetrating Terpenes	*Pungent Compounds*
Citrus Terpenes	*Unique Compounds*

CREATING SPICE PAIRINGS AND BLENDS

In most instances, spices work well together because they share one or more flavour compounds. In this book, the Periodic Table of Spices and blending science of each spice profile have been devised to help you understand spices through their flavour compounds. Below is a step-by-step guide for how to use this information to create your own unique spice mixes.

Step 1

CHOOSE MAIN FLAVOUR GROUP(S)

Consider the flavour groups of the Periodic Table when choosing the main flavours of your dish. Do you want it to be spicy, fruity, earthy, zesty, or something else? You can have one or several main flavours, such as a zesty citrus dessert or a meat dish that's warming and smoky.

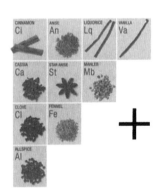 +

▲ *Sweet Warming*   ▲ *Penetrating Terpenes*
  Phenols

EXAMPLE
You may want to bring a strongly fragrant sweetness to a bean or lentil dish using spices in Sweet Warming Phenols, counterbalanced with an equally strong, but fresher, clean-tasting spice from Penetrating Terpenes. You will now be picking one or two spices from each of these groups to convey these key flavours.

Step 2

CHECK THE BLENDING SCIENCE

Read through the blending science in the relevant spice profiles to get to know the range of flavour compounds that each spice would bring to the dish. Try to make connections through shared compounds, especially between spices in different flavour groups; spices with no flavour compound link are more likely to clash.

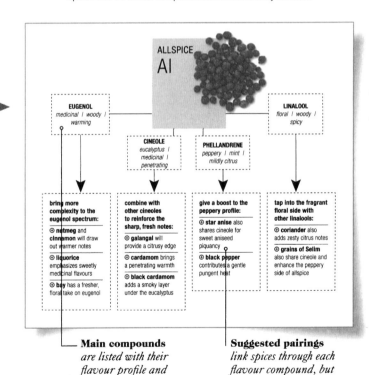

Main compounds
are listed with their flavour profile and other qualities

Suggested pairings
link spices through each flavour compound, but are not exhaustive

"

Complexity increases with each extra spice, and so will pleasure – research shows that the greater the range of flavours and mouth sensations in a dish, the tastier it will be.

"

Step 3

Step 4

PICK YOUR PRIMARY SPICES

Having reviewed the different flavour compounds in each spice, now settle on the specific spices that will convey the main flavours of the dish. Consider using two spices from the same flavour group to add depth and complexity: they will tend to blend well but bring different nuances for a more rounded base flavour.

ADD COMPLEXITY

Develop the blend by bringing in spices from further flavour groups, again selecting through shared flavour compounds. In addition to the spice profiles, use the table on pp214–217 to explore the full range of main flavour compounds.

ALLSPICE
Al

STAR ANISE
St

+

GALANGAL
Gg

>

+

CORIANDER
Co

Eugenol *is the main compound and has a warm, medicinal flavour*

Anethole *has a liquorice flavour and dominates star anise*

Cineole *is eucalyptus-like and vital to the taste of galangal*

Linalool *is the main compound in coriander and has a lilac aroma*

EXAMPLE
Allspice and star anise link together powerfully because they belong to the same flavour group, bringing warmth and sweetness with aniseed overtones. These spices are a particularly great pair because they also share some minor compounds: peppery phellandrene and cineole. Galangal brings a new flavour dimension and since it also contains cineole, the trio harmonize together incredibly well.

EXAMPLE
Coriander shares floral linalool with both allspice and star anise. This link helps coriander harmonize with the primary spices and will also reinforce their floral aspects that might otherwise be lost. Another connection is made through its camphene compound, which is related to the penetrating camphor in galangal.

world of | SPICE

Explore the main regions of the spice world via ancient trade routes and modern-day maps, discover the key spices in each cuisine, and recreate signature blends.

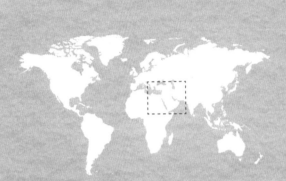

World of Spice

MIDDLE EAST

The Middle East has been at the heart of
the East–West spice trade for millennia.
The spice palette is bright and green on
the eastern shores of the Mediterranean,
and drier and more intense across the
deserts of Arabia, while Iran's fertile lands
brim with sweeter, fresher flavours.

SPICE REGIONS

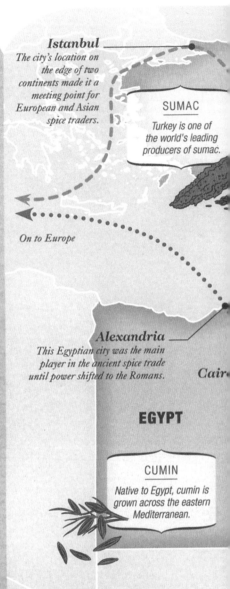

Istanbul
*The city's location on
the edge of two
continents made it a
meeting point for
European and Asian
spice traders.*

SUMAC
Turkey is one of
the world's leading
producers of sumac.

On to Europe

Alexandria
*This Egyptian city was the main
player in the ancient spice trade
until power shifted to the Romans.*

Cair

EGYPT

CUMIN
Native to Egypt, cumin is
grown across the eastern
Mediterranean.

Spices from Asia

From 700 to 1450 CE,
global commerce in spices
was dominated by Arab
merchants, who sailed the
trade winds to bring goods
from India and Southeast
Asia, including turmeric,
black pepper, cloves,
nutmeg, and nigella.

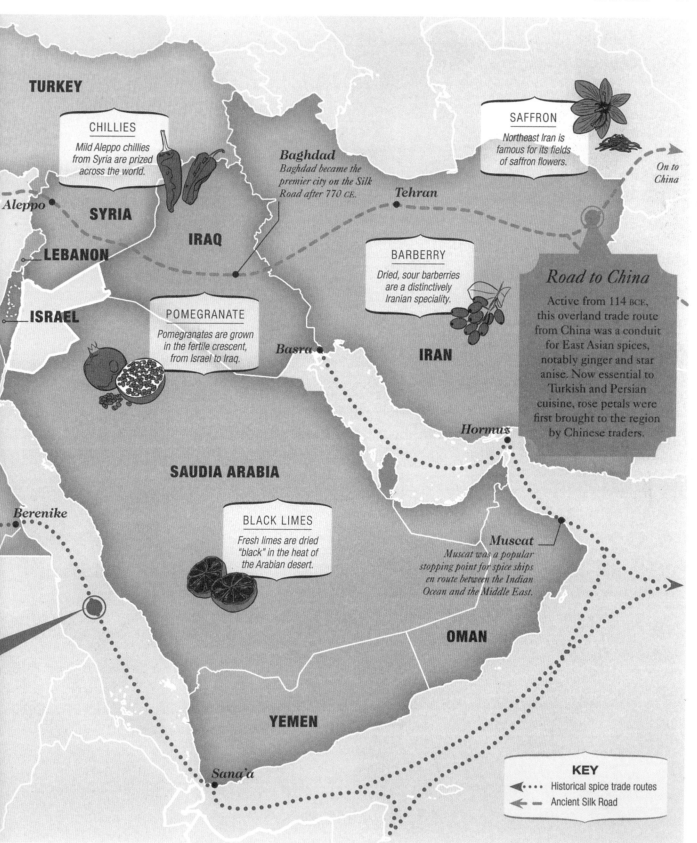

TURKEY

CHILLIES
Mild Aleppo chillies from Syria are prized across the world.

Baghdad
Baghdad became the premier city on the Silk Road after 770 CE.

SAFFRON
Northeast Iran is famous for its fields of saffron flowers.

On to China

Aleppo

SYRIA

Tehran

LEBANON

IRAQ

BARBERRY
Dried, sour barberries are a distinctively Iranian speciality.

ISRAEL

POMEGRANATE
Pomegranates are grown in the fertile crescent, from Israel to Iraq.

Basra

IRAN

Road to China
Active from 114 BCE, this overland trade route from China was a conduit for East Asian spices, notably ginger and star anise. Now essential to Turkish and Persian cuisine, rose petals were first brought to the region by Chinese traders.

Hormuz

SAUDIA ARABIA

Berenike

BLACK LIMES
Fresh limes are dried "black" in the heat of the Arabian desert.

Muscat
Muscat was a popular stopping point for spice ships en route between the Indian Ocean and the Middle East.

OMAN

YEMEN

Sana'a

KEY
•••• Historical spice trade routes
— — Ancient Silk Road

SPICE PALETTE

sumac

Aleppo pepper

Signature

Aleppo pepper, sumac, allspice, black pepper, garlic
The palette gets its mild, salty heat from the Aleppo pepper, a tang from its native sumac, and a mellow piquancy from allspice.

Supporting

Safflower, cumin, cinnamon, cardamom, nigella, sesame
Syrians have a more sensitive taste for spice than the Turkish or Lebanese, choosing the milder safflower over saffron to flavour and colour rice dishes.

Supplementary

Tamarind, nutmeg, caraway, anise
Tamarind paste adds a sweet-sourness to the palette, while nutmeg, caraway, and anise are used to bring richness and liquorice spice to cakes and desserts.

SYRIA

Fruity | Warm | Sour

Often overlooked in favour of the cuisines of its better known neighbours, Turkey and Lebanon, it's a bitter irony that Syria's vibrant food culture is making a name for itself only as its people scatter from conflict in the area. The country has plenty to offer: a rich natural larder bursting with fresh herbs, cherries, dates, pomegranates, and nuts, laced with a fragrant and mild spice palette.

> "
> *Star of the Syrian spice rack is Aleppo pepper, a mild form of chilli flakes produced around the ancient Silk Road town of Aleppo.*
> "

LOCAL SPICE BLEND

Za'atar

This nutty, earthy blend of dried herbs and spices is a versatile seasoning for hummus, labneh, cheeses, meats, and fish.

2 tbsp cumin seeds
1 tsp sea salt
2 tbsp sesame seeds
2 tbsp dried oregano
2 tbsp sumac

Dry-roast the cumin in a frying pan, over a low heat, until fragrant, then grind with the salt. Dry-roast the sesame seeds until golden and stir into the mixture with the oregano and sumac.

Baharat – simply meaning "spices" – is the blend that defines the Middle East, its smoky mix varying from region to region.

Lamb kofte with *baharat*, see p210. ➤

SPICE PALETTE

urfa biber

cumin

Turkish baharat

Use in meat kofte, pilafs, or with roast vegetables, especially aubergine.

2 tbsp black peppercorns
2 tbsp cumin seeds
2 tbsp coriander seeds
1 tsp cloves
½ tbsp cardamom seeds
1 tbsp ground nutmeg
pinch of ground cinnamon
1 tbsp dried mint

Finely grind the whole spices and combine with the remaining ingredients. Makes approximately 9 tablespoons.

TURKEY

Fresh | Mild | Smoky

At the crossroads of Europe, Asia, and the Middle East, Turkey has long been a hub for the trading of exotic spices. In the halls of Istanbul's domed Spice Bazaar, sacks of Iranian saffron and Sichuan pepper sit alongside Turkish specialities such as *pul biber*, a mild, coarsely ground chilli used as a table condiment, or the darker, smokier *urfa biber*. Dishes from the Aegean and Mediterranean coast tend to use more fresh herbs and less spice than those from eastern areas, where heavier spicing and sweetness bring a more Middle Eastern flavour.

SPICE PALETTE

Signature

Pul biber, black pepper, cumin, garlic, sumac
Turkish spicing is surprisingly subtle, with dishes characterized by the mild heat of *pul biber* and black pepper.

Supporting

Urfa biber, paprika, allspice, nigella, cinnamon
Paprika, allspice, and *urfa biber* impart warmth and richness to meat dishes and soups, while cinnamon is added to sweet dishes, especially in eastern Turkey.

Supplementary

Fenugreek, clove, nutmeg, coriander, cardamom
Look closely, and you'll find spices from all over the world in Turkish cooking – Asian flavours are particularly common.

SPICE PALETTE

paprika

sumac

Signature
Sesame, sumac, cumin, garlic, paprika
If Israel's palette can be characterized by any blend of flavours, it's this Mediterranean-Middle Eastern flush of warm, sour, and spicy-sweet.

Supporting
Caraway, chilli, fenugreek, nigella, black pepper, cinnamon, cardamom, coriander
Spices are particularly popular in Israel's famous breads: aniseedy caraway in Jewish rye bread, as well as nigella seeds in pittas.

Supplementary
Turmeric, hibiscus, rose, saffron, bay
The melting pot of flavours in Israeli cuisine is mirrored in its range of spices, some of which you won't find elsewhere in the Middle East, such as earthy-sweet dried hibiscus flowers.

ISRAEL
Varied | Earthy | Sweet

Although Israel shares much of its menu with neighbouring Lebanon, the country draws its sprawling, ever-evolving spice palette from across the globe: fiery chilli pastes from Yemen, paprika from Russia and eastern Europe, harissa from North Africa, and, increasingly, flavours from further afield thanks to Israeli travellers returning with Korean, Thai, and Mexican spice blends. The influx of fresh new flavours won't dampen Israel's devotion to its spice traditions, however: you'll still find its *zhug* green chilli condiment served alongside falafels, grilled meats, sandwiches, soups, and egg dishes.

***Hibiscus** flowers are steeped in water or ground to powder to release their sharp, cranberry-like fruitiness.*

◄ Sautéed squash and potatoes with poached egg and *zhug*.

LEBANON
Bright | Warm | Aniseedy

The Middle East's most famous export, traditional Lebanese mezze, can be found across the Levantine region, often resulting in fierce disputes over origin: hummus, for example, which is steadfastly claimed by both Israel and Lebanon. The country's cooks deploy spices liberally, whether on their own or in the ubiquitous seven-spice *baharat*, a staple in every kitchen for use in mezzes, marinades, soups, and stews.

> " *This volatile heartland of the eastern Mediterranean punches way above its weight in its spectrum of spices.* "

SPICE PALETTE

allspice

ginger

nutmeg

Signature

Coriander, cinnamon, black pepper, allspice, clove, ginger, nutmeg
A *baharat* blend of these seven spices is used to flavour beef and lamb dishes, such as *kibbeh* beef croquettes, *kafta* skewers, and stuffed vegetables.

Supporting

Garlic, sumac, paprika, cumin, cardamom, sesame, fenugreek
Lebanon's spectrum of warm, nutty, earthy, and sour spices adds depth to meats and salads. Cardamom brings a distinctive sweetness to tea and sweets.

Supplementary

Saffron, turmeric, caraway, anise
The sweet-toothed Lebanese are particularly fond of dishes spiced with aniseed flavours; *meghli* rice pudding or *sfouf* tea cake are especially popular.

LOCAL SPICE BLEND

Zhug

This bright, intensely spicy chilli paste is the national condiment of Israel.

1 tsp cardamom seeds
1 tsp coriander seeds
1 tsp cumin seeds
2 green chillies, chopped
2 garlic cloves, chopped
1 large bunch coriander, chopped
1 large bunch flat-leaf parsley, chopped
2 tbsp olive oil
salt and pepper, to taste
juice of ½ lemon

Toast the dry spices in a frying pan over medium heat, then grind. Pound to a paste with the chillies and garlic. Combine with the herbs and 1 tbsp oil. Season and set aside for 10 minutes. Stir in the lemon juice and loosen with more olive oil.

LOCAL SPICE BLEND

Taklia

A versatile, savoury blend usually added to soups and stews just before serving.

3 cloves garlic, peeled and sliced
2 tbsp olive oil
1 tsp ground coriander
a good **pinch** of cayenne
½ tsp sea salt

Fry the garlic gently in the oil, then when it is fragrant but not coloured, pour it into a mortar with the coriander, cayenne, and salt, and grind to a paste.

cardamom

cinnamon

Signature

Black pepper, cardamom, cinnamon, cumin
Black pepper is the preferred seasoning and the other rich, warm spices are paired with lamb, Iraq's favourite meat, in kebabs and stews.

Supporting

Allspice, garlic, turmeric, tamarind, saffron, dried lime
Sour flavours play an important role in Iraqi spicing: tamarind and turmeric, for example, which characterize the traditional dish of *masgûf* (grilled carp).

Supplementary

Fenugreek, cassia, paprika, coriander, ginger
Additional spices are drawn from across the globe, with influences creeping in from Latin America, China, Southeast Asia, and India.

IRAQ
Sweet | Fragrant | Sour

Spices have been woven throughout Iraq's rich history and were first cultivated by the rulers of ancient Mesopotamia. The palette was enlivened by the fresh, fruity spices of the Persians, and further added to by traders on the Silk Road and Spice Route, who brought the sweet-and-sour flavours of Chinese cassia and the heady cardamom, turmeric, and fenugreek of South Asia.

> "
> *Spices are so central to Iraqi home cooking that families have their own unique baharat blended for them at the local market.*
> "

LOCAL SPICE BLEND

Arabic baharat

This Iraqi version of the regional blend is sweet and fragrant, and can be used as an all-purpose rub, marinade, or seasoning.

1 tbsp black peppercorns
1 tbsp allspice
1 tsp cloves
1 tsp coriander seeds
1 tsp cumin seeds
1 tbsp cinnamon
1 tsp grated nutmeg

Grind the whole spices and combine with the cinnamon and cumin.

Saffron *is the most expensive spice in the world, and Iran is responsible for over 90 per cent of its production.*

Persian rice pudding with *advieh*, see p210. ➤

Advieh

A heady blend of Persian spices to sprinkle over savoury rice, rub over meats, or add to stews. It is good on Persian rice pudding, too.

2 tbsp dried rose petals
2 tbsp cardamom seeds
1 tbsp cumin seeds
2 tbsp ground cinnamon
2 tbsp ground ginger

Grind the whole spices and combine with the cinnamon and ginger.

IRAN
Floral | Musky | Sour

Iran's spice palette and cuisine are as rich and exciting as its history. In this sprawling intersection between east and west – the centre of the Persian Empire and the Silk Road, invaded by Greeks, Arabs, Turks, Mongols, and Uzbeks – you'll find caviar and Chinese noodles, smoked fish and hot-and-sour prawns, and a natural larder brimming with pistachios, pomegranates, mint, walnuts, and the prized Iranian saffron, grown in the northeast. Stews and pilafs are underpinned by Iran's sweet-and-sour spices – sumac, dried limes, barberries, and tamarind – while fragrant rose petals give spice mixes and sweets a hint of the exotic.

SPICE PALETTE

saffron

rose

Signature
Saffron, sumac, rose
Iran's famous burnt-red saffron strands – never powder – give seafood and poultry a rich, slightly bitter flavour and rice dishes their vibrant amber colour.

Supporting
Dried lime, barberry, angelica, cinnamon, cumin, ginger, turmeric, garlic
Iranian cuisine owes its fruity tang to its dried fruits and sour, citrusy spices, with a rich baseline of fragrant and earthy cinnamon, cumin, and ginger. Turmeric is used to colour and add a musky depth to savoury dishes.

Supplementary
Fenugreek leaves, curry powder, paprika, tamarind
The subtle bitterness and warmth of fenugreek leaves and drier spices balance the sweetness and sour flavours of Iran's fresh ingredients.

SPICE PALETTE

cumin

cinnamon

Signature
Cumin, cinnamon
The go-to spice for savoury dishes is cumin, while cinnamon is used just as liberally to add depth to Egypt's array of sweet dishes.

Supporting
Garlic, black pepper, chilli, coriander
Tomato sauces are perked up with a fresh palette of garlic, black pepper, and chilli flakes, while coriander provides a mellow, citrusy partner to cumin.

Supplementary
Ginger, cloves, bay, cardamom, allspice
You will often find an additional spice or two to partner the main flavour, but Egyptians keep their spicing relatively simple, or reach for the *baharat*.

EGYPT
Fresh | Earthy | Nutty

Flanked by the Red Sea and the Mediterranean, Egypt's ports became the gateway to the riches of the East long before its mercantile heyday in the Middle Ages. Despite its spice-rich history, the modern Egyptian palette is simpler than that of other Levantine countries. Indigenous cumin is the prevailing flavour – its rich, nutty notes enliven the relatively humble ingredients of Egypt's vegetable soups, meat stews, and grain dishes such as *koshari*. Cumin, along with hazelnuts, sesame seeds, and coriander, is also a key flavouring in *dukkah*, a distinctively Egyptian condiment that varies in content from house to house.

LOCAL SPICE BLEND

Dukkah

An everyday blend of spices and nuts that is often served with olive oil and bread or used to season roasted meats or hummus.

150g (5½oz) hazelnuts
150g (5½oz) whole almonds
1 tbsp coriander seeds
1 tbsp cumin seeds
3 tbsp sesame seeds
pinch of salt

Preheat the oven to 200°C (400°F/ Gas 6). Spread the nuts on separate baking sheets. Roast the almonds for 8 minutes and the hazelnuts for 10 minutes, shaking the trays every 3 minutes. Dry-fry the seeds over a high heat for 3 minutes, tossing constantly. Grind together the cooled nuts, seeds, and salt.

▲ Hummus and flatbreads served with *dukkah*.

Ancient Egyptians founded the spice trade, importing spices from Africa and Arabia as early as 3000 BCE.

ARABIAN PENINSULA
Rich | Dry | Musky

The Arabian spice palette shares many of its rich, fragrant flavours with its northern neighbours: the Levantine trinity of cumin, coriander, and cinnamon, as well as dried limes and saffron from Iran. But as the Arabian peninsula stretches down to Yemen and Oman, with Africa and Asia beyond, the flavours and heat of its food intensify with the climate and terrain. In come cloves and black pepper, masala mixes, turmeric and coconut dishes from Asia, and hot chillies from Africa.

> "
> *Omani and Yemeni cuisines are justifiably famous for their heady blend of fiery flavours.*
> "

LOCAL SPICE BLEND
Hawaij

A curry-like Yemeni blend, popular in slow-cooked meat dishes and soups and as a spice rub. A sweeter version replaces the pepper and cumin with ginger, cloves, cinnamon, or fennel, and is added to coffee and desserts.

1 tbsp black peppercorns
7 tsp cumin seeds
1 tbsp cardamom seeds
1 tbsp coriander seeds
2 tbsp ground turmeric

Grind the whole spices and combine with the turmeric.

SPICE PALETTE

dried lime

bay

Signature
Baharat, dried lime, bay
The signature flavours of Arab *baharat*, dried limes, and bay leaves give slow-cooked dishes and spice mixes a distinctive sour, musky flavour.

Supporting
Saffron, cardamom, clove, cinnamon, cumin, coriander, garlic, chilli, black pepper
Lamb and rice dishes are a firm fixture on Saudi menus, and the palette is full of piquant, citrusy spices that cut through the richness of the meat.

Supplementary
Turmeric, nutmeg, caraway
Sweet and slightly bitter, turmeric gives a brightness to the flavour and colour of Yemeni spice blends and Omani fish soups.

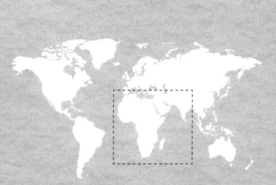

World of Spice

AFRICA

Africa's cuisine is as diverse as the land is vast. From Casablanca to the tip of the Cape, you will find spices that tell a complex story: of kingdoms and empires, of overland and maritime spice routes, of slave trades, of European colonization, and of migration within Africa.

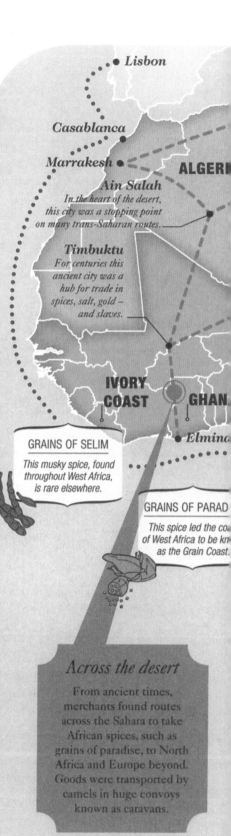

● *Lisbon*

Casablanca

Marrakesh ●

ALGER

Ain Salah
In the heart of the desert, this city was a stopping point on many trans-Saharan routes.

Timbuktu
For centuries this ancient city was a hub for trade in spices, salt, gold – and slaves.

IVORY COAST **GHAN**

● *Elmina*

GRAINS OF SELIM
This musky spice, found throughout West Africa, is rare elsewhere.

GRAINS OF PARAD
This spice led the coa of West Africa to be kn as the Grain Coast.

Across the desert
From ancient times, merchants found routes across the Sahara to take African spices, such as grains of paradise, to North Africa and Europe beyond. Goods were transported by camels in huge convoys known as caravans.

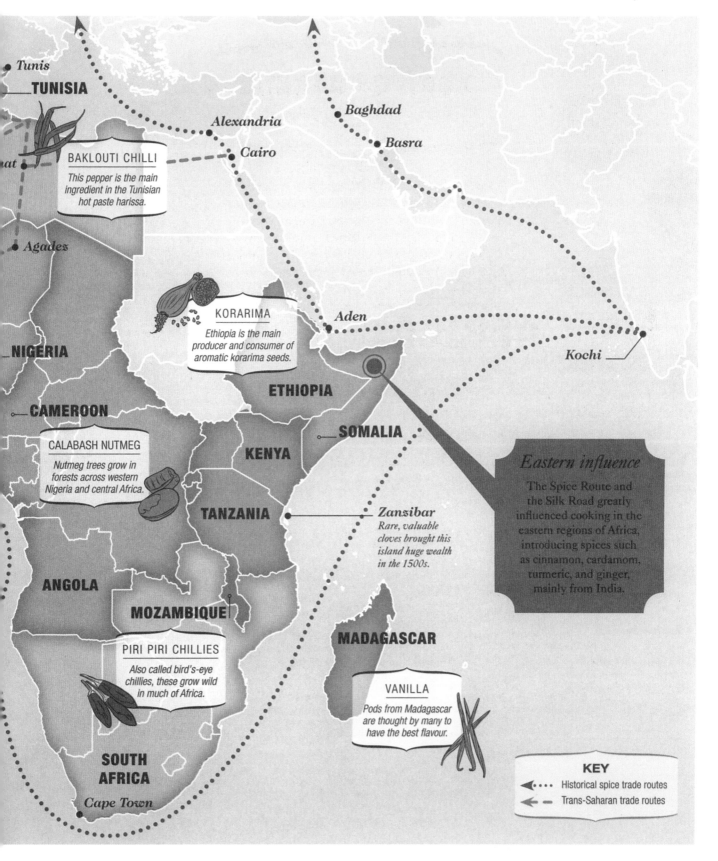

TUNISIA

Tunis

Alexandria

Cairo

Baghdad

Basra

BAKLOUTI CHILLI
This pepper is the main ingredient in the Tunisian hot paste harissa.

Agades

KORARIMA
Ethiopia is the main producer and consumer of aromatic korarima seeds.

Aden

Kochi

NIGERIA

CAMEROON

CALABASH NUTMEG
Nutmeg trees grow in forests across western Nigeria and central Africa.

ETHIOPIA

SOMALIA

KENYA

Eastern influence
The Spice Route and the Silk Road greatly influenced cooking in the eastern regions of Africa, introducing spices such as cinnamon, cardamom, turmeric, and ginger, mainly from India.

TANZANIA

Zanzibar
Rare, valuable cloves brought this island huge wealth in the 1500s.

ANGOLA

MOZAMBIQUE

MADAGASCAR

PIRI PIRI CHILLIES
Also called bird's-eye chillies, these grow wild in much of Africa.

VANILLA
Pods from Madagascar are thought by many to have the best flavour.

SOUTH AFRICA

Cape Town

KEY
···◄ Historical spice trade routes
◄ – – Trans-Saharan trade routes

SPICE PALETTE

fenugreek

cardamom

Signature

Korarima, fenugreek, chilli pepper, cardamom, cumin, coriander
Also called false or Ethiopian cardamom, *korarima* is native to Ethiopia and has a similar but milder flavour to true cardamom. The spice is notably used to flavour *kifto*, a type of steak tartare dish.

Supporting

Turmeric, ginger, garlic, nigella, clove
Cloves added to the hottest chillies, cardamom or *korarima*, and salt comprise the *mitmita* spice blend. Other supporting spices help to flavour the many interesting vegetable sides and relishes of the region.

Supplementary

Cinnamon, nutmeg, ajwain, timiz
Before the chilli pepper arrived, the local species of long pepper (*Piper capense*), known as *timiz*, provided the main source of pungent heat.

HORN OF AFRICA

Fiery | Aromatic | Smoky

Ethiopia's capital, Addis Ababa, is home to Africa's largest spice market – a sign of this region's spice diversity. The ubiquitous *berbere* mix and its less complex sister blend *mitmita*, both shared by Ethiopia and Eritrea, are dominated by red hot piri piri chillies. Yet the quintessential taste of Ethiopian cooking comes from bittersweet fenugreek and smoky floral *korarima*. Somalian cuisine, meanwhile, is defined by the fruitiness of coriander, cleanness of cardamom, and earthiness of cumin.

> " *Spices are among the few external influences brought to bear on the unique flavours of Ethiopian cooking.* "

LOCAL SPICE BLEND

Niter kibbeh

This spiced clarified butter is used as the flavoursome base fat for many regional dishes, including hearty *wat* meat stews.

500g (1lb 2oz) unsalted butter	**1 tsp** ground cumin seeds
1 medium onion, finely chopped	**1 tsp** *korarima* or cardamom seeds
2 garlic cloves, finely chopped	**½ tsp** turmeric powder
1 tbsp grated fresh root ginger	**1 tsp** dried oregano
	6 basil leaves
1 tsp fenugreek seeds	**4** sage leaves

Melt the butter in a pan over a medium-low heat. Add the remaining ingredients and cook, stirring, for 20 minutes. Strain through muslin into a sterilized jar.

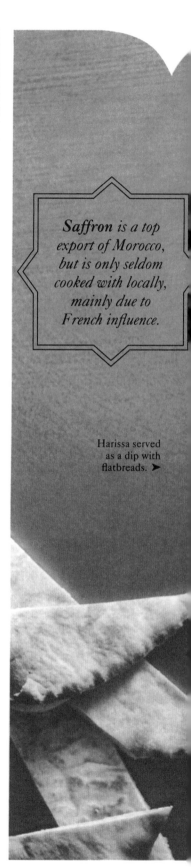

Saffron is a top export of Morocco, but is only seldom cooked with locally, mainly due to French influence.

Harissa served as a dip with flatbreads. ➤

LOCAL SPICE BLEND

Harissa

Harissa paste is used as a condiment, a dip for bread, or as the main flavouring for stews and sauces.

100g (3¹/₂oz) dried red chillies, Baklouti if you can get them, or other moderately hot chillies, such as Kashmiri
3 or 4 fat cloves of garlic
1 tsp salt
1–2 tbsp lemon juice
½ tsp cumin seeds, ground
½ tsp coriander seeds, ground
½ tsp caraway seeds, ground
1 tbsp olive oil

Deseed the chillies and soak in hot water for 30 minutes. Drain, combine with the other ingredients, and pound or blend to a paste.

THE MAGHREB
Earthy | Rich | Mild

The collective of countries known as the Maghreb is the portal where Africa meets the Middle East and Europe. The region's cuisine has been shaped by cultural exchange between indigenous Berbers and their conquerors through the centuries – Arabs, Ottomans, and French – as well as from the period when Islamic Berbers themselves ruled most of the Iberian peninsula as Al-Andalus. Spicing is sweet and mild for the most part, with cumin the everyday choice, and cinnamon bringing its aromatic notes to rich, fruit-laden tagines. The chilli heat of Tunisia's harissa paste is a sweat-inducing exception.

SPICE PALETTE

cumin

paprika

Signature
Cumin, cinnamon, ginger, chilli
Cumin gives the dishes of the Maghreb their mild and earthy undertones, while cinnamon and ginger add an aromatic edge to tagines, soups, and stews.

Supporting
Coriander, turmeric, clove, paprika, allspice
Arab traders introduced further exotic spices from the East – coriander, turmeric, and cloves – and in the other direction, paprika and allspice were introduced from the Americas.

Supplementary
Pepper, nutmeg, cardamom, fenugreek
These lesser spices tend not to feature on their own and are more usually encountered in the blend *ras el hanout*, a broad combination of spices with local variations that brings together most if not all of the above palette of spices.

SPICE PALETTE

cardamom

bay

coriander

Signature

Ginger, cardamom, garlic, cinnamon, clove
Ginger gives East African cuisine piquancy and heat. Kenyan and Ugandan dishes are fairly mild, but ginger is used liberally. Cardamom, clove, and cinnamon add their sweet aromas to the local version of chai tea.

Supporting

Bay, black pepper, cumin, coriander
Pepper and cumin bring heat and earthiness to various blends. Bay and coriander are added to meaty versions of pilau, alongside the standard masala.

Supplementary

Tsiperifery, turmeric, chilli, sesame
Tsiperifery is a variety of pepper native to Madagascar, more pungent and citrusy than ordinary black pepper. Crushed sesame features in Ugandan cooking, often partnered with spinach.

Spices for an East African pilau masala blend. ➤

EAST AFRICA

Zingy | Sweet | Fragrant

Thanks to the legendary spice islands of the Zanzibar Archipelago, Tanzania has historically been the epicentre of East Africa's spice trade and continues to play the role of dominant influencer in the region's cuisine. Over 2,000 years of trade with Arabia, Persia, and India saw the introduction of warming spices such as cloves, ginger, pepper, cinnamon, and cardamom. Ginger and cardamom travelled furthest inland, making them the most widely used spices of the region. In coastal areas, cooking draws on turmeric and coriander to bring fresh, tropical notes when combined with coconut.

LOCAL SPICE BLEND

Pilau masala

Introduced to the region via India and Arabia, pilau rice is a one-pot dish made with meat or vegetables and spiced with the following masala blend.

½ **tsp** cumin seeds
½ **tsp** whole black peppercorns
½ **tsp** cloves
¼ **tsp** cardamom seeds
¼ **tsp** ground cinnamon

Grind the whole spices and combine with the cinnamon. The masala is usually added when frying the onions.

SPICE
PALETTE

CENTRAL AFRICA
Nutty | Pungent | Local

With the exception of chillies introduced in the 15th century by Portuguese explorers, the cuisine of Central Africa has remained true to its indigenous spice cupboard. Seeds and bark of the *bobimbi* tree are the region's equivalent to garlic, used in almost every local dish, and three native pungent spices provide lingering heat and hints of citrus: Ashanti pepper (*Piper guineense*), grains of Selim, and *mbongo* (*Aframomum citratum*).

> " *Confusingly, 'grains of paradise' is a name applied locally to four different spices: Ashanti, mbongo, grains of Selim, and grains of paradise!* "

Zanzibar was once the world's largest producer of cloves, a trade established by Omani settlers to the island.

LOCAL SPICE BLEND
Mbongo mix

Use to flavour Cameroonian "black stew" *mbongo tchobi*, most often made with white fish.

4 tsp ground *mbongo* or black cardamom
1 tsp *bobimbi* or **1 handful** wild garlic or garlic chives
30 *njangsa* seeds or **1 handful** unsalted peanuts
2 calabash nutmeg seeds or **1 tsp** grated nutmeg
1 tsp grains of paradise
4 garlic cloves
1 onion, roughly chopped

Grind the whole spices, combine with the garlic and onion in a blender, add 4 tbsp water, and process until smooth.

Scotch bonnet chilli

ginger

Signature
Bobimbi, njangsa, mbongo
Njangsa are the oil-rich seeds of the *Ricinodendron* tree, bringing a nutty flavour and thickening property to dishes, with a particular affinity for fish.

Supporting
Calabash nutmeg (*Monodora myristica*), chilli (Scotch bonnet), ginger, grains of paradise
Milder than ordinary nutmeg, indigenous calabash nutmeg found its way to the Caribbean – where it is called Jamaican nutmeg – via the European slave trade. Ginger, chilli, and grains of paradise are regular additions to soups.

Supplementary
Garlic, bay, black pepper, curry powder
The region is gradually embracing non-native spices, with garlic, pepper, and bay leaf used to season local versions of the jollof rice dish, and curry powder employed as a flavour shortcut in Cameroonian curries.

SPICE PALETTE

grains of Selim

grains of paradise

Signature

Chilli, ginger, garlic
Most savoury dishes begin with these backbone spices, almost always used together. Chillies tend to be at the hot end of the scale, used fresh, dried, or powdered.

Supporting

Grains of Selim, grains of paradise, *iru*, *prekese*, nutmeg, bay
Grains of Selim and grains of paradise both bring pepperiness. *Prekese* are the sweetly fragrant pods of a pea-like plant, also known as "soup perfume". *Iru* are the fermented seeds of the locust bean tree, with a strong ammonia smell, used as a condiment.

Supplementary

Turmeric, Ashanti pepper, clove, anise
Ashanti pepper (see p35) is most important in soups, notably *banga* (palm nut), peanut, or pepper soups. Clove-spiced sour millet porridge is a popular breakfast dish in Accra.

WEST AFRICA

Hot | Pungent | Smoky

West Africa is a region of diverse landscapes and peoples, and equally varied culinary traditions. It can, however, be useful to consider the cuisine divided according to its two major language groups: French and English. In Francophone countries, the use of mustard paste and souring agents such as vinegar or lemon juice is widespread, notably in the popular chicken dish *poulet yassa*. Anglophone countries, by contrast, bring intense depth of flavour to dishes through smoked, fermented, and dried ingredients, pepping up almost any savoury dish with dried or smoked and ground crayfish, or fermented locust beans.

> **Originally from Senegal, the spicy rice dish jollof is raising the profile of West African cuisine across the world.**

LOCAL SPICE BLEND

Yaji

This is the spice mix used to marinate the meat for *suya*, West Africa's street food kebabs.

10 strands of grains of Selim	**5 tbsp** ginger powder
1 tbsp whole Ashanti pepper	**2 tbsp** cayenne pepper flakes
5 tbsp crushed *kuli-kuli* or peanut puffs, e.g. Osem Bamba	**1** dry stock cube, crumbled
	½ tsp salt
	black pepper, to taste

Break up the grains of Selim and grind with the Ashanti pepper; you may need to sieve out any fibres. Combine with the remaining ingredients and mix well.

Durban is known as the biggest Indian city outside India, and Victoria Street Market is famed for its spices.

Beef bunny chow made with Durban curry masala, see p211. ➤

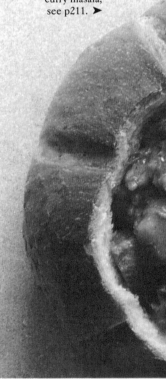

LOCAL SPICE BLEND

Durban curry masala

This blend from South Africa's third city is characterized by bold heat with a touch of sweetness.

2 tsp coriander seeds
2 tsp cumin seeds
1 tsp cardamom seeds
½ tsp fenugreek seeds
2 cloves
5cm (2in) cinnamon stick
6 tsp mild chilli powder
1 tsp cayenne pepper
½ tsp ground ginger

Toast the whole spices in a frying pan over a medium heat until fragrant, then grind and combine with the remaining spices.

SOUTHERN AFRICA

Hot | Sweet | Diverse

If South Africa is known as the Rainbow Nation, the country's cuisine encompasses a similarly broad diversity of spices, largely determined by the colonial past. Early Dutch colonization has left a legacy of Indonesian-influenced spicing in Cape Malay dishes, while the influx of Indian labourers under British rule makes Durban a contender for the premier curry city in the world. Mozambique is the fiery quarter of Southern Africa with its Portuguese-influenced piri piri chilli blends. By contrast, flavours within landlocked Botswana and Zimbabwe are much milder, with spices used carefully and sparingly.

SPICE PALETTE

cinnamon

turmeric

Signature

Cinnamon, turmeric, coriander, chilli, garlic
Regional cooks don't hold back if chilli is called for, but turmeric is often used for a milder curry-like flavour. Cinnamon enlivens the Dutch-derived custard dessert *melktert*, and coriander adds fruitiness to *biltong*, a dry-cured meat.

Secondary

Clove, black pepper, cumin, ginger, cardamom, bay
Further combinations of Asian spices produce a variety of Indonesian- or Indian-inspired masala blends, while bay leaf flavours the savoury custard topping of *bobotie*, South Africa's national dish.

Supporting

Nutmeg, anise, allspice
These three sweet, fragrant spices are sometimes used alongside coriander in regional variations of *biltong*.

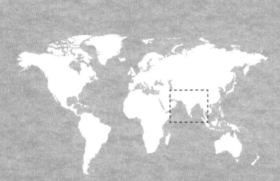

World of Spice

SOUTH ASIA

Each of South Asia's diverse communities has its own distinctive seasonings, from a simple sprinkle of cumin to complex spice blends. Native spices, such as cardamom and cinnamon, are central to many cuisines, while chilli and coriander, once non-local, are now valuable exports.

SPICE REGIONS

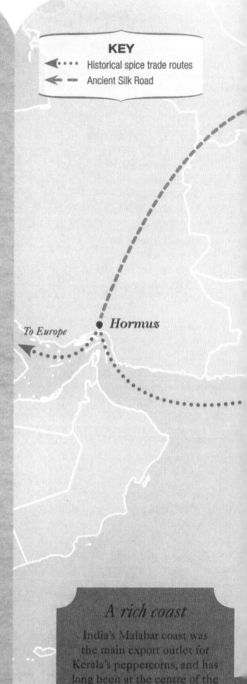

KEY

◄···· Historical spice trade routes
◄— Ancient Silk Road

To Europe • *Hormus*

A rich coast

India's Malabar coast was the main export outlet for Kerala's peppercorns, and has long been at the centre of the global spice trade. In the 16th century Portugal was the first European nation to enrich itself by trading peppercorns from this area.

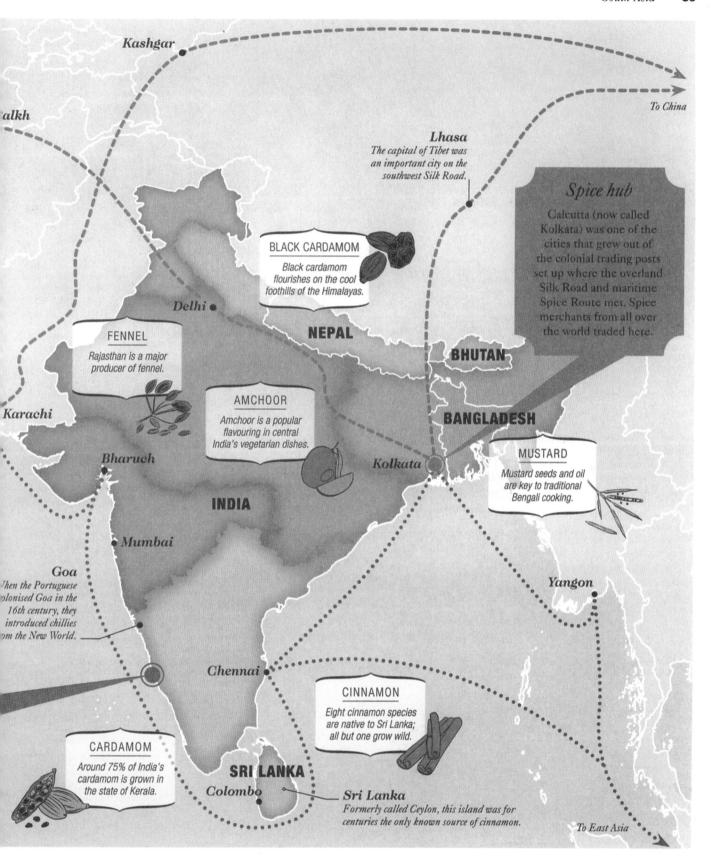

Kashgar

Balkh

To China

Lhasa
*The capital of Tibet was
an important city on the
southwest Silk Road.*

Spice hub
Calcutta (now called
Kolkata) was one of the
cities that grew out of
the colonial trading posts
set up where the overland
Silk Road and maritime
Spice Route met. Spice
merchants from all over
the world traded here.

BLACK CARDAMOM
*Black cardamom
flourishes on the cool
foothills of the Himalayas.*

Delhi

NEPAL

FENNEL
*Rajasthan is a major
producer of fennel.*

AMCHOOR
*Amchoor is a popular
flavouring in central
India's vegetarian dishes.*

BHUTAN

Karachi

BANGLADESH

Bharuch

MUSTARD
*Mustard seeds and oil
are key to traditional
Bengali cooking.*

Kolkata

INDIA

Mumbai

Goa
*When the Portuguese
colonised Goa in the
16th century, they
introduced chillies
from the New World.*

Yangon

Chennai

CINNAMON
*Eight cinnamon species
are native to Sri Lanka;
all but one grow wild.*

CARDAMOM
*Around 75% of India's
cardamom is grown in
the state of Kerala.*

SRI LANKA

Colombo

Sri Lanka
*Formerly called Ceylon, this island was for
centuries the only known source of cinnamon.*

To East Asia

SPICE PALETTE

turmeric

cumin

chilli

Signature
Cumin, turmeric, chilli, ginger, garlic
The foundation of essential masala mixes and pastes, these versatile spices are often used together and provide an obliging base for main ingredients.

Supporting
Cassia, clove, cardamom, Indian bay, fennel
These sweet spices bring warmth and fragrance. Indian bay is from the same family as cinnamon, and tastes like a mix of cloves, cinnamon, and allspice.

Supplementary
Black cumin, anardana, peppercorn, saffron
Smoky, tart, warming, and sweet, these spices grab the senses with their distinctive personalities, and perform well as solo seasonings or as part of a blend.

Chickpea curry spiced with garam masala, see p211. ➤

NORTH INDIA
Complex | Earthy | Fragrant

From no-frills rustic cooking in Punjabi homes, to the refined flavours of Mughal palace kitchens, and kebabs and hearty dhals finished with sizzling cumin at roadside cafés, this food is as widely travelled as the spices that have earned it such international acclaim. During the heyday of princely Maharajas and Nawabs, royal chefs created flamboyant spice blends for sophisticated dishes, many of which featured a dozen or more aromatic seasonings. Home cooks also draw on a versatile spice box, preferring the warming nature of garam masalas over brute chilli heat.

LOCAL SPICE BLEND
Garam masala
Many households have their own variation of this warming spice blend, which is used in the same way as you would a seasoning.

25g (scant 1oz) black cardamom seeds
25g (scant 1oz) cassia, broken into pieces
25g (scant 1oz) black peppercorns
10g (¼oz) black cumin seeds
2 blades mace
10g (¼oz) cloves
⅛ nutmeg, chopped

Grind all the spices to a fine powder and sieve to remove any fibres.

HIMALAYAN BELT

Astringent | Fiery | Warming

Cooking in the Himalayas is shaped by nature's harvest in the foothills along with frugal high-altitude pickings. There's an emphasis on wholesome pulses, often finished with a *tarka* of warming fried cumin seeds, chillies, and ginger. Spices tend to be basic, and in areas such as Bhutan, chillies are elevated to a main ingredient. Ginger-spiced steamed dumplings, chilli-laden Tibetan broths, and Chinese noodles coexist with such Punjabi staples as parathas, naans, and homely dhals.

> " *Longevity of food is of primary focus, and spiced pickles and preserves perk up meals during the cold winter months.* "

LOCAL SPICE BLEND

Timur ko chhop

The Himalayan equivalent of salt and pepper: use as a seasoning for soups, a dip for fried meats, or as a fiery pick-me-up over fried potatoes, noodles, and curries.

1 tsp *timur* or Sichuan pepper
2 tbsp red chilli powder
1 tsp salt

Dry-roast the *timur* in a frying pan, over a low heat, until fragrant, stirring all the time. Mix with the chilli and salt, and grind to a powder.

SPICE PALETTE

fenugreek

timur

Signature
Fenugreek, chilli, *timur*, ginger, garlic
The bitterness of fenugreek seeds contrasts with the nuttiness of lentils and pulses, while *timur* (a type of Sichuan pepper) lends a more citrusy, but still astringent flavour to Nepali masalas.

Supporting
Black cardamom, asafoetida, turmeric
Asafoetida's sulphurous aroma is softened to mellow sweetness after cooking, which complements the earthiness of smoky black cardamom and turmeric.

Supplementary
Coriander, ajwain, clove, cumin
Ajwain seeds and cloves have robust and bitter flavours to enliven everyday meals, along with more discreet coriander and cumin.

SPICE PALETTE

dried red chillies

coriander

Signature
Coriander, cumin, dried red chillies, turmeric, ginger
The key spices of central India provide depth of flavour and richness to everyday vegetables, lentils, and pulses, and although they are used across South Asia, their versatility is very much centre stage here.

Supporting
Asafoetida, fennel, nigella
These bold seasonings play a significant role in pickles and preserves, and their feisty character complements and contrasts with main ingredients, too.

Supplementary
Ajwain, amchoor
With its thyme-like flavour, ajwain is often used with fish and starchy vegetables, while amchoor cuts through richness with its fruity tartness.

CENTRAL INDIA
Tart | Nutty | Assertive

Influenced by the culture of neighbouring Rajasthan, Gujarat, and Maharashtra, India's central states transform vegetarian staples into memorable dishes with a creative use of contrasting spices. A well-known simple seasoning is a trio of fried nigella, fenugreek, and fennel seeds, which lends a pickled flavour to softened vegetables and meaty masalas. Meat eaters are catered for with predominantly Mughal-style dishes. In Bhopal, Madhya Pradesh's capital city, cafés serve biryanis, kebabs, and aromatic curries spiced with garam masala emboldened with plenty of pounded coriander seeds.

> " *A sprinkling of amchoor mango powder can elevate fried potatoes to star status in central India.* "

LOCAL SPICE BLEND
Chaat masala

A seasoning sprinkled over street snacks, fruit salads, and kebabs.

2 tbsp cumin seeds	**1 tsp** ground ginger
1 tsp coriander seeds	**½ tsp** asafoetida
1 tbsp black peppercorns	**1 tbsp** kala namak (Himalayan black salt)
3 tbsp amchoor	**1 tsp** salt

Dry-roast the whole spices in a frying pan, over a medium heat, until fragrant. Leave to cool and then mix with the other ingredients and grind to a powder.

Panch phoran translates as "five spices". Bengali versions substitute local spice radhuni for mustard seed.

Panch phoran

This whole spice mix is a Bengali and Bangladeshi speciality, and is particularly good for flavouring dhals and vegetable dishes.

2 tsp cumin seeds
2 tsp brown mustard seeds
2 tsp fennel seeds
1 tsp nigella seeds
1 tsp fenugreek seeds

Simply mix together the whole spices. To use, fry a teaspoonful in oil or ghee at the start of cooking, or temper a dish just before serving.

EAST INDIA AND BANGLADESH

Pungent | Sweet-sour | Mustardy

Cooks in the river delta of West Bengal and Bangladesh embrace complex spice blends, which work especially well with fish and seafood. For religious reasons, many Hindus in Kolkata don't cook with onions and garlic, preferring the distinctive nature of nutty-tasting poppy seed paste, popped mustard seeds, ginger, and the aromatic five-spice mix of *panch phoran*. Bangladeshi Muslims favour more strident seasonings in such dishes as Mughal-style biryanis and beef curries infused with whole spices.

SPICE PALETTE

mustard

ginger

Signature

Chilli, mustard, turmeric, cumin, ginger, garlic
Although chillies get top billing in hilly regions, flavourings in the plains are characterized by contrasting spice combinations cooked in mustard oil.

Supporting

Poppy, black cardamom, fennel
Taking the edge off the more assertive signature spices is a cast of "carrier" seasonings, which provide depth of flavour and richness to classic dishes.

Supplementary

Coriander, fenugreek, nigella
Fried nigella seeds lend a nutty and pickled flavour to vegetable and meat dishes, and their piquancy is complemented and balanced by bitter fenugreek and citrusy coriander seeds.

Masor tenga fish curry featuring *panch phoran*, see p211. ▼

SPICE PALETTE

mustard

dried red chilli

curry leaf

Signature
Kokum, dried red chilli, cumin, turmeric, mustard, ginger, garlic
These spices form the backbone of most cooking in this region, although garlic is shunned by the Jain community for religious reasons.

Supporting
Fenugreek, curry leaf, black pepper
Dishes from this region show restraint in their use of fenugreek seeds and curry leaves, but there's no holding back when peppercorns are roasted and ground into warming masalas.

Supplementary
Asafoetida, sesame
Sesame seeds are so much more than a garnish: they add richness and a nutty character when roasted and ground, and are good vehicles for sulphurous asafoetida.

➤ Vindaloo paste ready for use in a pork or chicken curry, see p212.

WEST INDIA
Bitter | Sour | Sweet

The use of spices in western India reflects varied landscapes and cultures. The arid climate of Rajasthan and parts of Gujarat differs from the tropical atmosphere of Maharashtra and Goa, and the cooking styles are equally distinct. Savoury dishes in Gujarat are characterized by sweet-sour flavours underpinned by jaggery and pungent spices such as fenugreek seeds and dried red chillies. Royal Rajasthani dishes are acclaimed for their richness and chilli-laden masalas, while along the Konkan coastline, hot and sour fish curries, balanced by creamy coconut masalas, are emblematic. Goa is famed for accommodating vinegary and garlicky Indo-Portuguese dishes.

LOCAL SPICE BLEND

Vindaloo paste

The Goans adopted and adapted this fiery, sweet-sour mix from the Portuguese.

1½ tsp cumin seeds
15–20 dried Kashmiri chillies, whole
1 tsp black peppercorns
2 tsp black mustard seeds
1 tsp fenugreek seeds
6 cloves
1 tsp cardamom seeds
5cm (2in) piece of cassia
½ star anise
6 tbsp cider vinegar or palm vinegar
1 tsp fine salt
2 tsp jaggery or date palm sugar

Toast the spices in a frying pan over a medium heat until fragrant, then grind. Transfer to a bowl, add the vinegar, salt, and jaggery, and mix to a stiff paste.

tamarind

cardamom

SOUTH INDIA AND SRI LANKA

Fresh | Zesty | Robust

From the cardamom hills of Kerala to Sri Lanka's cinnamon plantations and Andhra Pradesh's renowned chilli harvest, this region's culinary traditions come from centuries of trading in spices. Influences from the Portuguese, French, Dutch, Southeast Asians, and British have been adapted to suit local tastes, but it's the stalwarts of *sambhar* (tart lentils with vegetables), rice in all its guises, and sour fish masalas that give distinction to this region's cuisine.

Kokum is the dried rind of a fruit in the mangosteen family, used like tamarind to impart a sour flavour.

Signature

Tamarind, mustard, fenugreek, cumin, cardamom, ginger, garlic, curry leaf, chilli
Dishes are characterized as mild and mellow or bold and fiery depending on whether the spices have been dry-roasted, fried, pounded, or left whole.

Supporting

Cassia, cinnamon, black pepper, nutmeg, asafoetida
Cassia is stronger and harsher in flavour than cinnamon, and lends itself to boldly seasoned masalas. Both spices work well with the warmth of peppercorns, nutmeg, and chillies.

Supplementary

Sesame, star anise, mace
It's likely that star anise was introduced to this region by Chinese traders, since very little is grown in South Asia. Its fennel-like sweetness is well matched with the nuttiness of toasted sesame seeds and aromatic mace.

LOCAL SPICE BLEND

Gunpowder

Sprinkle this distinctly southern condiment over rice dishes, *dosa* (lentil and rice pancakes), and *idli* (steamed rice cakes). When moistened with a little oil, it makes a robustly spiced dip.

25g (scant 1oz) chana dhal or split yellow lentils

25g (scant 1oz) split urad dhal or black gram lentils

25g (scant 1oz) fresh or desiccated coconut

1 tbsp black sesame seeds

2 tbsp curry leaves (about 20)

6–8 red chillies, mild or hot according to taste

1 tbsp tamarind pulp

¼ tsp asafoetida

2 tsp jaggery or date palm sugar

Toast the lentils in a dry pan over low heat for 7–10 minutes, stirring continuously, until coloured. Transfer to a bowl and leave to cool. Toast the coconut for 3–4 minutes in the same way. When it turns pale golden, add the sesame seeds, curry leaves, and chillies, and continue cooking until the chillies have darkened.

Stir in the tamarind pulp and asafoetida, and toast for 1 minute before adding the sugar. Turn off the heat and stir until the sugar has melted. Scrape all these ingredients into the lentils and leave to cool, before grinding to a coarse powder. Spread on a tray to dry for 1 hour.

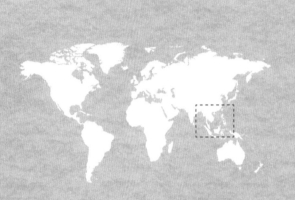

World of Spice

SOUTHEAST ASIA

When Portuguese traders brought the chilli pepper to Southeast Asia, they started a culinary revolution: it now dominates spice palettes across the region, along with characteristic fresh spices, such as garlic, ginger, and lemongrass.

SPICE REGIONS

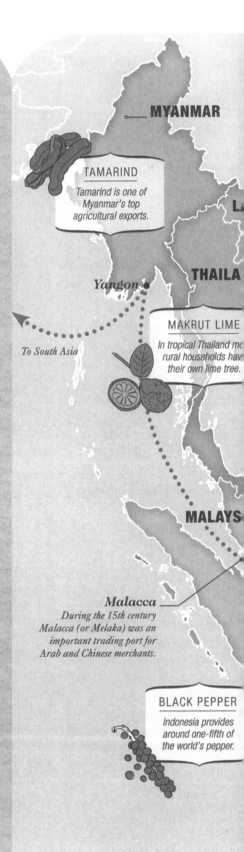

MYANMAR

TAMARIND
Tamarind is one of Myanmar's top agricultural exports.

L...

Yangon

THAILA...

MAKRUT LIME
In tropical Thailand m... rural households hav... their own lime tree.

To South Asia

MALAYS...

Malacca
During the 15th century Malacca (or Melaka) was an important trading port for Arab and Chinese merchants.

BLACK PEPPER
Indonesia provides around one-fifth of the world's pepper.

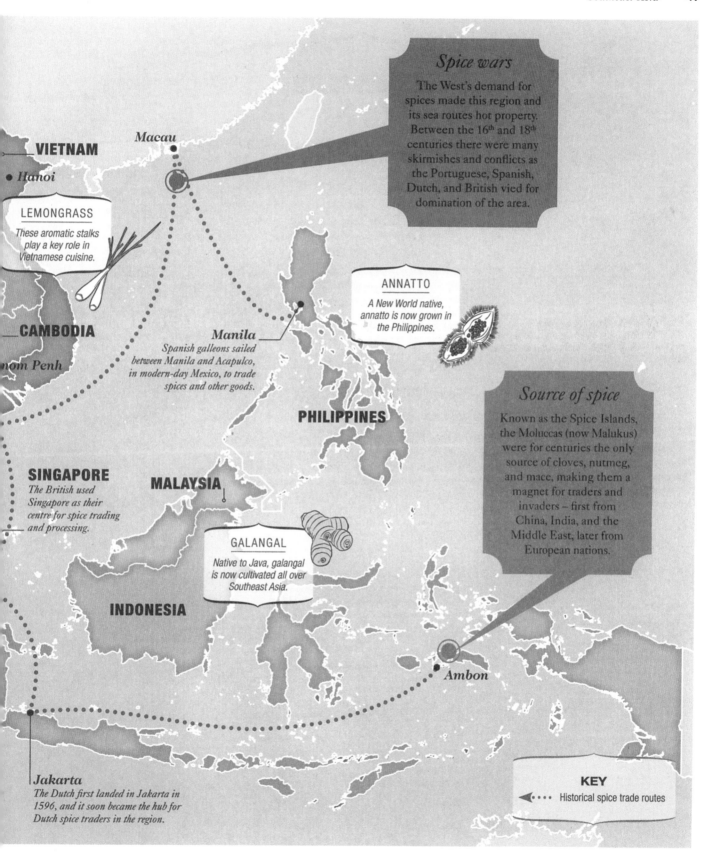

VIETNAM

• *Hanoi*

Macau

LEMONGRASS

These aromatic stalks play a key role in Vietnamese cuisine.

CAMBODIA

nom Penh

Manila
Spanish galleons sailed between Manila and Acapulco, in modern-day Mexico, to trade spices and other goods.

ANNATTO

A New World native, annatto is now grown in the Philippines.

PHILIPPINES

Spice wars

The West's demand for spices made this region and its sea routes hot property. Between the 16th and 18th centuries there were many skirmishes and conflicts as the Portuguese, Spanish, Dutch, and British vied for domination of the area.

Source of spice

Known as the Spice Islands, the Moluccas (now Malukus) were for centuries the only source of cloves, nutmeg, and mace, making them a magnet for traders and invaders – first from China, India, and the Middle East, later from European nations.

SINGAPORE
The British used Singapore as their centre for spice trading and processing.

MALAYSIA

GALANGAL

Native to Java, galangal is now cultivated all over Southeast Asia.

INDONESIA

• *Ambon*

Jakarta
The Dutch first landed in Jakarta in 1596, and it soon became the hub for Dutch spice traders in the region.

KEY

◀ ••• Historical spice trade routes

SPICE PALETTE

ginger

garlic

Signature

Ginger, garlic, chilli
Early Chinese, and more
recent Thai, influences
have had a lasting impact
on the Burmese spice palette:
few savoury dishes omit the
base notes from this trio of
fresh spices.

Supporting

**Garam masala, mild curry powder,
sesame, coriander, lemongrass,
turmeric, cumin**
Centuries of trade across
the Bay of Bengal have
seen Indian flavours
well integrated into local
recipes, with garam masala
a particularly popular blend.

Supplementary

**Black pepper, star anise,
cinnamon, curry leaf,
tamarind, poppy**
Spices that pack a punch
without flooring other flavours
are valued in Myanmar: the
aromatic warmth of pepper,
star anise, and cinnamon;
sulphurous curry leaves;
sour tamarind; and richly
nutty poppy seeds.

MYANMAR
Punchy | Fragrant | Savoury

Varied terrain, climate, and ethnicity bring eclectic
flavours to the Burmese table, where dry spices from
India and Bangladesh are used sparingly to enhance
the flavour of freshly pounded spice pastes. The
cuisine is less sweet than that of neighbouring
Thailand, with sour notes popular, and a preference
for subtle pungency over pure heat. Fresh, fragrant
leaves (both cultivated and wild) find their way into
most dishes, as do various fermented fish products.

> **"**
>
> *Influences from over 100
> indigenous groups, and from
> powerful neighbours, feed into
> Myanmar's rich bank of
> traditional recipes.*
>
> **"**

LOCAL SPICE BLEND

Burmese garam masala

India's most famous spice mix is also popular
in Myanmar. Use as the basis for spicing a dish,
or like a seasoning added at the end of cooking.

1 tsp coriander seeds	**1 tsp** cardamom pods
1 tsp black peppercorns	**1 tsp** cloves
1 tsp cumin seeds	**2.5cm (1in)** cinnamon stick
2 dried bay leaves	**2** star anise

Dry-roast all the spices in a frying pan, over a low heat, until
fragrant. Leave to cool before grinding into a fine powder.

*Pandan leaves
are used to impart
a vanilla-like
flavour, particularly
to coconut-based
sweet dishes.*

Thai salad of sliced
steak, chilli and
lime dressing,
and *khao kua*. ▼

black pepper

lemongrass

LOCAL SPICE BLEND
Khao kua

This ground roasted rice powder, infused with fresh spices, is a key ingredient in both Laotian *larb* and Thai beef salad. Its unique texture means nothing else can be used as a substitute.

5 tbsp uncooked glutinous ("sticky") rice
1 lemongrass stalk, sliced
1 thumb-sized piece of galangal, sliced
3 makrut lime leaves, roughly torn

Dry-roast all the ingredients in a frying pan, over a medium heat, stirring frequently, until the rice turns golden brown. Leave to cool, then pick out the spices and pound the rice using a pestle and mortar until coarsely ground.

THAILAND, LAOS, AND CAMBODIA
Hot | Fresh | Clean

No other country along the spice route embraced the chilli pepper as enthusiastically as Thailand. It's impossible to imagine Thai cuisine without liberal quantities of chilli, though the blander flavours of the Cambodian kitchen do hint at what pre-chilli Thai food would have tasted like. Other spice staples were less eagerly adopted and, like cooks in land-locked Laos, Thai chefs still prefer freshly pounded spice pastes. Cambodian cuisine, meanwhile, draws its more subtle heat from the black pepper that has been grown in the country since the 13th century.

Signature
Chilli, garlic, coriander root, lemongrass
All four fresh spices are near ubiquitous in Thai and Laotian cuisine. Cambodian cooks use less chilli but get enthusiastically stuck into the rest.

Supporting
Lime leaf, galangal, ginger, *krachai* (wild ginger), black pepper, tamarind
Several roots in the ginger family, along with makrut lime leaves, provide further fresh flavours, while tamarind is drawn on for sour notes, and black or white pepper for slow-burning heat.

Supplementary
Turmeric, clove, nutmeg, cinnamon, fennel, cardamom, pandan leaf, green pepper
Although widely available throughout the region, dry spices tend to find their way into a limited number of dishes rather than everyday cooking.

SPICE PALETTE

lemongrass

star anise

Signature

Ginger, garlic, chilli
A Chinese influence can
be seen in this trio of fresh
spices, which provide the
foundation that supports
all the herbs so beloved
by Vietnamese cooks.

Supporting

**Lemongrass, coriander root,
star anise, allspice, turmeric,
dill, pandan leaf, black pepper**
Aromatic spices add a rich
flavour profile to broths and
stews, while black pepper
provides background heat in
dishes deemed too delicate
for chilli.

Supplementary

**Cardamom, liquorice,
fennel, cinnamon, clove**
Rarely centre stage, these
spices are often used to
bring in background notes
of sweetness and warmth.

VIETNAM
Fresh | Warm | Delicate

While not as influenced by the spice trade as Malaysia
or Indonesia, Vietnam nevertheless keeps a well-
stocked spice cupboard. Most dishes carry some vital
base notes from dried aromatics, but, on the plate, it
tends to be the abundance of fresh herbs that stands
out more. Southern Vietnamese cuisine is more richly
spiced than its northern counterpart, while sour,
salty notes are prevalent throughout the country.
To an already well-balanced Vietnamese kitchen,
French colonialists brought a delicate way with more
European spices, such as dill, fennel, and liquorice.

LOCAL SPICE BLEND

Nuoc cham

No Vietnamese table setting
is complete without a bowl
of *nuoc cham* dipping sauce,
used for dunking anything
from spring rolls to grilled
meats and seafood.

2 bird's eye chillies,
roughly chopped
1 garlic clove, roughly chopped
2 tsp palm sugar
juice of **½** a lime
2 tbsp Vietnamese fish sauce
(*nuoc mam*)

Place the chilli, garlic, and sugar
in a pestle and mortar, and pound
into a paste. Squeeze in the lime
juice, add 2 tablespoons of water
and the fish sauce, then mix well.

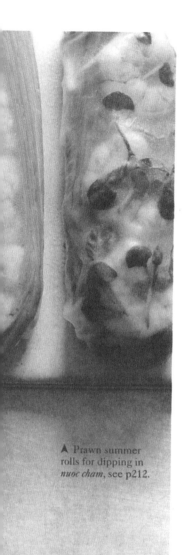

▲ Prawn summer rolls for dipping in *nuoc cham*, see p212.

Bird's eye chillies are popular in Vietnam and were probably introduced in the 16th century by the Portuguese.

MALAYSIA AND SINGAPORE

Complex | Rich | Fusion

The southern Malay port of Melaka was ideally placed to become a major trading hub, both for ships plying the Indo-Chinese seas, and those bound for more distant destinations on the spice route. As a result, throughout Malaysia and Singapore, significant Chinese, Indian, and Muslim communities endure to this day, and the regional cuisine is distinguished by a willingness to embrace such varied cultural influences and experiment with new flavours. The concept of fusion food, as we know it, was arguably born in Melaka, where Chinese, Indian, Arabic, and European ingredients often find themselves in the same cooking pot.

LOCAL SPICE BLEND

Malaysian fish curry paste

Layering a fresh base of galangal, garlic, and shallots with an Indian-style dry spice masala, this classic fusion paste can be used to make a quick fish curry by mixing it with coconut milk and simmering with chunks of any firm white fish.

2 tsp coriander seeds	**thumb-sized piece** of galangal, peeled and roughly chopped
1 tsp cumin seeds	
½ tsp fennel seeds	
½ tsp black peppercorns	**3 fat garlic cloves,** roughly chopped
4 medium-sized dried chillies	
½ tsp turmeric	**50g (1¾oz)** shallots, roughly chopped

Lightly toast the whole dry spices in a frying pan, leave to cool, then grind to a powder along with the turmeric. In a food processor or using a hand blender, blitz together the galangal, garlic, and shallots with a splash of water to form a purée. Mix the dry masala with the fresh purée to form the curry paste.

Signature

Ginger, garlic, chilli
The classic Southeast Asian flavour trilogy forms the base of most savoury recipes in Malaysia and Singapore, but the three are rarely used on their own.

Supporting

Cardamom, turmeric, dried chilli, black pepper, clove, coriander seed and root, cumin, cinnamon, curry leaf, lemongrass, galangal, tamarind, pandan leaf, lime leaf
Dried spice mixes add warm, earthy base notes to support the fresh aromatics of the likes of lemongrass, makrut lime, and curry leaves.

Supplementary

Fennel, anise, star anise, dried ginger, cassia, Sichuan pepper, sesame
Malay cooks were enthusiastic adopters of most new arrivals along the Spice Route, creating richly flavoured dishes with multi-layered spicing.

SPICE PALETTE

ginger

garlic

Signature

Garlic, ginger, shallot
Indonesian cooks draw on
a wide range of spices, but
few are used as extensively as
this trio, which form the base
notes for countless recipes.

Supporting

**Nutmeg, mace, clove, salam leaf,
galangal, lemongrass, pandan
leaf, lime leaf, tamarind, chilli,
turmeric, cumin, cinnamon**
Indigenous nutmeg, mace,
and cloves mingle with
fresh, aromatic leaves
and roots – including
sour, astringent salam
leaf – and the warm notes
of Spice Route imports.

Supplementary

**Black pepper, coriander, curry
leaf, cardamom, curry powder,
Sichuan pepper, caraway, anise**
Further spices from India,
along with Sichuan pepper
from China, and caraway
and anise from the
Mediterranean, complete
Indonesia's broad-ranging
arsenal of flavours.

INDONESIA

Vibrant | Complex | Diverse

Spread across an archipelago of more than 17,000
islands with strong natural resources and long-
established trade routes, Indonesia enjoys a spice
palette that's as eclectic as the heritage of its people.
The traditional saying "if your eyes do not water, the
food is not good" hints at a nation that fully embraced
the 16th-century arrival of the chilli pepper, but there
is more to Indonesian cuisine than eye-watering
heat. Fragrant local spices mix with exotic imports
from Persia, India, and China to create dishes with
complex depth of flavour.

LOCAL SPICE BLEND
Bumbu

Many Indonesian recipes are based on some
kind of *bumbu* (spice paste). Every region –
and cook – has their own favourite version.
This one's quite classic.

1 tsp coriander seeds
3 cloves
½ tsp white peppercorns
1 pinch grated nutmeg
1.5cm (½in) galangal, peeled
and roughly chopped
2.5cm (1in) fresh turmeric,
peeled and roughly chopped

6 shallots, roughly chopped
3 garlic cloves,
roughly chopped
2 red chillies, roughly chopped
1 tsp shrimp paste
1 tbsp vegetable oil, for frying

You can use a blender, but the best flavour is achieved by
pounding using a pestle and mortar: start with the dry spices,
then add fibrous galangal and turmeric, followed by the
remaining fresh ingredients, finally mixing in the shrimp paste.

Heat the oil in a wok or frying pan, add the spice mixture,
and cook over a high heat, stirring frequently,
for approximately 5 minutes, or until the paste
turns golden. Cool before using.

*Adobo is a Spanish
term applied by
colonists to the native
Filipino technique of
preserving meat with
vinegar and spices.*

The simple
selection of
spices for *adobo*
marinade. ➤

LOCAL SPICE BLEND

Adobo marinade

Filipino recipes often start with a simple marinade, usually with coconut vinegar in a starring role. Use this recipe to marinate chicken or pork overnight. See pp208–09 for a spiced-up version of *adobo*.

100ml (3½fl oz) coconut vinegar
50ml (1¾fl oz) soy sauce
3 garlic cloves, crushed
1 tsp black peppercorns
2 bay leaves

Place all the ingredients in a small saucepan and bring the mixture to the boil. As soon as it boils, remove from the heat and allow to cool down to room temperature before using.

PHILIPPINES

Mild | Colourful | Aromatic

Given how important food is to the Filipino way of life (five meals a day is the norm), dishes are surprisingly unadventurous with their spicing. Most classic recipes use no more than two or three spices, and very few would classify as "spicy" in the hot sense. Despite more than 300 years of Spanish rule, which clearly left their mark on a spice palette that feels more European than Asian, the Philippines didn't take to the chilli pepper in anywhere near the same way as the Spanish and their trading partners along the Spice Route.

SPICE PALETTE

bay

black pepper

Signature

Bay, black pepper, garlic
This "holy trinity" of Filipino cuisine is in nearly every savoury recipe, including the unofficial "national dish" *adobo*.

Supporting

Annatto, turmeric, ginger, lemongrass, pandan leaf
Spices are rarely used to add heat, but often as natural food colouring (red from annatto, yellow from turmeric) or for their aromatic properties.

Supplementary

Chilli powder, paprika, tamarind
When Filipinos do reach for the hot stuff, they tend to choose powder over fresh chillies, or opt instead for paprika. Tartness is valued over heat, and tamarind is the main flavour constituent of the popular *sinigang* broth.

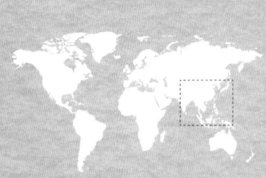

World of Spice

EAST ASIA

Despite being at the far eastern edge of
the Old World, East Asia has influenced the
global spice trade hugely, from key stops on
15th-century trade routes to being the
world's fourth-largest spice producer today.
Most of the spices here are mild; Sichuan
pepper is a tongue-tingling exception.

SPICE REGIONS

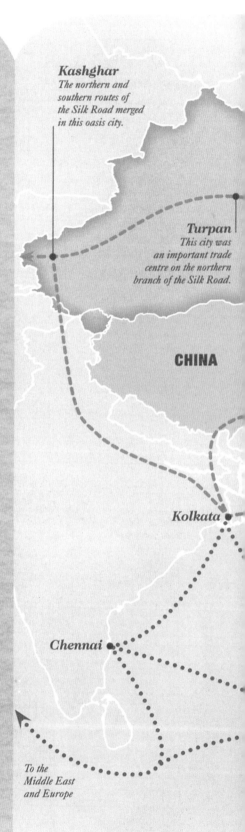

Kashghar
*The northern and
southern routes of
the Silk Road merged
in this oasis city.*

Turpan
*This city was
an important trade
centre on the northern
branch of the Silk Road.*

CHINA

Kolkata

Chennai

*To the
Middle East
and Europe*

The road begins

The Silk Road was the world's greatest trade thoroughfare until the 15th century, when faster sea routes were found. The Chinese city of Chang'an (now Xi'an) marked the start of this 6,400-km (4,000-mile) network.

Xi'an
The Western Market in the old city of Chang'an was a meeting place for traders from all over the world.

Beijing

PERILLA SEEDS
Also known as shiso, perilla is grown mainly in central Japan.

SESAME
Grown widely in East Asia, sesame is one of the world's oldest crops.

GINGER
Ginger from China's Shandong region is prized for its high quality.

JAPAN

SOUTH KOREA

SICHUAN PEPPER
This key spice is a distinguishing feature of East Asian cuisine.

Yeosu

Shanghai

Nagasaki
Portuguese traders made Nagasaki their Japanese base in the late 16th century.

LIQUORICE
Liquorice gives meat marinades in southern China a sweet-salty tang.

TAIWAN

CASSIA
This sweet spice grows in the tropical climate of southern China.

Macau

Yangon

Manila

Chengdu
The city's market is known worldwide for the quality of its Sichuan peppercorns.

Flavour exchange

The spice trade between China and the West went both ways: spices such as cassia travelled west to Central Asia and Europe, whilst ginger and saffron went east and became integral to cooking in many regions of China.

KEY
◄···· Historical spice trade routes
◄─ ─ Ancient Silk Road

SPICE PALETTE

red chilli

garlic

Signature

Sesame, red chilli, garlic
Korean spicing is full-bodied and robust, but subtle, too, with the pungency of chillies and garlic often balanced by the rich, toasty flavours of sesame, or mellowed through fermentation in dishes such as kimchi.

Supporting

Ginger, black pepper, perilla seeds
Supporting spices such as ginger and pepper add deeper notes of pungency, with hints of mint and liquorice from the perilla seeds.

Supplementary

Green chilli, cinnamon
While red chillies provide the fire in fermented dishes, green chillies and cinnamon bolster the pungent and sweet aspects of Korean dishes.

SOUTH KOREA
Fiery | Warm | Pungent

Korean cooking has only recently become as popular across the world as other long-established Asian flavours, but with its intoxicating blend of heat and acidity in a cuisine that is complex, robust, and subtle, it has quickly come to be a firm favourite. Unsurprisingly, given Korea's location and history of colonization by China and Japan, influences and spices from these neighbours abound, with chillies, ginger, and garlic playing important roles. Yet the key techniques of fermentation and preservation in which they are employed create flavours and dishes that are unique to this country.

LOCAL SPICE BLEND
Yangnyeomjang

A very popular and deeply flavoured, pungent seasoning sauce. It also makes a great dipping sauce and marinade.

2 tsp white sesame seeds
3 tbsp soy sauce
1 tbsp toasted sesame oil
½ tsp rice vinegar
2 tsp *gochugaru* (dried chilli peppers)
½ tsp caster sugar or honey
1 garlic clove, crushed
1 spring onion, sliced

Dry-roast the sesame seeds in a frying pan, over a high heat, stirring until just golden. Mix with the other ingredients and keep in the fridge for up to a week.

◄ Pan-fried tofu with spring onions and *yangnyeomjang.*

JAPAN

Fresh | Mild | Bright

For a relatively small archipelago, Japan is surprisingly diverse in its cooking and spicing. The southern "barbarian" cuisine was developed in the 16th and 17th centuries through interaction with the few foreigners who were allowed to visit the island. The Portuguese introduced deep-frying, chillies, and vinegar, the Chinese brought ramen, gyoza, and dumplings, and the British introduced curry. This Western-influenced cuisine contrasts with the more subtle *washoku* (Japanese cuisine) found elsewhere in the country.

"

All Japanese cooking shares an emphasis on the natural world, with seasonality at the heart of everything.

"

LOCAL SPICE BLEND

Shichimi-togarashi

This aromatic mixture can be used as a table condiment or for flavouring curries, grilled meats, and noodle dishes.

2 tbsp *sanshō* or Sichuan pepper, finely ground

2 tbsp dried orange, yuzu, or lemon peel

4 tbsp chilli powder

2 tbsp nori seaweed flakes

2 tsp black sesame seeds

2 tsp hemp seeds, flax seeds, or chia seeds

2 tsp garlic powder

Simply mix together all the ingredients.

SPICE PALETTE

sesame

star anise

ginger

Signature

Sesame, *sanshō*, ginger
The richness of sesame, citrus heat of *sanshō* (similar to Sichuan pepper), and fresh zing of ginger are representative of a cuisine that manages to be both pungent and subtle.

Supporting

White pepper, chilli, garlic, star anise
Additional levels of heat come from the fire of chillies and the slow burn of white pepper, while garlic and star anise bring complex aromas of sulphur and liquorice.

Supplementary

Clove, allspice, cinnamon, black pepper
These stronger spices are used sparingly, their aim being to layer flavours without overwhelming the key Japanese elements of freshness and brightness.

SPICE PALETTE

Sichuan pepper

sesame

Signature
Ginger, sesame, Sichuan pepper
Freshness and simplicity are
at the heart of this region's
dishes, in which spices are
used sparingly alongside
lamb, beef, fish, and wheat.

Supporting
Star anise, garlic
Tofu and fresh vegetable
dishes in Shandong cooking
make use of fragrant star
anise, while among Beijing's
Muslim population garlic is
combined with lamb and beef.

Supplementary
Cumin, chilli
Having originated in
the kitchens of Chinese
Muslims, *yangrou chuan*
(lamb skewers) are coated
in cumin and chilli and are
a favourite in Beijing.

NORTH CHINA
Salty | Sour | Light

In a country as vast as China there are great
variations in cuisine, but when it comes to
spicing it's a more integrated picture, with
most of the country incorporating the gentle
spices used in the Shandong, Henan, and Beijing
cuisines of northern China. Shandong cooking
is characterized by subtle flavours that preserve
rather than dominate the main ingredients.
Henan features more delicate but harmonious
flavours, and Beijing draws influences from both,
with an emphasis on sour notes provided by the
dark vinegar used throughout the region.

> **"**
> *Shandong is regarded as
> the primary cuisine of China's
> eight major regional cuisines.*
> **"**

LOCAL SPICE BLEND
Shandong spice bag

This collection of spices is used to infuse the
master stock for many northern Chinese chicken
stews, such as Dezhou- or Daokou-style.

10 cardamom pods
2 star anise
½ tbsp whole Sichuan pepper
½ tbsp cloves
½ tbsp ground cumin

7.5cm (3in) cinnamon stick
10–12cm (4–5in) piece
of liquorice root
dried peel of an orange
or tangerine

Place all the ingredients in a piece of muslin or spice bag,
tie tightly, and drop into the cooking water.

△ Muslin and
ingredients ready
to make a Nanjing
spice bag.

*Lotus seeds have
a mild, sweet
flavour reminiscent
of fresh almonds
and pine nuts.*

SPICE PALETTE

ginger

white pepper

Signature

Ginger, white pepper, Sichuan pepper, sesame
The signature spices of this region never dominate; rather they are used to bring out the flavours of the fish or meat component of a dish.

Supporting

Star anise, cinnamon, lotus seed
The four styles of Jiangsu's cuisine use sweet aromatics like star anise and cinnamon in dishes such as Wuxi spare ribs. Desserts like lotus porridge are another favourite.

Supplementary

Black cardamom, fennel, cumin, liquorice
Suzhou's pastries are made with a wide range of spices and spice-based ingredients that offer smoky, sweet, salty, and nutty flavours, as well as powerful aromatics.

LOCAL SPICE BLEND

Nanjing spice bag

These spices are combined with sliced fresh ginger and Shaoxing wine to flavour the stock for the renowned Nanjing salted duck (see p212).

6 cloves
4 star anise
1 tsp whole white pepper, crushed
6 bay leaves
dried peel of a tangerine
1 tsp liquorice root powder
1 tsp salt

Place all the ingredients in a piece of muslin or spice bag, tie tightly, and drop into the cooking water.

EAST CHINA
Subtle | Aromatic | Sweet

Eastern Chinese cuisine is a contrasting mix of flavours determined largely by the varying terrain. Inland, the Yellow Mountains and the Huangshan area are the preserve of unique foraged ingredients in Anhui cuisine, which is often sweetened with sugar to create hearty peasant food. The coast, by contrast, taking in Jiangsu, Zhejiang, and Shanghai, has a refined gourmet cuisine whose emphasis is on subtly aromatic flavours that highlight the abundant sea and river food of the region.

SPICE PALETTE

ginger

garlic

Signature
Garlic, ginger, chilli, sesame
South China's signature spices intensify and enhance the techniques that are geared towards preserving the flavour, colour, and texture of the main ingredients.

Supporting
Black pepper, *shajiang*, five-spice powder
Woody black pepper and camphorous *shajiang* powder add a kick to many dishes, while five-spice is used to enhance sweetness and fragrance.

Supplementary
White pepper, liquorice
Liquorice root replaces five-spice where a more lingering, bitter, aniseed flavour is desired. In Taiwan, white pepper is often partnered with pork belly.

SOUTH CHINA
Sour | Aromatic | Sweet

If there's one Chinese cuisine that has travelled throughout the world, it's the Cantonese food from Guangdong, the most southerly of the country's eight great food traditions. Thanks to extensive emigration from this largely coastal region, cooking techniques such as steaming and stir-frying travelled the world. Simple condiments and spicing – light soy sauce, garlic, ginger, and sesame oil – dominate in Canton cooking, but other parts of south China's cuisines, notably Hunan, Fujian, and Taiwan, offer more intense flavours – spicy, sour, sweet, and bitter – via techniques such as drying and preserving and a wider use of spices.

LOCAL SPICE BLEND
Five-spice powder
Yes, you can buy this in any supermarket, but homemade is truly a million times better. Use as a rub for roasting meats, or add to stir-fries and stews.

2 star anise
1 tsp fennel seeds
1 tsp cloves
5cm (2in) cinnamon stick
1 tbsp whole Sichuan pepper

Simply grind all the spices to a fine powder, sieving out any fibres if necessary.

Prawn stir-fry flavoured with five-spice, see p213. ▼

> *Shajiang is also known as sand ginger, and has the same fresh heat as ginger, with a mildly medicinal edge.*

WEST CHINA
Fruity | Warm | Earthy

The Silk Road introduced the Sichuan region to less familiar spices brought by travellers from neighbouring western and central Asia. The result was a wide blend of flavour sensations, including sour, sweet, bitter, salty, hot, and spicy, especially in the far-west region of Xinjiang. Here, where the population is more than 50 per cent Muslim, spices such as cumin and saffron, as well as dried fruits, feature heavily in lamb, chicken, and vegetable dishes from Uyghur and Kazakh cuisine.

> "
> *Western Chinese cuisine is dominated by Sichuan pepper, used in the region's cooking for more than 2,000 years.*
> "

LOCAL SPICE BLEND
Chilli black bean sauce

This is a homemade version of *doubanjiang*, the Sichuan fermented bean paste. Use as a marinade, dip, or in stir-fries.

200g (7oz) red bird's eye chillies, finely chopped

50g (1¾oz) fermented black beans, rinsed and chopped

2 tbsp vegetable oil

1 tbsp rice wine

2 tsp dark rice vinegar

1 tbsp sugar

3 garlic cloves

7.5cm (3in) piece of ginger, chopped

Fry the chillies and beans in the oil for 1 minute. Add the wine and vinegar and simmer for 3 minutes. Add the sugar and simmer for 10 minutes. Then add the garlic and ginger, and cook until the oil floats on the surface. Store in the fridge for up to 3 weeks.

SPICE PALETTE

Sichuan pepper

bird's eye chilli

Signature
Bird's eye chilli, Sichuan pepper, garlic
In classic Sichuan dishes such as beef in chilli broth, this trio of spices often dominates the flavour.

Supporting
Star anise, ginger, sesame, black cardamom
Used in both Sichuan and Xinjiang cuisine, star anise, ginger, sesame, and black cardamom add complexity to dishes such as bang bang chicken and hotpot.

Supplementary
Cumin, saffron, cinnamon
In Kashgar, the market is filled with the flavours that made their way to this Uyghur region from the Middle East, including cumin, cinnamon, and saffron.

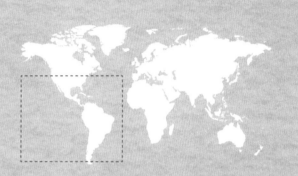

World of Spice

THE AMERICAS

An amalgamation of flavours and textures from mountains high, valleys low, seas and oceans, forests and islands – plus an array of influences from all corners of Asia and Europe – the spice map of the Americas is eclectic, bold, and complex.

SPICE REGIONS

To Asia

Two-way traffic

Spices travelled in both directions between continents. Cloves, pepper, and cinnamon reached the New World by sea from Asia; in return, chillies, vanilla, and cocoa beans were all transported back to the Old World.

To Asia

KEY

◄···· Historical spice trade routes

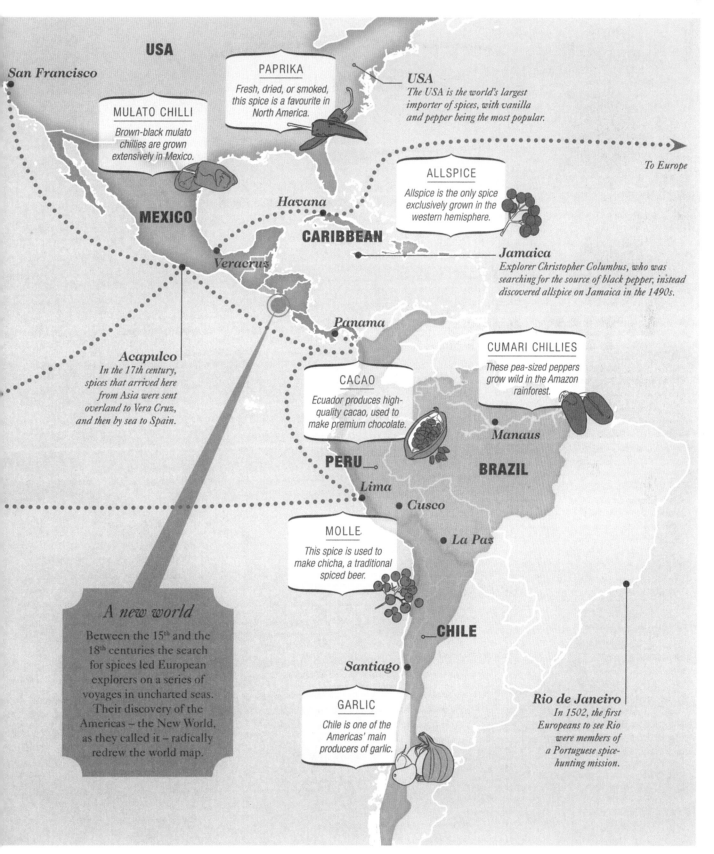

USA

San Francisco

PAPRIKA
Fresh, dried, or smoked, this spice is a favourite in North America.

USA
The USA is the world's largest importer of spices, with vanilla and pepper being the most popular.

MULATO CHILLI
Brown-black mulato chillies are grown extensively in Mexico.

To Europe

ALLSPICE
Allspice is the only spice exclusively grown in the western hemisphere.

Havana

MEXICO

CARIBBEAN

Veracruz

Jamaica
Explorer Christopher Columbus, who was searching for the source of black pepper, instead discovered allspice on Jamaica in the 1490s.

Panama

CUMARI CHILLIES
These pea-sized peppers grow wild in the Amazon rainforest.

Acapulco
In the 17th century, spices that arrived here from Asia were sent overland to Vera Cruz, and then by sea to Spain.

CACAO
Ecuador produces high-quality cacao, used to make premium chocolate.

Manaus

PERU

BRAZIL

Lima

Cusco

La Paz

MOLLE
This spice is used to make chicha, a traditional spiced beer.

A new world
Between the 15th and the 18th centuries the search for spices led European explorers on a series of voyages in uncharted seas. Their discovery of the Americas – the New World, as they called it – radically redrew the world map.

CHILE

Santiago

GARLIC
Chile is one of the Americas' main producers of garlic.

Rio de Janeiro
In 1502, the first Europeans to see Rio were members of a Portuguese spice-hunting mission.

SPICE PALETTE

Scotch bonnet chilli

clove

allspice

Signature

Scotch bonnet chilli, allspice, clove, ginger, nutmeg, cinnamon
Bar Scotch bonnet, these staples are used across both sweet and savoury recipes, with native allspice joined by fragrant spices from Asia.

Supporting

Black pepper, cumin, garlic, paprika, habanero chilli
Mainly used to create greater depth in one-pot dishes, these spices bring flavours from South Asia, the Mediterranean, and Central America.

Supplementary

Turmeric, coriander, fenugreek, cayenne chilli, nigella
The first three spices are integral to West Indian curry powder, cayenne is used in hotter jerk blends, and roasted nigella seeds flavour breads and vegetable dishes.

THE CARIBBEAN

Adventurous | Bold | Spicy

When European explorers went looking for the Indies, they found instead the Caribbean Islands. Centuries of empire-building ensued, almost wiping out the indigenous peoples and turning the West Indies into a new trading hub on the Spice Route. Such forces made Caribbean cuisine into the melting pot that it is today, fusing Amerindian, African, Creole, Spanish, Dutch, Portuguese, British, Latin American, Persian, South Asian, and Indonesian cuisines.

> "
> *The Caribbean's varied cultural influences make for adventurous spicing, including sweet, sour, hot, tangy, and earthy flavours.*
> "

LOCAL SPICE BLEND

Jamaican jerk rub

A dry seasoning used to marinate chicken, fish, pork, and beef. Invented in Jamaica and adapted around the Caribbean.

2 tsp allspice	**1 tsp** ground ginger
1 tsp whole black peppercorns	**½ tsp** ground cinnamon
½ tsp cloves	**2 tsp** onion powder
1 tsp chipotle or cayenne powder	**2 tsp** garlic powder
1 tsp paprika	**1 tsp** dried thyme
1 tsp grated nutmeg	**2 tsp** brown sugar
	2 tsp sea salt

Grind the whole spices and combine with the rest of the ingredients. Flavour intensity depends on marinating time.

Mexican oregano has pronounced citrus and aniseed notes. Dried, it is added to chilli powder blends.

Roast vegetables served with *mole* sauce. ▼

LOCAL SPICE BLEND

Mole mix

Each country has its own version, always made with three different chillies.

2 each dried ancho, pasilla, and mulato chillies
3 tbsp cacao nibs
1 tbsp sesame seeds
2cm (¾in) piece of cinnamon stick
¼ tsp cumin seeds
¼ tsp anise seeds
¼ tsp whole black peppercorns
¼ tsp cloves
¼ tsp dried thyme
¼ tsp dried marjoram
1 dried bay leaf, crumbled

Toast the whole spices in a dry frying pan over a medium heat, stirring, until fragrant. Mix with the remaining ingredients and grind. Stir into fried onions and garlic, then simmer with chopped tomatoes for a mole sauce.

MEXICO AND CENTRAL AMERICA

Hot | Toasted | Complex

The range of spices used in everyday Mexican and Central American dishes is as complex as the region's historical culinary influences. Cultural fusion is key: Belizean cuisine draws from the Maya, the Garifuna, Creole, and even the British, while Mexico's dishes can thank Mayan, Aztec, and Spanish-colonial influences. The Mayans frequently made use of red and green jalapeño chillies; the Aztecs used chipotle chillies, cacao, and vanilla. All of these spices made their way round the world via the Spanish conquistadores, who in return brought cumin, pepper, cloves, and cinnamon.

SPICE PALETTE

paprika

cumin

Signature

Chilli (ancho, jalapeño, pasilla, mulato, chipotle, *chile de arbol*), paprika, cumin
For that fiery kick, any of 60 different chillies offering varying degrees of heat are used, either fresh, whole dried, or powdered, while cumin is essential to chilli powder mix.

Supporting

Black pepper, garlic, cinnamon, clove, vanilla
Black pepper is usually slow cooked to draw out its complex pungency. Savoury and sweet dishes draw on the latter three spices, with cinnamon traditionally flavouring local chocolate bars.

Supplementary

Cacao, sesame, allspice, Mexican oregano, coriander, annatto
The first three spices all contribute to *mole* sauce, while Mexican oregano and coriander seeds bring extra complexity to chilli blends. Annatto is mainly used for colouring meats, rices, and stews.

turmeric

garlic

Signature

Chilli (*ají amarillo, rocoto/locoto, merquén*), cumin, garlic
Chillies lead Andean cuisine, offering heat, freshness, and colour, and often starring as the main ingredient. Spicy sauces pep up any slow-cooked dish.

Supporting

Pepper (white and black), *molle* (pink pepper), turmeric, cinnamon, paprika (sweet and smoked)
These warming spices tend to be added to slow-cooked stews and soups to create depth of flavour and colour.

Supplementary

Annatto, coriander, mustard
More usually seen in Mexico and Central America, annatto brings colour to Andean dishes, too. Coriander and mustard seeds add subtly aromatic and warming touches.

THE ANDES

Warming | Earthy | Piquant

Spanning some 4,500 miles, the Andes mountain range traces a route from Argentina and Chile, crossing through Bolivia, Peru, and Ecuador, up to Colombia and Venezuela. People who live in or close to the Andes at 1,000 to 3,000m (3,250 to 10,000ft) or more above sea level usually slow cook hearty dishes such as stews and soups. Chillies play a dominant role; *ají amarillo* (yellow chilli) has been cultivated for more than 8,000 years and was a key ingredient in Inca cuisine. In Andean Peru, *uchucuta* is a spicy salsa made from *rocoto* chilli and herbs; *llajua* is the Bolivian and Argentine equivalent.

LOCAL SPICE BLEND

Chimichurri

A popular fresh spice and herb sauce, widely served with sausages and steak.

1 tsp chilli powder
½ tsp dried chilli flakes
½ tsp paprika
2 garlic cloves, finely chopped
1 onion, finely chopped
4 tsp finely chopped parsley or coriander
1 tsp finely chopped oregano
3 tsp white or red wine vinegar
6 tbsp olive oil
salt and black pepper, to taste

Place all the ingredients in a bowl and stir well to combine them.

▲ Slices of steak dressed with *chimichurri*.

Molle are the dried pink berries of the Peruvian peppertree. They are similar to peppercorns, but the plants are unrelated.

AMAZON BASIN

Exotic | Mysterious | Hot

Ranging across nine different countries, the Amazon is the world's largest rainforest. Ancestral influence, convergence between the rainforest's three key countries – Brazil, Peru, and Colombia – plus an array of European influences, most significantly from Portugal and Spain, all play their part in this extensive larder. Amazon chillies are some of the world's hottest, and are often used – along with garlic, cumin, and turmeric – to marinate meat and fish.

> **"**
> *Dominating the spice wheel are chillies, grown here since pre-Columbian times.*
> **"**

LOCAL SPICE BLEND

Tucupí

A Brazilian broth-like sauce made from cassava root and served with duck, pork, or fish.

2kg (4½lb) sweet cassava root, peeled and roughly chopped
2 garlic cloves, finely chopped
3–4 hot, fresh red chillies, finely chopped (or more to taste)
1 tsp whole black pepper, ground

Blend the cassava with 750ml (1¼ pints) water in a food processor to form a thick purée. Transfer to a muslin cloth placed over a bowl and squeeze out the starchy juice.

Leave to settle, then strain off the liquid into a jug, discarding the sediment. Cover the liquid and leave at room temperature for 24 hours to ferment. Pour into a pan, stir in the spices, bring to the boil, and simmer for 30 minutes.

SPICE PALETTE

black pepper

cumin

Signature

Black pepper, chilli (*ají amarillo, ojito de pez, pinguita de mono, pucunucho, cumari, malagueta, cayenne*), garlic, cumin
With hundreds of native chilli species, in all shapes and sizes, and ranging from mild to fiery hot, it's little wonder that they cross the spectrum to be used in many dishes.

Supporting

Annatto, açaí berries, *jambú*, tonka beans, turmeric
Jambú is a flower whose numbing effect leads to its nickname of "toothache plant". It is used in *tacacá*, one of Brazil's most popular soups.

Supplementary

Priprioca, guaraná*, ginger, cinnamon, clove, paprika, vanilla, *copoazú, macambo
The dried roots of *priprioca* (a type of sedge grass) offer up a peppery hit, while *guaraná* seeds are used as a stimulant more than for their flavour, but are very common. *Copoazú* and *macambo* are relatives of cacao.

SPICE PALETTE

pepper

vanilla

Signature

Chilli (jalapeño, poblano, ancho, cayenne), garlic, pepper (black and white), vanilla
After garlic and chillies, pepper and vanilla are the most common spice imports, adding everyday warmth to savoury and sweet dishes, respectively.

Supporting

Paprika, mustard, ginger, nutmeg, cinnamon, cloves
Milder forms of mustard are used particularly in table condiments, while nutmeg, cinnamon, and cloves are the spices of choice for sweet baking.

Supplementary

Anise, sesame, cumin, paprika, turmeric, mace
These diverse spices are used in dishes drawn from the cuisines of the Middle East and Asia, which have an increasingly strong influence on the North American food scene.

NORTH AMERICA
Hot | Sweet | Eclectic

European settlers brought a limited range of spices with them to North America, mainly as a way to preserve food for the long journey. Gradually spices from Central America (chilli, annatto), the Caribbean (allspice), and South America (*molle*) left their mark, though only chilli has enjoyed an enduring popularity thanks to the proximity of Mexico. Today, North American cuisine is a true fusion, in which dishes from Mexican fajitas to Indian curries and Japanese ramen form part of the everyday diet.

"

The eclectic spice palette of contemporary North America reflects the diverse migration that defines the region.

"

LOCAL SPICE BLEND
BBQ rub

A dry spice blend for barbecued meat, with many regional variations. This recipe takes brown sugar from Kansas City and paprika from the Memphis rub.

1 tbsp ground cumin
1 tbsp chilli powder
1 tbsp ground black pepper
1 tbsp onion powder
1 tbsp garlic powder

½ tbsp cayenne pepper
3 tbsp brown sugar
2 tbsp smoked paprika
2 tbsp sea salt

Mix together all of the ingredients to create a dry rub for barbecued meat, from steak or brisket to pulled pork and chicken wings.

Aji limo is a hot chilli with a strong lemony flavour, although it takes its name from the Lima region.

Ceviche of raw white fish marinated in *leche de tigre*. ➤

LOCAL SPICE BLEND

Leche de tigre

Translating as "tiger's milk", this is the marinating liquid for ceviche, the raw fish dish originally from Peru and now enjoyed all along the Pacific coast.

½–1 *ají limo*, habanero, or other hot chilli, finely chopped
1 fat garlic clove, crushed
2.5cm (1in) piece of ginger, coarsely grated
1 tbsp fresh coriander stalks, finely chopped
½ small red onion, finely chopped
juice of **5** limes
salt, to taste

Combine all the ingredients and refrigerate for 1 hour before using to marinate fresh white fish. *leche de tigre* is traditionally drunk after the fish has been eaten.

PACIFIC SOUTH AMERICA

Fresh | Spicy | Citrus

From the Gulf of Panama to the tip of Patagonia, the vast coastline of South America naturally draws from its waters for sustenance: all manner of seafood is fried, grilled, or stewed. Indigenous culture, Spanish colonization, the slave trade, and Asian and Arab migrations have all influenced dishes, from delicate chilli and coconut fish soups to hearty *charquicán* (beef and vegetable stew). Chillies are key to the spice mix, often used fresh in ceviche, while dishes in the Nikkei tradition – a fusion of Japanese and Peruvian cooking – draw on flavourings such as ginger, sesame, tamarind, and *umeboshi* (pickled plum) paste.

ginger

coriander stalks

Signature
Chilli (*ají limo, panca, chombo*), garlic, coriander stalks
Chillies, usually used fresh, are extremely prevalent and usually add zip to seafood dishes, while coriander stalks bring a slightly floral flavour.

Supporting
Cumin, chilli powder, ginger, fresh lime, turmeric
Cumin is used as a seasoning, while chilli powder provides a milder alternative to fiery whole chillies. Fresh, clean ingredients, such as ginger and lime, are added to soups and stews.

Supplementary
Annatto, sesame, tamarind
Tangy tamarind adds both sweet and sour touches, sesame lends a nutty richness, and annatto's bright red hue colours soups and stews.

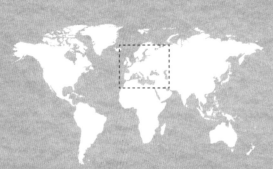

World of Spice

EUROPE

Despite the diversity of European cuisine, the continent has few native spices. Almost everything used across the region was introduced via the global spice trade, the legacy of which is that European spice palettes are broadly similar – though interesting regional variations still occur.

SPICE REGIONS

European empires

Competition between the nations of Europe to control global trade, including in spices, led to these countries setting up colonies in Africa, Asia, and the Americas. By the end of the 19th century, Europe controlled 85 per cent of the world's land.

GREAT BRITAIN

London

FRAN

ESPELETTE CHILLI
This mild chilli is used to spice traditional French Basque dishes.

PORTUGAL

FRAN

SPAIN

Lisbon

To Asia and the Americas

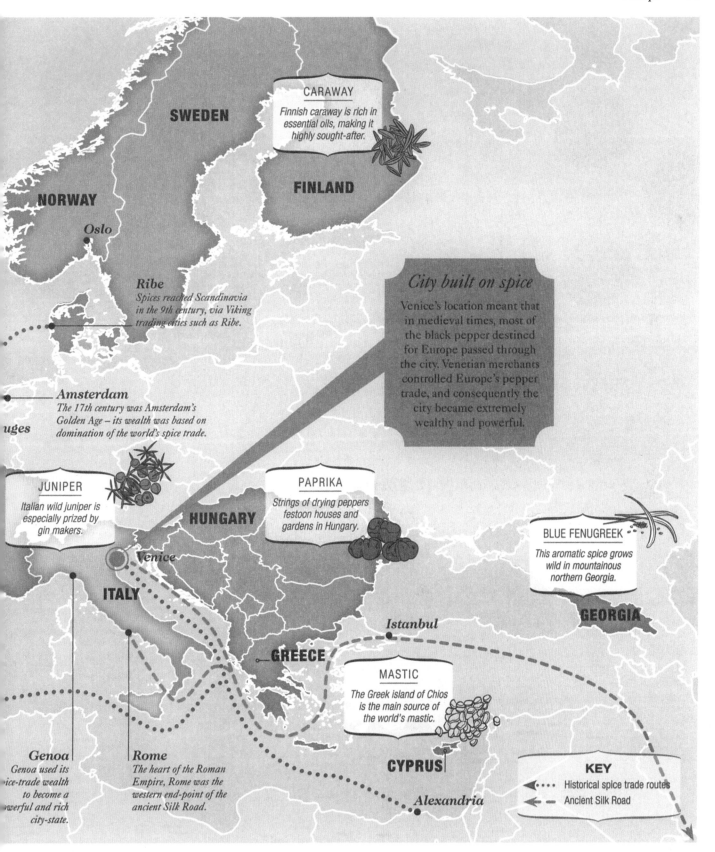

CARAWAY

Finnish caraway is rich in essential oils, making it highly sought-after.

SWEDEN

FINLAND

NORWAY

Oslo

Ribe
Spices reached Scandinavia in the 9th century, via Viking trading cities such as Ribe.

City built on spice

Venice's location meant that in medieval times, most of the black pepper destined for Europe passed through the city. Venetian merchants controlled Europe's pepper trade, and consequently the city became extremely wealthy and powerful.

Amsterdam
The 17th century was Amsterdam's Golden Age – its wealth was based on domination of the world's spice trade.

uges

JUNIPER
Italian wild juniper is especially prized by gin makers.

PAPRIKA
Strings of drying peppers festoon houses and gardens in Hungary.

HUNGARY

BLUE FENUGREEK
This aromatic spice grows wild in mountainous northern Georgia.

Venice

ITALY

GEORGIA

Istanbul

GREECE

MASTIC
The Greek island of Chios is the main source of the world's mastic.

Genoa
Genoa used its ~ice-trade wealth to become a ~werful and rich city-state.

Rome
The heart of the Roman Empire, Rome was the western end-point of the ancient Silk Road.

CYPRUS

Alexandria

KEY
•••• Historical spice trade routes
– – Ancient Silk Road

SPICE PALETTE

nutmeg

dill

caraway

Signature
Cardamom, cinnamon, caraway, dill, nutmeg
Cardamom is king, although cinnamon runs a close second, while caraway is more popular in Finland. Dill seeds are common in pickling solutions.

Supporting
Ground ginger, clove, allspice, liquorice, mustard, saffron, juniper
Ginger, cloves, and allspice are used for more seasonal sweet bakes, although allspice is also paired with pickled herring and pork. Salty liquorice is a unique Scandinavian treat.

Supplementary
Angelica, bitter orange powder, dried rosehips, fennel
Angelica and powdered orange peel are common in Finland – the latter is added to biscuits, cakes, and the traditional Easter dessert, *mämmi*. Rosehips are used to flavour jelly, jams, oil, and tea.

SCANDINAVIA
Sweet | Earthy | Aromatic

The clean, refined fare of the Nordic countries has some of the most distinctive spicing in all of Europe. Most notable is the use of cardamom, supposedly brought north by the Vikings from Constantinople 1,000 years ago. Danish pastries and other Nordic bakes would be lost without the festive flavours of cinnamon, cloves, ginger, and allspice. The region's love of pickling and preserving sees a profusion of aromatics such as dill seed and the native juniper, which also appears with game and in Finland's *sahti* beer. Brown mustard is common both as a condiment and as a whole spice.

LOCAL SPICE BLEND

Finnish gingerbread spice

A fragrant, warming spice mix and the perfect base for the classic Finnish gingerbread biscuits known as *piparkakut*.

1 tbsp bitter orange powder
2 tsp ground cloves
2 tsp ground ginger
2 tsp ground cinnamon
1 tsp ground cardamom

Simply mix all the ingredients together. Enough to flavour the dough for around 30 biscuits.

▲ Biscuit shapes cut from Finnish *piparkakut* dough, see p213.

Bitter orange powder is made from the dried peel of Seville oranges, and imparts a sour citrus flavour.

GREAT BRITAIN
Warming | Gutsy | Festive

One of the culinary legacies of the British Empire is a taste for South Asian spicing, often amalgamated into all-purpose curry powders. These are used liberally in the eponymous "national dish", as well as a gravy-like sauce for chips, the vegetable preserve known as piccalilli, and the summer buffet staple Coronation chicken. Dating further back to Britain's medieval past is a love of warming aromatic spices for flavouring sweet bakes and alcoholic drinks consumed in the cold winter months; to a Brit, cloves, cinnamon, nutmeg, ginger, and mace are all immediately evocative of the festive season.

LOCAL SPICE BLEND

Mulling spice

Warm red wine or cider is infused with this collection of whole sweet spices and traditionally drunk at winter celebrations, from Bonfire Night to orchard wassails on Twelfth Night.

2 cinnamon sticks
6 cloves
6 allspice berries
½ nutmeg
2 bay leaves

Add the spices to a pan of red wine or cider and heat to simmering point, or tie them up first in a piece of muslin for easy retrieval. Add sugar or honey, orange and/or lemon slices, and rum or sloe gin to taste. Enough for two bottles of red wine or 1.75 litres (3 pints) of still cider.

Signature

Curry powder, allspice, clove, cinnamon
Curry powder is a mix of spices including fenugreek, turmeric, ginger, and cumin. Allspice is used in a myriad of sweet dishes and also in salted beef.

Supporting

Mustard, cayenne pepper, nutmeg, mace, ginger, juniper
Potent English mustard is an essential accompaniment to cooked meats, fiery cayenne is used in devilled kidneys, and juniper is most often used in game dishes.

Supplementary

Saffron, white pepper, coriander, anise, turmeric
Historically, saffron and white pepper were popular, but their traditional use has largely dwindled to Cornish buns and preserved meats, respectively. In addition to use in pickling spice, coriander seeds flavour Lancastrian Goosnargh cakes.

SPICE PALETTE

garlic

mustard

Signature
Garlic, mustard, fennel, nutmeg
French cooking and garlic are utterly inseparable. Whether smoked, fresh, or green, for many it is the defining taste of Gallic food.

Supporting
Caraway, vanilla, anise, white pepper, juniper, saffron
White pepper is essential to the *quatre épices* mix, and you'll find juniper used in Alpine regions, and saffron for the southern fish stew *bouillabaisse*. Caraway, vanilla, and anise flavour creams and cakes.

Supplementary
Angelica, tonka bean, clove, mace
The French kitchen utilizes a number of more unusual spices: angelica stalk is added to sweets and *digestif* liqueurs, while the powerful tonka bean is infused into creams and custards.

FRANCE
Pungent | Fragrant | Comforting

France doesn't immediately spring to mind as a country with a spice-rich cuisine, yet the word itself is derived from Old French *espice* (meaning "seasoning"), and it was the 18th-century French botanist Pierre Poivre who broke the Dutch stranglehold on clove and nutmeg with smuggling raids to the Moluccas Spice Islands. Indeed, it's hard to imagine a classic Dauphinoise potato without the warmth of nutmeg, Provençal cookery without the aniseedy notes of fennel, or innumerable French dishes without garlic or Dijon and Bordeaux mustards.

> "
> *French cooking tends to draw heat from garlic and pepper, but chillies feature in Basque and Provençal dishes.*
> "

LOCAL SPICE BLEND
Quatre épices

This "four spices" mix is often used to season terrines. Proportions can be tweaked and, confusingly, cinnamon added as a fifth spice.

1 tbsp white peppercorns
1 tsp cloves
1 tsp ground nutmeg
1 tsp ground ginger

Grind the whole spices and combine with the nutmeg and ginger. To make a mix for sweet bakes, replace the white pepper with allspice or cinnamon.

LOCAL SPICE BLEND
Paella mix

Saffron and *pimentón* are essential to the flavour of paella, Spain's versatile rice-based dish.

2 pinches of saffron
3 tbsp *pimentón* (a mixture of smoked and sweet)
2 tsp garlic powder
2 tsp onion powder
1 tsp cayenne pepper
1 tsp ground black pepper
1 tsp dried oregano
1/2 tsp dried parsley
1/2 tsp ground cloves
1/2 tsp ground cumin

Grind the saffron threads using a pestle and mortar, and combine with the remaining ingredients. Makes approximately 6 tablespoons.

SPAIN AND PORTUGAL
Smoky | Sweet | Piquant

Brought back from the Americas by Columbus in the late 1400s, sweet and chilli peppers are inescapable in this region. Spanish cooks often reach for the mildness of *pimentón*, while the Portuguese brave the heat of malagueta chillies. Dried nora peppers are essential to the Catalan romesco sauce for fish, and green *guindilla* chillies are used in a hot sauce from the Canaries. Saffron abounds in Andalusian cuisine and the Valencian classic, paella, while cinnamon laces sweet Portuguese dishes.

Spice mix and ingredients ready for paella, see p213. ▼

SPICE PALETTE

Pimentón

piri piri chilli

Signature

Pimentón, chilli (malagueta)
Spain's vivid red *pimentón* (paprika) comes in three varieties: *dulce* (sweet), *agridulce* (bittersweet), and *ahumado* (smoked). Hot malagueta chillies are popular in Portuguese stews and other meat dishes.

Supporting

Pimentón picante, dried nora peppers, chilli (piri piri), garlic, saffron
Pungent *pimentón picante* is less popular than its milder variants, but makes a regular appearance in the Canaries and Galicia. Piri piri is used interchangeably with malagueta in Portugal.

Supplementary

Dried choricero peppers, chilli (*guindilla*, *alegrías*), cacao, anise, cloves, cinnamon
Cacao nibs are occasionally used in game and beef stews. Fragrant anise is paired with chestnuts in Portugal and with dried figs in Catalonia.

SPICE PALETTE

vanilla

black pepper

fennel

Signature

Chilli (*peperoncino*), black pepper, fennel
Hot peppers have long been popular in southern Italy, although their appeal is increasingly spreading north. More than anywhere else in Europe, black pepper transcends being a mere seasoning in Italy.

Supporting

Coriander, nutmeg, garlic, saffron, clove, vanilla
Coriander seeds are a popular flavouring for meat dishes, and it can seem as if almost every Italian cheese dish features nutmeg.

Supplementary

Ginger, cacao, liquorice, cinnamon, anise
Ginger is used sparingly, while cacao nibs may feature in the sweet and sour *agrodolce* sauce. Calabrians pair liquorice with game and use it to flavour liqueurs.

➤ Penne pasta with *arrabiata* sauce, Parmesan, and fresh basil.

ITALY

Punchy | Rustic | Warming

Italy played a key role in the story of spice when the Republic of Venice dominated the trade from the 8th to 15th centuries. Today, varied regional palettes reflect Italy's history as a collection of separate states, but fennel, nutmeg, and saffron are popular countrywide for flavouring meats, cheeses, pasta dishes, and risottos. The fiery food of Calabria uses the hot *peperoncino* chilli to spice cheese, salami, and oil. Cloves, too, are prevalent both in sweet dishes – the compact Sienese *panforte* tart, for instance – and in rustic savoury ones.

LOCAL SPICE BLEND

Arrabiata sauce

Translating as "angry", this quick pasta sauce gets its fiery reputation from liberal quantities of chilli and black pepper.

1 tbsp hot red chilli flakes
1 tsp dried oregano
1 tsp garlic powder
1 tsp salt
1 tsp ground black pepper
1 tbsp olive oil
50g (1¾oz) cubed pancetta
1 onion, finely chopped
2 x 400g cans chopped tomatoes

Combine the first five ingredients and set aside. Heat the oil and fry the pancetta and onion for 5 minutes. Add the spice mix and tomatoes, and simmer for 10 minutes. Serve with penne pasta.

SOUTHEAST EUROPE
Unusual | Earthy | Generous

The food of these eastern Mediterranean and former communist states is far from spice heavy, and Greek food in particular tends to favour herbal flavouring. That said, Hungarian paprika (introduced by the Turks in the 17th century), and Georgian blue fenugreek represent two of Europe's most distinctive flavours. Chillies appear often in Balkan cooking, but rarely for heat; what warmth there is tends to come from black pepper. Caraway is often paired with cabbage in Hungary and occasionally with fish in the Balkans, and cinnamon is popular in Romania. The food of Cyprus is often laced with coriander seeds and, unusually, pine-like mastic.

blue fenugreek

paprika

Signature
Blue fenugreek, black pepper, paprika
Blue fenugreek, almost exclusively used in Georgian cuisine, tastes a little like hay and burnt sugar. Both seeds and pods are ground to a powder.

Supporting
Cinnamon, caraway, fennel, chilli
As well as providing the warm spice notes of Greek moussaka, cinnamon features heavily in Romanian cookery, which is otherwise spice light. Caraway is sometimes added to the Greek orange-flavoured *loukaniko* sausage.

Supplementary
Dill, carob, vanilla, mastic
Dill seeds are often paired with fish in Eastern Europe. Carob is popular as an alternative to chocolate, and is used in Greek carob cake; Hungarian creams and cakes are often infused with vanilla.

Peverino is a peppery biscuit from Venice dating from the city's heyday as the European centre of the spice trade.

LOCAL SPICE BLEND

Khmeli-suneli

Universally popular in Georgia, *khmeli-suneli* is used as a meat rub or in hearty stews, although it is highly palatable sprinkled on almost anything.

1 tbsp coriander seeds
1 tsp black peppercorns
2 dried bay leaves
1 tbsp blue fenugreek leaves
1 tbsp blue fenugreek seeds
1 tsp garlic powder

½ tsp chilli powder
2 tbsp dried marigold
2 tbsp dried savory
2 tbsp dried marjoram
1 tbsp dried mint
1 tbsp dried dill
1 tsp dried hyssop

Grind the whole spices and combine with the rest of the ingredients.

SPICE | *profiles*

Discover all you need to know about the world's top spices with in-depth science and practical advice, and begin your culinary adventure with innovative recipes.

CINNAMON

Sweet | Aromatic | Warm

BOTANICAL NAME
Cinnamomum verum

ALSO KNOWN AS
Ceylon cinnamon, "true" cinnamon.

MAJOR FLAVOUR COMPOUND
Cinnamaldehyde.

PARTS USED
Dried bark of tender shoots.

METHOD OF CULTIVATION
Trees are coppiced at 18–24 months of age and the stump covered, causing it to grow like a bush. New shoots are removed at the base and stripped for their bark.

COMMERCIAL PREPARATION
Inner layers of bark are dried in the sun and rolled together by hand into long "quills", which are graded and cut.

NON-CULINARY USES
In perfumery and as a natural antiseptic.

The plant
Cinnamon is a small evergreen tree in the laurel family, found in the wild growing in wet tropical forests.

Young shoots *are harvested for their bark every two years*

Powder
Ground spice quickly loses its flavour. Buy it in small quantities, keep in an airtight container in a cool, dark place, and use within 6 months.

Whole
Cinnamon sticks will keep their flavour for up to a year. Lighter brown, thinner, more fragile sticks are higher quality.

Spice story

From 1600 BCE, ancient Egyptians used a type of cinnamon for incense and as an embalming spice, importing it from Asia via African traders. It is not known for certain whether this was cinnamon from Sri Lanka or Chinese cassia. From the 8th century CE, Arab merchants dominated the trade and invented tall tales to protect their sources and high prices. In one such myth, giant birds were said to gather the bark from an unknown land, using it to make nests on high cliffs, and the only way to collect it was to lure the birds away with large pieces of meat. The real source remained a mystery to Europeans until the Portuguese found cinnamon trees growing in Sri Lanka in the early 1500s, and promptly occupied the island. They in turn were ousted by the Dutch, who then fought the British for centuries over control of the territory and lucrative trade.

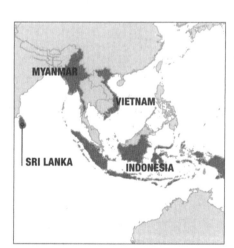

Region of cultivation
Cinnamon is native to the island of Sri Lanka and is now also notably cultivated in Myanmar, Vietnam, Indonesia, and the islands of the Seychelles off the coast of East Africa.

Kitchen creativity }

Cinnamon does not in itself taste sweet, but rather it enhances the perception of sweetness in other ingredients. This makes it perfect for sweet bakes and desserts, and for drawing out sweet notes in savoury dishes.

BLENDING SCIENCE

Cinnamaldehyde is the main flavour compound and is sensed by temperature receptors on the tongue, giving cinnamon a warming quality that makes it a good partner for other warming spices. Make further connections through the woodiness of caryophyllene, the penetrating aroma of eugenol, and the floral notes of linalool.

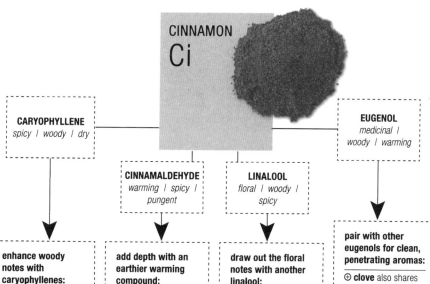

CINNAMON
Ci

CARYOPHYLLENE
spicy | woody | dry

EUGENOL
medicinal | woody | warming

CINNAMALDEHYDE
warming | spicy | pungent

LINALOOL
floral | woody | spicy

enhance woody notes with caryophyllenes:

⊕ **allspice** shares eugenol, for warming spiciness

⊕ **peppercorn** adds pungent heat from piperine

add depth with an earthier warming compound:

⊕ **cumin** contributes the equally warming and tenacious cuminaldehyde

draw out the floral notes with another linalool:

⊕ **cardamom** brings complex citrus, floral, and penetrating eucalyptus aromas

pair with other eugenols for clean, penetrating aromas:

⊕ **clove** also shares caryophyllene and should be used sparingly

⊕ **anise** and **star anise** will enhance the sweetening effect of cinnamon and add liquorice notes

FOOD PARTNERS

⊕ **Fruit** Mix cinnamon powder with sugar and scatter over peaches, figs, apples, and pears before baking or grilling, or add to the batter for a plum or cherry clafoutis.

⊕ **Sweet bakes** Use ground cinnamon to flavour Nordic buns, Italian *panforte*, or French *pain d'épices*.

⊕ **Tomatoes and aubergines** A cinnamon-infused tomato sauce makes an excellent topping for baked aubergines.

⊕ **Red meats** Add a stick or two to a lamb tagine, an Iranian *khorak* beef stew, or the stock of a fragrant Vietnamese beef *pho* noodle soup.

⊕ **Pigeon** Cinnamon is the main flavouring in Moroccan *pastilla* pigeon pie with filo pastry.

BLENDS TO TRY

Use and adapt these recipes for classic blends featuring cinnamon:

Advieh p27
Burmese garam masala p48
Jamaican jerk rub p64
Mole mix p65
Mulling spice p73

RELEASE THE FLAVOUR

The taste components in cinnamon need time to escape from its woody matrix, and the critical flavour compound, cinnamaldehyde, does not dissolve in water.

Add early in cooking to give flavours time to suffuse the dish.

Fat and alcohol will help disperse cinnamaldehyde.

Steam is also a carrier of cinnamaldehyde, so boil vigorously with a lid on the pan.

CASSIA

Sweet | Peppery | Astringent

BOTANICAL NAME
Cinnamomum cassia, C. loureirii, C. burmanii

ALSO KNOWN AS
Chinese cinnamon (*C. cassia*), Vietnamese/
Saigon cinnamon (*C. loureirii*), Indonesian/
Java/Korintje cinnamon (*C. burmanii*).

MAJOR FLAVOUR COMPOUND
Cinnamaldehyde.

PARTS USED
Dried bark, unripe fruits ("buds").

METHOD OF CULTIVATION
The bark is harvested every second year
in the monsoon season from trees that are
at least four years old.

COMMERCIAL PREPARATION
Strips of inner bark are dried in the sun
and curl up naturally, forming thick shards;
buds are dried.

NON-CULINARY USES
In perfumes; in Chinese medicine to treat
diarrhoea and dyspepsia.

The plant
Cassia comes from
an evergreen tree
in the laurel family,
and is closely related
to cinnamon.

**Leaves and
buds** *are also
aromatic,
unlike "true"
cinnamon*

Bark *is
coarse and
greyish brown*

Buds
The dried unripe fruits resemble
cloves and are used in the Far East
as a pickling spice.

Bark
The bark is darker,
thicker, more loosely
coiled, and harder to
snap than that of
cinnamon. It carries
a stronger aroma
and more intense
flavour.

Spice story

Cassia was used for medicinal purposes
in ancient China from 2700 BCE, and
was among the first spices to reach the
Mediterranean via the ancient trade
routes. The Egyptians used cinnamon
as a culinary spice and for its health
properties, but it is unclear whether
they used cinnamon or cassia. Persians
knew cassia and cinnamon as *darchini*,
and used them in savoury and sweet
dishes. By the 5th century BCE, cassia
had been identified as distinct from
cinnamon. Medieval English and
French cookbooks referred to cassia
and cinnamon as "canella", but cassia's
coarser flavour saw its status demoted:
in his 15th-century book of manners,
Bok of Nurture, John Russell wrote
that "Synamone is for lords, canelle
for common people". Today, cassia
accounts for nearly 50 per cent of the
world's cinnamon supply, and is a key
spice in China and Southeast Asia. It is
popular in North America, where most
"ground cinnamon" is actually cassia.

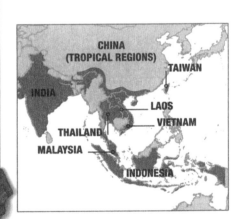

Region of cultivation
Cassia is native to the wet tropical forests
of southern China. It is cultivated across
southern and eastern Asia, but mainly in
southern China, Vietnam, and Indonesia.

Kitchen creativity }

Cassia has a sweet, warming taste, but is bitter and lacks the floral, citrus notes of cinnamon. Its deeper, spicier, less subtle flavour is best suited to robustly flavoured savoury dishes, although the spice can be used in sweet baking.

BLENDING SCIENCE

Cassia's flavour profile is dominated by cinnamaldehyde, the compound that gives cinnamon and cassia their recognisable taste. Tannins, which give a mouth-puckering astringency, are also present and it contains coumarin, a phenol absent in "true" cinnamon, as well as eucalyptus-scented cineole.

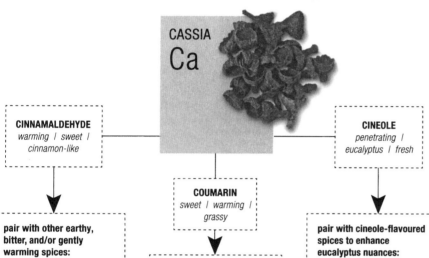

CASSIA
Ca

CINNAMALDEHYDE
warming | sweet | cinnamon-like

COUMARIN
sweet | warming | grassy

CINEOLE
penetrating | eucalyptus | fresh

pair with other earthy, bitter, and/or gently warming spices:

⊕ **carob** is sweet, earthy and contains cinnamaldehyde

⊕ **cumin** contributes an earthy, slightly bitter warmth

⊕ **star anise** adds herbal, earthy, and floral notes, and an undercurrent of liquorice

⊕ **ginger** brings pungent warmth and sweet citrus notes

combine with other sweet spices for a broader profile:

⊕ **mahleb** shares coumarin and gives an almond flavour

⊕ **nutmeg** is a star match, adding bittersweet woodiness

⊕ **vanilla** is honey sweet and slightly nutty

⊕ **anise** intensifies sweetness and adds herby notes

pair with cineole-flavoured spices to enhance eucalyptus nuances:

⊕ **cardamom** adds a sweet minty background

⊕ **bay** is rich in cineole and introduces a complex, piney, and floral freshness

⊕ **allspice** provides a sweet peppery warmth

⊕ **grains of Selim** has a medicinal flavour and adds pine, floral, and woody notes

FOOD PARTNERS

⊕ **Beef, pork** Include a piece of cassia bark with other warming spices in an Italian beef or oxtail ragu, beef rendang, or pork vindaloo.

⊕ **Pulses, grains** Add a piece of cassia bark to the base aromatic ingredients for a pilaf, dhal, or curry.

⊕ **Baking** Create the unmistakable aroma of American iced cinnamon rolls by using ground bark; add ground buds to Christmas confections, fruit cake, and spiced biscuit dough.

⊕ **Preserves** Infuse cucumber pickling brine, tomato chutney, or a barbecue sauce with cassia buds.

BLEND TO TRY

Use and adapt this classic blend featuring cassia:

Garam masala p40

Coumarin caution

Sweet-tasting coumarin can cause temporary liver damage if consumed in excessive amounts. Regular consumers of cinnamon-flavoured foods should therefore choose "true cinnamon" rather than cassia.

Children
3.5g (⅛ oz)

Adults
7g (¼ oz)

Medical authorities have recommended maximum weekly quantities of cassia, above which it should not be consumed for a long period.

RELEASE THE FLAVOUR

Most flavour compounds in cassia, including dominant cinnamaldehyde, do not dissolve in water and can struggle to escape from woody bark's matrix.

Cassia bark is best ground in an electric grinder

Grind cassia just before use to minimize the loss of flavour oils by evaporation.

Include fats and/or alcohol in a dish to help disperse flavour compounds.

Steam disperses cinnamaldehyde and a water-based dish can be infused with flavour if boiled in a lidded pan.

CLOVE

Sweet | Astringent | Camphorous

BOTANICAL NAME
Syzygium aromaticum

ALSO KNOWN AS
Nail spice: the common name in many languages translates as "nail spice", due to its shape.

MAJOR FLAVOUR COMPOUND
Eugenol.

PARTS USED
Flower bud.

METHOD OF CULTIVATION
Twice a year, the flower buds are picked by hand when they have just turned pinky-red and are almost ready to open.

COMMERCIAL PREPARATION
The buds are dried in the sun until they turn dark brown and harden.

NON-CULINARY USES
To flavour *kretek* cigarettes in Indonesia; in some dental products; and to treat nausea, indigestion, and inflammation.

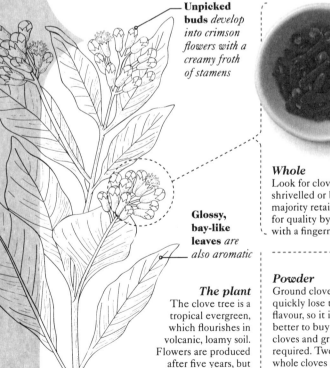

Unpicked buds *develop into crimson flowers with a creamy froth of stamens*

Glossy, bay-like leaves *are also aromatic*

The plant
The clove tree is a tropical evergreen, which flourishes in volcanic, loamy soil. Flowers are produced after five years, but the tree can remain productive for 100 years.

Round tops *are the unopened petals of the flower*

Whole
Look for cloves that are plump, not shrivelled or broken, and where the majority retain their rounded tops. Test for quality by pressing the "stem" with a fingernail: oil should ooze out.

Powder
Ground cloves quickly lose their flavour, so it is better to buy whole cloves and grind as required. Twelve whole cloves are roughly equivalent to a teaspoon of ground.

Spice story

The Moluccas (now Maluku) of Indonesia were once renowned as the Spice Islands thanks to a trio of indigenous spices – cloves, nutmeg, and mace – which were cultivated there, and nowhere else, for almost two millennia. Courtiers addressing the Emperor during the Chinese Hang dynasty (206 BCE–220 CE) used cloves to sweeten their breath, and the Romans, who named the spice *clavus* (Latin for nail), used it as an incense and perfume. In the Middle Ages, clove took off as a culinary spice in the West. At first the Republic of Venice had a virtual monopoly of the lucrative trade, but the Portuguese, Dutch, Spanish, and English fought a series of wars to seize control, with the Dutch eventually winning out. In the 18th century, Frenchman Pierre Poivre managed to smuggle clove seedlings to Mauritius.

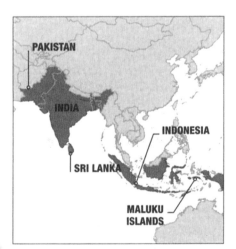

Region of cultivation
Indonesia is the largest producer of cloves, although most of the crop is used by the local *kretek* cigarette industry. Other major producers are Madagascar and Tanzania, with lesser amounts from India, Sri Lanka and Pakistan.

Kitchen creativity }

Clove's powerful flavour is usually tamed by blending it with other similarly warming spices to soften its dominance. Antiseptic properties make it a common spice for pickling, but use sparingly.

BLENDING SCIENCE

Clove has the highest eugenol content of any spice; this perfumed, warming phenol compound has a eucalyptus-like scent and a sweetening effect on the tongue. Woody caryophyllene is the other compound useful for pairing, and the flavour profile is rounded off with green banana-like methyl amylketone and minty methyl salicylate.

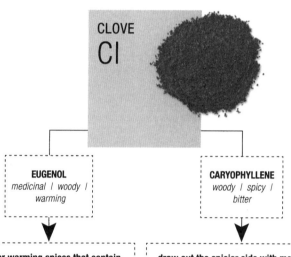

CLOVE
Cl

EUGENOL
medicinal | woody | warming

CARYOPHYLLENE
woody | spicy | bitter

pair with other warming spices that contain some eugenol:

⊕ **allspice** provides a sweet, peppery warmth

⊕ **liquorice** contributes sweetness and eucalyptus-like notes

⊕ **nutmeg** or **cinnamon** used sparingly adds warm spicy notes

⊕ **bay leaf** and **fenugreek** offer excellent savoury pairings

draw out the spicier side with more caryophyllene-carrying spices:

⊕ **grains of paradise** bring a peppery warmth and penetrating spiciness

⊕ **black pepper** lends warmth as well as woody notes

⊕ **cacao** adds rich, roasted, bitter flavours

FOOD PARTNERS

⊕ **Tomatoes and red cabbage** Add a pinch to tomato sauce or when braising red cabbage.

⊕ **Peaches** The fruit shares eugenol, making it a natural partner. Preserve in a sugar syrup infused with cinnamon, fresh ginger, and whole cloves (2–3 per peach).

⊕ **Beef and pork** Season a beef stew, pork braise, or classic French *pot-au-feu* with a few whole cloves, or use them in the masala for a Keralan beef curry.

⊕ **Milk** Add a clove or two to milk before scalding it to make a white sauce or an Indian *kheer* or *payasam* pudding.

⊕ **Hot drinks** Infuse tea or coffee with a whole clove for sweetness without the calories. Cloves are also an essential aromatic in mulled wine or cider.

BLENDS TO TRY

Try these recipes for classic blends featuring clove, or why not adapt them with some blending science?

Pilau masala p34

Vindaloo paste p44

Finnish gingerbread spice p72

RELEASE THE FLAVOUR

Clove's main flavour compounds, eugenol and caryophyllene, are oil based. They evaporate very quickly once released, and barely dissolve in water.

Use whole cloves or grind just before adding to the recipe.

Add early to give ample time for the flavour to diffuse out of the woody matrix.

Alcohol   *Oil*

Some oil/fat and/or alcohol is needed to distribute the flavour compounds.

ALLSPICE

Warm | Peppery | Sweet

BOTANICAL NAME
Pimenta dioica

ALSO KNOWN AS
Jamaican pepper, clove pepper, pimento.

MAJOR FLAVOUR COMPOUND
Eugenol.

PARTS USED
Dried berries; occasionally fresh leaves.

METHOD OF CULTIVATION
Twigs bearing bunches of berries are handpicked from trees in summer, when the berries are mature but still green.

COMMERCIAL PREPARATION
Berries are "sweated" (see vanilla curing, p100) and then dried for several days in the sun, or artificially, before being picked.

NON-CULINARY USES
Essential oil in perfumes and cosmetics; flavouring agent in medicines; pesticide and fungicide; antiseptic and digestive aid.

Spice story

The Mayans of Central America were using allspice from at least 2,000 BCE to embalm their dead, alleviate arthritis, and flavour chocolate beverages, while the indigenous peoples of the Caribbean used it to preserve meat and fish. Christopher Columbus was the first European to encounter the spice, in Jamaica in 1494, but mistook it for a variety of pepper, hence its Spanish name *pimento*. From the outset, Europeans were enamoured of its preservative powers, and the spice is used as a preservative in the Scandinavian fishing industry to this day. When Russia was invaded by Napoleon in the early 19th century, the Russian troops crushed allspice berries inside their boots to ward off bacterial and fungal foot infections.

The plant
Allspice is an evergreen tree in the myrtle family. It starts fruiting by the age of 7 or 8 years, and continues for up to 100 years.

Powder
Ground allspice quickly loses its potency. Buy in small quantities and keep sealed in a cool, dark place for up to 6 months.

Berries *ripen to dark purple if left on the tree, but lose most of their aroma*

Whole
The dried berries retain their flavour well and will keep almost indefinitely sealed in a cool, dark place.

Rough surface *contains tiny oil glands*

Most flavour *is concentrated in the wrinkled husk (or "pericarp"), not the seeds*

Glossy leaves *are used in the Caribbean for stuffing meat*

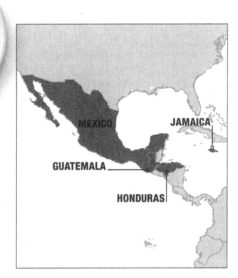

Region of cultivation
Native to the West Indies, Mexico, and Central America, allspice is mainly cultivated in Jamaica, but also in Honduras, Mexico, Guatemala, Hawaii, and Tonga.

Kitchen creativity }

True to its name, this full-bodied, versatile spice suits both sweet and savoury dishes, and blends comfortably with other spices. Allspice forms the backbone of Jamaican cuisine and is a key component of jerk seasoning.

BLENDING SCIENCE

Allspice partners with other spices that share the phenolic compound eugenol, which carries a strongly medicinal aroma. Other cineole-bearing spices with a eucalyptus-like, penetrating quality also pair well. Lesser amounts of the lighter terpenes phellandrene, linalool, myrcene, and pinene round off the taste profile.

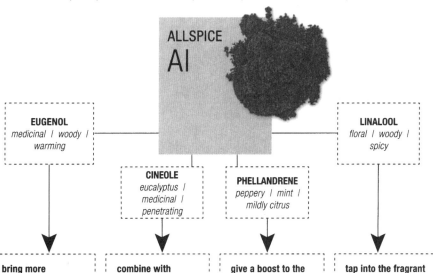

ALLSPICE
Al

EUGENOL
medicinal | woody | warming

CINEOLE
eucalyptus | medicinal | penetrating

PHELLANDRENE
peppery | mint | mildly citrus

LINALOOL
floral | woody | spicy

bring more complexity to the eugenol spectrum:
- ⊕ **nutmeg** and **cinnamon** will draw out warmer notes
- ⊕ **liquorice** emphasizes sweetly medicinal flavours
- ⊕ **bay** has a fresher, floral take on eugenol

combine with other cineoles to reinforce the sharp, fresh notes:
- ⊕ **galangal** will provide a citrusy edge
- ⊕ **cardamom** brings a penetrating warmth
- ⊕ **black cardamom** adds a smoky layer under the eucalyptus

give a boost to the peppery profile:
- ⊕ **star anise** also shares cineole for sweet aniseed piquancy
- ⊕ **black pepper** contributes a gentle pungent heat

tap into the fragrant floral side with other linalools:
- ⊕ **coriander** also adds zesty citrus notes
- ⊕ **grains of Selim** also share cineole and enhance the peppery side of allspice

FOOD PARTNERS

⊕ **Raw fish** Combine with mustard seeds as a pickling spice for raw fish, such as herring, or in Mexican *escabeche*.

⊕ **Sweet vegetables** To bring out the natural sweetness in vegetables, try it in a tomato sauce or soup, a beetroot *borscht*, or puréed sweet potato.

⊕ **Red meats** Stir ground spice into beef stews (particularly tomato-based) and pork or game pâté mixtures.

⊕ **Stone fruit and rhubarb** Sprinkle a pinch of ground allspice into the pan when poaching plums, apples, pears, or rhubarb.

⊕ **Sweet bakes** Add a pinch to biscuit dough, ginger cake, milk puddings, or steam puddings.

BLENDS TO TRY

Try these recipes for classic blends featuring allspice, or why not adapt them with some blending science?

Arabic baharat p26
Jamaican jerk rub p64
Mulling spice p73

RELEASE THE FLAVOUR

Extra layers of smoky, roasted aromas from pyrazines can be created by cracking and toasting the whole spice before grinding.

Before toasting, crush the berries lightly in a pestle and mortar to crack the shells.

Flavour compounds are concentrated in the shell

Cracking the shells helps to release the flavour oils, which are stored in tiny glands.

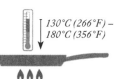

130°C (266°F) – 180°C (356°F)

Toast in a dry frying pan. New flavour compounds, such as pyrazines, form above 130°C (266°F), but at 180°C (356°F) burnt flavours dominate.

ANISE

Camphorous | Sweet | Warming

BOTANICAL NAME
Pimpinella anisum

ALSO KNOWN AS
Aniseed, sweet cumin, white anise.

MAJOR FLAVOUR COMPOUNDS
Anethole, anisyl alcohol.

PARTS USED
Fleshless fruits housing small seeds.

METHOD OF CULTIVATION
Grown as an annual crop, plants are pulled
up or mown when the fruits ripen.

COMMERCIAL PREPARATION
Fruits are left to dry for a week, then
threshed to separate the flower heads.

NON-CULINARY USES
The essential oil is used in cough
medicine, perfumes, and soaps. Also
known as a traditional remedy for
trapped wind and headaches.

Spice story

Records show ancient Egyptians using
anise as a cure for snake bites, but it
was the Romans who really developed
a fondness for its intensely sweet,
liquorice-like taste, drawing on anise to
flavour everything from the provisions
of a lowly centurion to the spiced wine
conditum and rich cake *mustaceoe*
served at special banquets. Anise
endured as a popular kitchen garden
plant into the Middle Ages, especially
in the Pyrenees, where monks produced
an anise-flavoured liqueur that the
French drank as an aperitif and also
added to stews and stocks. Today,
several liqueurs are still flavoured
with anise's essential oil, including
French *pastis*, Greek *ouzo*, Turkish
raki, and Arab *arrak*. Anise has also
long been regarded as an effective aid
to digestion; in India today the fruits are
commonly chewed whole after meals.

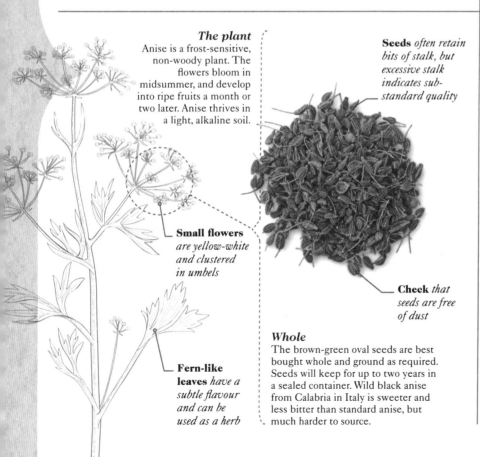

The plant
Anise is a frost-sensitive,
non-woody plant. The
flowers bloom in
midsummer, and develop
into ripe fruits a month or
two later. Anise thrives in
a light, alkaline soil.

Small flowers
*are yellow-white
and clustered
in umbels*

**Fern-like
leaves** *have a
subtle flavour
and can be
used as a herb*

Seeds *often retain
bits of stalk, but
excessive stalk
indicates sub-
standard quality*

Check *that
seeds are free
of dust*

Whole
The brown-green oval seeds are best
bought whole and ground as required.
Seeds will keep for up to two years in
a sealed container. Wild black anise
from Calabria in Italy is sweeter and
less bitter than standard anise, but
much harder to source.

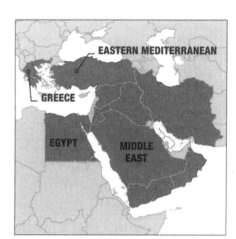

Region of cultivation
Anise is cultivated widely in its native region
of the eastern Mediterranean, Egypt, and the
Middle East, and commercial crops are now
grown as far afield as the Baltic countries and
Latin America. Cultivation has also spread east
to India, China, and Japan.

Kitchen creativity }

Anise is most frequently used to flavour sweet bakes, but has many savoury applications as well. Anise and fennel seeds are largely interchangeable in Asian cooking. If using an anise-based liqueur, add the lightest drizzle to avoid overwhelming a dish.

BLENDING SCIENCE

The unmistakable herby liquorice flavour of anise derives from the powerful anethole compound. Spice pairings can be made through the other, more subtle compounds – anisyl alcohol for its hints of cherry, vanilla, and chocolate, as well as estragole and traces of pinene and limonene.

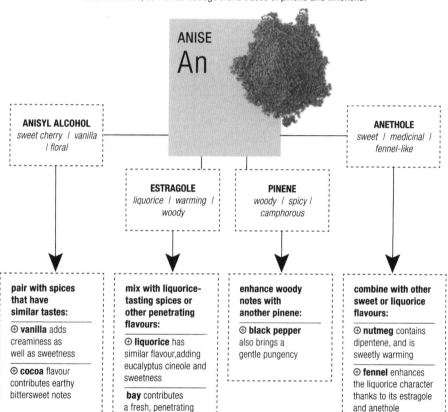

ANISE
An

ANISYL ALCOHOL
sweet cherry | vanilla | floral

ANETHOLE
sweet | medicinal | fennel-like

ESTRAGOLE
liquorice | warming | woody

PINENE
woody | spicy | camphorous

pair with spices that have similar tastes:
⊕ **vanilla** adds creaminess as well as sweetness
⊕ **cocoa** flavour contributes earthy bittersweet notes

mix with liquorice-tasting spices or other penetrating flavours:
⊕ **liquorice** has similar flavour, adding eucalyptus cineole and sweetness
bay contributes a fresh, penetrating herbiness

enhance woody notes with another pinene:
⊕ **black pepper** also brings a gentle pungency

combine with other sweet or liquorice flavours:
⊕ **nutmeg** contains dipentene, and is sweetly warming
⊕ **fennel** enhances the liquorice character thanks to its estragole and anethole

FOOD PARTNERS

⊕ **Celeriac** Add ground anise to a rich dressing for celeriac remoulade.

⊕ **Potatoes** Fry chopped onions with whole anise, curry leaves, and mustard seeds to flavour a potato and pea curry.

⊕ **Fish** Stir a teaspoonful into a South Indian-style coconut fish soup or tomato-based Mediterranean fish stew.

⊕ **Pork** Add the toasted seeds to sausage meat used for meatballs or stuffing.

⊕ **Fruit** Incorporate the seeds into a sweet pastry dough for a lemon, quince, or apple tart, or fry them in a batter for apple or banana fritters.

RELEASE THE FLAVOUR

Anethole dissolves in alcohol and oil but not in water. Fry gently in oil or other fats before mixing into the rest of the dish, or use alcohol (e.g. from rice wine or fermented soy sauce) in a liquid-based dish to disperse.

Alcohol   *Oil*

BLENDS TO TRY

Try these recipes for classic blends featuring anise, or why not adapt them with some blending science?
Burmese garam masala p48
Shandong spice bag p58
Nanjing spice bag p59

The sweetness compound

Anethole comprises up to 90 per cent of the flavour oils in anise and conveys the spice's liquorice flavour. The compound also excites the sweetness receptors on human taste buds, making it sweeter than sugar – but without the calories. It is no surprise, then, that anise has long been the spice of choice for flavouring sweet confectionery and liqueurs, especially before the ready availability of sugar.

13 times sweeter than sugar

STAR ANISE

Liquorice | Sweet | Warm

BOTANICAL NAME
Illicium verum

ALSO KNOWN AS
Chinese anise, badian anise, Siberian anise.

MAIN FLAVOUR COMPOUND
Anethole.

PARTS USED
Seed pods, seeds.

METHOD OF CULTIVATION
The fruits are harvested before they ripen, from late summer through to early winter.

COMMERCIAL PREPARATION
The fruits are dried, typically in the sun, until hard and woody and the pods' points have split to expose the seeds.

NON-CULINARY USES
In soaps, perfumery, and cough mixtures; in Chinese medicine for stomach pain, headaches, and rheumatism.

The plant
Star anise is the fruit of a small Chinese evergreen tree, closely related to magnolia. Trees can bear fruit for 100 years or more.

Leaves *are large, fragrant, and waxy, forming in bunches*

Narcissus-like flowers *turn yellow just before fruiting*

Whitish trunk *is aromatic*

Ground
The seeds and woody carpels are used to make the ground spice. The flavour compounds evaporate fast, so it does not stay fresh for long.

Each "arm" *is a carpel that contains a seed*

Whole pods
The shiny seeds have less flavour than the carpels, where the fragrant defence compounds are concentrated.

Spice story

Star anise's Latin name *Illicium* means "allurement", referring to its sweet smell and pretty shape. It has been cultivated for more than 3,000 years for culinary and medicinal use in its native China and Vietnam. It symbolizes good fortune in Chinese culture, where finding a star with more than the normal eight arms is considered very good luck. From the late Middle Ages it was traded along the tea route from China via Russia, and for much of this time it was known as Siberian cardamom. Due to the relatively high price of anise, and increasing popularity of Asian cooking, star anise has never been more widely used than it is today. Indeed, shortages have occurred during international flu outbreaks because star anise contains shikimic acid, a chemical used to make the antiviral drug Tamiflu.

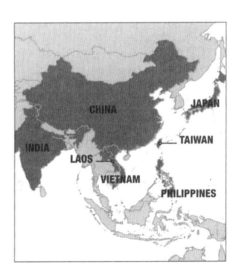

Region of cultivation
Native to southwest China and northeast Vietnam, star anise is cultivated in China, India, Laos, Vietnam, the Philippines, Japan, and Taiwan.

Kitchen creativity }

Star anise is essential to Chinese cuisine and indispensable to five-spice powder. In South India, it may be added to a biryani and used in versions of garam masala. Vietnamese *pho* would be incomplete without its distinctive flavour.

BLENDING SCIENCE

Star anise shares the anethole flavour compound with anise, fennel, and liquorice, even though they are from unrelated plants. Anethole is 13 times sweeter than table sugar, and gives the spice its sweetness. The overall flavour profile is more complex than that of other anethole spices, and features linalool's alluring floral flavour.

STAR ANISE
St

CINEOLE
eucalyptus | mildly medicinal | penetrating

PHELLANDRENE
green | peppery | citrus

ANETHOLE
sweet | liquorice | warming

draw out the underlying eucalyptus notes with more cineole spices:

⊕ **cardamom** also enhances floral notes through shared linalool

⊕ **bay** adds pine-like notes, and shares linalool for fresh, floral aromas and a slight bitterness

⊕ **black cardamom** and **grains of Selim** will lend an appetizing wood smoke aroma to the blend

⊕ **galangal** and **ginger** also make excellent, fresh, and zesty pairings

pair with similarly sweet and/or warming spices:

⊕ **nutmeg, mace,** and **allspice** possess eugenol that synergizes with anethole; nutmeg and mace also share terpineol for fresh, woody notes

⊕ **cinnamon** has a sweet, warming spiciness that complements anethole

add heft to traces of fresh, herbal tanginess by combining with more phellandrene spices:

⊕ **peppercorn** brings a lingering spicy heat

⊕ **dill** also features limonene for a stronger citrus edge

FOOD PARTNERS

⊕ **Vegetables** Add a pod to braised leeks, cabbage, or fennel; sprinkle the ground spice over pumpkin, root veg, and swede before roasting; add a pinch to sweet vegetable purées.

⊕ **Rice** Put a whole pod in the pan when cooking basmati or sticky Thai rice – its delicate, sweet flavour complements biryanis and pilaus.

⊕ **Beef, pork** Use the whole spice to add a freshness to an oxtail stew, or add to Chinese slow-braised pork.

⊕ **Seafood** Mix star anise, ginger, and peppercorns in the saucepan before adding clams or mussels and wine or a splash of sherry or Pernod for a Vietnamese-style dish.

⊕ **Fruit preserves** Combine with quince, figs, apples, apricots, and tropical fruits such as pineapple and mango to add a fresh liquorice taste.

BLENDS TO TRY

Try these recipes for classic blends featuring star anise, or why not adapt them with some blending science?

Vindaloo paste p44
Burmese garam masala p48
Shandong spice bag p58
Nanjing spice bag p59
Five-spice powder p60

RELEASE THE FLAVOUR

Much of the flavour is locked up in the hard carpels of the pods, which protect the seeds and contain concentrated flavour compounds that evolved to repel pests. There are various ways to release and enhance that distinctive flavour.

Use oil and alcohol (e.g. rice wine, fermented soy sauce) to disperse the anethole.

Dry fry at 130–180°C (266–356°F) to create nutty pyrazine compounds.

Cooking with alliums creates meaty flavours when sulphur reacts with the anethole.

Slow cook with whole pods to allow time for the flavours to escape the woody husk.

CHINESE STEAMED SALMON <u>WITH</u> CHILLI <u>AND</u> STAR ANISE

Simple and easy to prepare, this delicately spiced Chinese supper is given a piquant twist with star anise and Scotch bonnet chilli, adding depth to the dish without overpowering the mild flavour of the fish. It works especially well with lightly smoked salmon, but if you prefer you can use unsmoked fillets.

SPICE IDEAS

Swap in **different coloured peppers**: black pepper for a more aromatic, complex heat; green pepper for dominant herbaceous notes.

Be inspired by the fresh spices to **try alternatives to star anise**: allspice will pick out fruity esters in chilli; citrus-floral coriander will enhance the citral in ginger.

Replace **fresh chillies with dried** – rehydrated and sliced – for smoky, toasted flavours.

Serves 4

Prep time 30 mins

Cooking time 10 mins

4 lightly smoked salmon fillets, skinned

½ tsp ground white pepper

handful of star anise, broken up

1 tbsp Shaoxing wine or dry sherry

1 tbsp finely chopped fresh root ginger

1 Scotch bonnet chilli, deseeded and cut into around 12 strips

2 tsp light soy sauce

2 tsp dark soy sauce

3 spring onions, finely chopped

1 tbsp vegetable oil

2 tsp sesame oil

1 tsp chilli oil

1 Rub the salmon fillets with the white pepper. Arrange them in a single layer in a heatproof dish, placing one piece of star anise underneath and one piece on top of each fillet of fish.

2 Pour in the wine or sherry, scatter the ginger over the fish, and place a few strips of chilli on top of each salmon fillet.

3 Pour water to a depth of 2cm (¾in) into a steamer or deep pan with a trivet in the bottom, and bring to a simmer. Place the fish dish in the pan, cover the pan tightly with foil, and steam over a low–medium heat for 8–10 minutes, depending on the thickness of the fish. Add more hot water to the pan if necessary.

4 When the fish is cooked, take the dish from the pan and remove the star anise pieces. Pour the soy sauces over the fish and scatter with the spring onions.

5 Heat a wok or heavy pan over a high heat. Add the three oils and swirl them round the pan. When the oil is very hot and slightly smoking, remove from the heat and pour over the fish. Serve with steamed rice and stir-fried greens, such as pak choi.

FENNEL

Aniseedy | Warming | Bittersweet

BOTANICAL NAME
Foeniculum vulgare (bitter fennel),
F. v. var. dulce (sweet fennel)

ALSO KNOWN AS
Sweet cumin.

MAJOR FLAVOUR COMPOUND
Anethole.

PARTS USED
Fruits (misnamed seeds), pollen.

METHOD OF CULTIVATION
Plants are cut when the seeds have matured on the flowering umbels and taken on a sage green colour.

COMMERCIAL PREPARATION
Umbels bearing the fruits are dried, then threshed, cleaned, and graded.

NON-CULINARY USES
Essential oil in cough medicines, soaps, and perfumes. In herbal medicine to improve vision and aid digestion.

Spice story

Herbalists throughout the ages, from the Vedic tradition of India to the authors of Ancient Greek medical texts, have endorsed fennel for its sight-restoring powers and as an antidote to snake bites. The Greek for fennel is *maratho,* and the plains of Marathon, where the Greeks won a decisive battle against the Persians in 490 BCE, were named for their "fennel fields". The Romans introduced the spice to all the lands they conquered, and by the early medieval period its popularity was widespread across Europe, thanks in part to the King of the Franks, Emperor Charlemagne (742–814 CE), who demanded that it be cultivated on his Imperial farms. European colonists used fennel as a preservative and to disguise the flavour of meat past its best. They spread the plant to the Americas and Australia, where wild escapees are now considered noxious weeds.

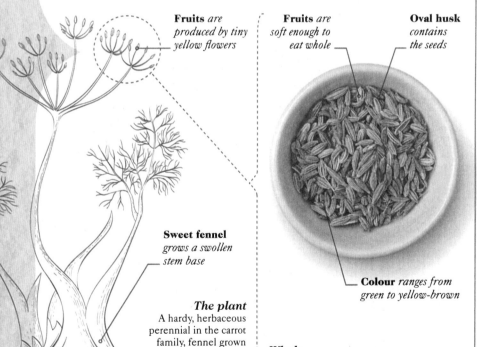

Fruits *are produced by tiny yellow flowers*

Fruits *are soft enough to eat whole*

Oval husk *contains the seeds*

Sweet fennel *grows a swollen stem base*

The plant
A hardy, herbaceous perennial in the carrot family, fennel grown for spice comes in two forms: wild bitter fennel and cultivated sweet fennel.

Colour *ranges from green to yellow-brown*

Whole
Bitter fennel has a mildy bitter taste a little like celery seed. Anise-like sweet fennel is more widely available.

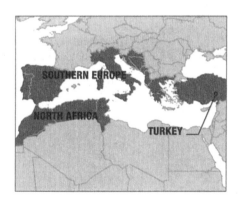

Region of cultivation
Native to the Mediterranean and cultivated throughout Europe, fennel is in fact mainly produced in India. Other notable growers include Turkey, Japan, Argentina, North Africa, and the USA (mostly California).

Kitchen creativity }

Fennel enhances both sweet and savoury foods with its mild aniseed character. The spice is most notable as a flavouring for Italian salami, and for its use in masala blends throughout South Asia, from Kashmir to Sri Lanka.

BLENDING SCIENCE

The main sweet aniseed flavour of fennel comes from powerful anethole, while penetrating fenchone contributes bitter pungency, and small amounts of citrusy limonene and pine-scented pinene are also present.

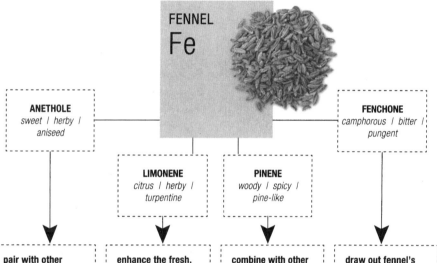

FENNEL
Fe

ANETHOLE
sweet | herby | aniseed

FENCHONE
camphorous | bitter | pungent

LIMONENE
citrus | herby | turpentine

PINENE
woody | spicy | pine-like

pair with other sweet spices containing liquorice-like compounds:

⊕ **anise** and **star anise** are dominated by anethole and add herby, floral aromas

⊕ **dill seed** brings minty, liquorice-like carvone and citrus notes of limonene

⊕ **nutmeg** is similarly sweetening; eugenol is a match for anethole

enhance the fresh, fruity side with another limonene:

⊕ **cardamom**'s penetrating eucalyptus-like cineole also helps to counterbalance anethole

combine with other pinenes to complement the woody spice notes:

⊕ **black pepper** adds a pungent warmth

⊕ **cumin** contributes an earthy, slightly bitter flavour

draw out fennel's penetrating, camphorous side:

⊕ **cassia**'s camphor will highlight the fenchone, but its sweetness will balance bitter notes

FOOD PARTNERS

⊕ **Plums and figs** Add toasted seeds when poaching or making jams and chutneys.

⊕ **Fruiting vegetables** Stir ground fennel into an aubergine, courgette, and tomato *caponata* stew.

⊕ **Pork and beef** Mix into meatballs or lightly crush with salt as a rub for roasting pork belly skin.

⊕ **Oily fish** Crush with a little pepper and salt and then sprinkle on top of fish fillets before frying.

⊕ **Almonds** Sprinkle sugar mixed with crushed fennel over warm almond biscuits.

RELEASE THE FLAVOUR

Fennel's flavour-containing oils are housed within hollow tubes (canals) just beneath the outer ridges of the fruits.

Grinding the seeds will break the canals and help the oils to escape.

Dry frying beforehand will create new roasted, nutty pyrazine flavours, which quickly combine with existing flavour compounds.

BLENDS TO TRY

Try these recipes for classic blends featuring fennel, or why not adapt them with some blending science?

Panch phoran p43
Five-spice powder p60

LIQUORICE

Sweet | Aniseedy | Warm

BOTANICAL NAME
Glycyrrhiza glabra

ALSO KNOWN AS
Sweetwood, Spanish
juice plant, *jethimadh*.

MAJOR FLAVOUR COMPOUND
Glycyrrhizin.

PARTS USED
Roots and rhizomes (underground stems).

METHOD OF CULTIVATION
Roots and rhizomes are harvested by digging
up the whole plant when it is 3–5 years old.

COMMERCIAL PREPARATION
The roots and rhizomes are cut off, cleaned
and trimmed, then dried for several months.

NON-CULINARY USES
Tobacco flavouring; ingredient of cough
medicines and lozenges; in traditional
medicine to treat inflammation, peptic
ulcers, and chest complaints.

Spice story

Ancient Assyrians, Babylonians,
Egyptians, Greeks, and Romans
all chewed liquorice to allay thirst,
freshen breath, and increase stamina.
The spice reached China, where it was
used as a stimulant and antidote to
poison, via the Silk Road over 2,000
years ago. By the 12th century,
liquorice extract was being widely
used in northern Europe, often
cultivated by monks and prescribed
for coughs, gastric ulcers, and chest
complaints. The first liquorice sweet
was made in 1760, and by the late
19th century sweets and liqueurs were
being manufactured across Europe,
particularly in Nordic countries. The
spice was also being used to flavour
tobacco, and today the majority of the
world's crop is grown for this purpose.
Its use as a spice remains localized to
China, India, and Scandinavia.

The plant
Liquorice is a
herbaceous perennial
in the pea and bean
family, with rhizomes
that form a branched,
spreading network.

**Bluish-purple
flowers** *produce
reddish-brown,
bristly seed pods*

Rhizomes *are
bright yellow and
pencil thick*

Powder
The ground dried root is available in
various shades and in "fine" or "raw"
varieties, depending on plant variety and
how it was processed.

Whole
Dried liquorice
root can be bought
in slices or in pieces
of up to 20cm (8in)
long, and will store
almost indefinitely
in a sealed container
in a cool, dry place.

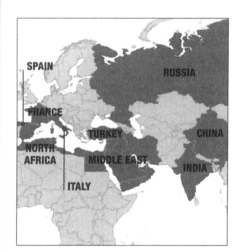

Region of cultivation
Liquorice is native to the Mediterranean region
and West Asia. It is cultivated mainly in Russia,
Spain, and the Middle East, but also in North
Africa, France, Italy, Turkey, North America,
India, and China.

Kitchen creativity }

The dried root or rhizome has an intense aniseed flavour and warm, lingering sweetness. It can be used to infuse sweet dishes, stocks, sauces, and stews, and it is added to spice blends such as Chinese five-spice. Use sparingly to avoid overwhelming the dish.

BLENDING SCIENCE

The powerful sweetening effect of liquorice root is produced by glycyrrhizin, a compound that is around 50 times sweeter than sugar. The warming, medicinal flavours of this spice are produced by three compounds – aniseed-like estragole, eucalyptus-like cineole, and clove-like eugenol. Small amounts of floral linalool, cucumber-like aldehydes, and oregano-tasting phenols give liquorice its rounded, complex taste.

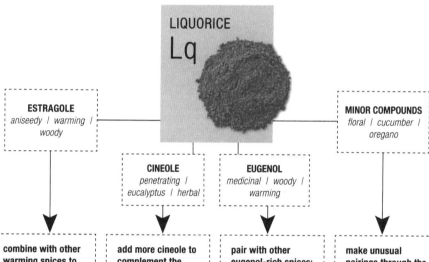

LIQUORICE
Lq

ESTRAGOLE
aniseedy | warming | woody

CINEOLE
penetrating | eucalyptus | herbal

EUGENOL
medicinal | woody | warming

MINOR COMPOUNDS
floral | cucumber | oregano

combine with other warming spices to reinforce the aniseed notes:

⊕ **anise** adds a herby flavour with hints of cherry, vanilla, and cacao alongside aniseed

⊕ **fennel** enhances the sweet flavour and adds complexity to the aniseed character

⊕ **star anise** has penetrating eucalyptus and peppery mint notes, alongside sweet anethole

add more cineole to complement the slightly herbal notes:

⊕ **bay** contributes a fresh, penetrating, herbal-floral flavour

⊕ **cardamom** intensifies eucalyptus flavours, adding some minty, lemony notes

pair with other eugenol-rich spices:

⊕ **clove** contributes sweet, astringent, camphorous notes

⊕ **cinnamon** and **cassia** are similarly sweet, and add woody and citrus notes spiciness

make unusual pairings through the minor compounds:

⊕ **coriander** enhances the floral notes of liquorice

⊕ **vanilla** has floral, leafy notes alongside anise-like anisaldehyde and creamy flavours

⊕ **nigella** and **ajwain** will partner with trace oregano-like compounds

FOOD PARTNERS

⊕ **Citrus** Sprinkle a little ground liquorice over a grapefruit and orange salad.

⊕ **Asparagus, fennel** Add to a butter dressing for grilled asparagus, or sprinkle over roasted fennel with lemon.

⊕ **Oily fish** Add ground liquorice to a cure for salmon or trout.

⊕ **Ham, beef** Infuse a braising liquid for a ham or beef brisket with liquorice root.

⊕ **Baking** Use ground in gingerbread dough, or steep liquorice root in the syrup for a steamed sponge pudding.

⊕ **Preserves** Use to flavour apple jelly and cherry jam, or with cardamom and coriander in a Scandinavian plum chutney.

RELEASE THE FLAVOUR

The glycyrrhizin in liquorice helps to disperse the flavours of both liquorice and any other spices in a dish by enabling oil and water to mix.

Oil droplets suspended in water

Added to water, glycyrrhizin can thicken to form a gel that allows oil and water to form a smooth mixture.

Add liquorice near the start of cooking to maximize the taste.

Steep the root in hot water first for dishes with a short cooking time or little liquid.

BLENDS TO TRY

Use and adapt these classic blends featuring liquorice.
Nanjing spice bag p59
Five-spice powder p60

MAHLEB

Bittersweet | Fruity | Woody

BOTANICAL NAME
Prunus mahaleb

ALSO KNOWN AS
Mahlab, *mehlepi*, rock cherry,
St Lucie cherry.

MAJOR FLAVOUR COMPOUND
Coumarin.

PARTS USED
The kernel (seed) within
the stone of the fruit.

METHOD OF CULTIVATION
The ripe cherries are harvested in the
autumn, when they have turned dark
purplish-black.

COMMERCIAL PREPARATION
The small, soft kernel is extracted by
cracking open the stone inside the
thin-fleshed cherry fruit. The seed is then
blanched, dried, and ground or sold whole.

NON-CULINARY USES
Essential oil is used in perfumery.

Spice story

Mahleb cherry stones have been found at Mediterranean and Middle Eastern prehistoric sites, but written evidence of their use in ancient times is scarce. The earliest perfume recipes listing kernels for their aromatic qualities date back only to the 12th century CE. There is some evidence, though, that mahleb may have been cultivated as early as the Sumerian era (4500–1900 BCE) in ancient Mesopotamia, around modern-day Iraq and Syria. In the native regions of the mahleb cherry tree, use of the dried, ground kernels as a culinary spice dates back centuries, popular in rich breads and cakes enjoyed at religious holidays. Mahleb is not commonly used outside Greece, Turkey, North Africa, and the Middle East, although Greek Americans often add it to their European-style yeast cakes and pastries.

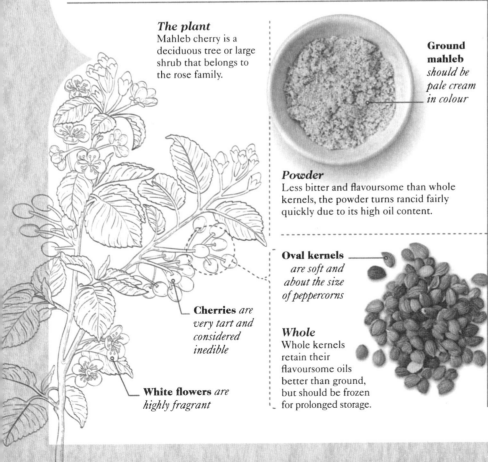

The plant
Mahleb cherry is a
deciduous tree or large
shrub that belongs to
the rose family.

Ground mahleb *should be pale cream in colour*

Powder
Less bitter and flavoursome than whole
kernels, the powder turns rancid fairly
quickly due to its high oil content.

Oval kernels *are soft and about the size of peppercorns*

Whole
Whole kernels
retain their
flavoursome oils
better than ground,
but should be frozen
for prolonged storage.

Cherries *are very tart and considered inedible*

White flowers *are highly fragrant*

Region of cultivation
Mahleb is native to the Mediterranean region,
parts of Central Asia, and Iran. It is mainly
cultivated in the Anatolia region of Turkey,
and in Syria and Iran.

Kitchen creativity }

Mahleb is luxuriously sweet and fruity, with an almond aroma and a woody cherry taste; whole kernels also release a bitterness when chewed. Mainly known as a baking spice, it can add fruit-and-nut notes to savoury dishes.

BLENDING SCIENCE

A lactone called coumarin produces mahleb's creamy taste, like sweet clover and apricot. Almond notes come from methoxyethyl cinnamate, and the spice also contains woody, peppery azulene and balsamic, fruity pentanol, as well as green-apple-like dioxolane. Bitterness in the fresh spice comes from phenols.

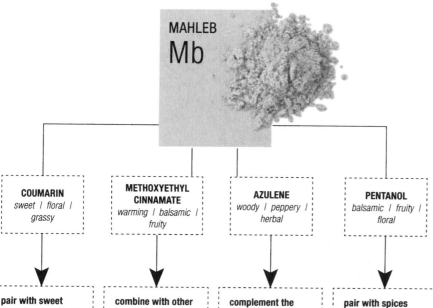

MAHLEB
Mb

COUMARIN
sweet | floral | grassy

pair with sweet spices or those with creamy nuances:

⊕ **clove** contributes sweet, astringent, camphorous notes

⊕ **nutmeg** adds warm spiciness

⊕ **liquorice** brings sweetness and eucalyptus-like notes, and sometimes contains coumarin-like substances

⊕ **vanilla** lends rich, mellow creaminess

METHOXYETHYL CINNAMATE
warming | balsamic | fruity

combine with other warming spices:

⊕ **cinnamon** and **cassia** contribute sweet, spicy, woody qualities

⊕ **galangal** contains a similar cinnamate compound and hints of cherry, adding a penetrating pungency

⊕ **ginger** adds hotness and sweet, citrusy notes

AZULENE
woody | peppery | herbal

complement the sweet woodiness of mahleb:

⊕ **sesame** brings harmonizing nutty and bready flavours; pale, unroasted seeds also have a creamy taste

⊕ **cacao** adds bitter chocolate notes, pairing well with the sweet coumarin

---

PENTANOL
balsamic | fruity | floral

pair with spices that either contain pentanol or enhance its flavour:

⊕ **poppy** seeds contain pentanol and add earthiness

⊕ **lemon myrtle** has distinctive green odours from the fruity tasting heptanone, and adds a powerful lemon-lime flavour

---

FOOD PARTNERS

⊕ **Stone fruit** Use ground mahleb to thicken a sweet cherry sauce, add it to a plum crumble topping, or sprinkle it over roasted apricots or peaches.

⊕ **Meat** Add to a Turkish dry spice rub for roast duck legs, pork, or lamb.

⊕ **Baking** Include mahleb with other warm spices in festive bakes, or add it to the sweet dough for an apricot tart.

⊕ **Ice cream** Sprinkle into cherry ice cream and top with candied pistachios.

⊕ **Tonka beans** Partner with vanilla-like tonka beans, which are similarly high in coumarin, in sweet recipes.

RELEASE THE FLAVOUR

Of mahleb's flavour compounds, only dioxolane and some bitter phenols are soluble in water to any great extent. Cooking in a water-based liquid will therefore result in a "green" and bitter taste and should be avoided.

Grind kernels to release short-lived oils. Leave for a few minutes before use to let bitter phenols evaporate.

Add to fats before mixing into a recipe to allow sweet and woody flavours to come to the fore.

Application of heat will decrease the bitter flavours and allow hints of cherry fruitiness to emerge.

VANILLA

Sweet | Musky | Woody

BOTANICAL NAME
Vanilla planifolia

MAJOR FLAVOUR COMPOUND
Vanillin.

PARTS USED
"Pods" (which are really fruits).

METHOD OF CULTIVATION
Plants are trained up posts or trees and the flowers pollinated by hand. Pods are picked before fully ripe.

COMMERCIAL PREPARATION
Pods are scalded or steamed, then sweated in sealed containers to make them release defensive phenol molecules. These react with the air and destructive plant enzymes to disintegrate into dark, flavourful compounds. Pods are then dried until black and shrivelled to one-fifth their original weight.

NON-CULINARY USES
In perfumes and cosmetics.

The plant
Vanilla is the fruit of a perennial, vine-like tropical orchid that bears bunches of green-yellow flowers.

Flowers
must be pollinated by hand

Fresh pods
are 15–25cm (6–10in) long and look like French beans

Extract
This is made by macerating pods in alcohol. Find labels saying "natural extract" and stating around 35 per cent alcohol.

Dark, plump *appearance is a sign of good sweating and maturing*

Whole pods
Brittleness is a sign of age, but pods can keep their flavour for up to 4 years. Frosting is caused by exposure to air.

Spice story

Vanilla was first cultivated for its scent 1,000 years ago on the eastern coast of Mexico by the Totonac people. The first recorded use as a flavouring dates to the 15th century CE, when the Aztecs conquered the Totonacs, discovered the bean-like fruit, and used it to flavour cacao drinks. The Spanish conquistador Cortés was served just such a drink by the Aztec king in 1519 and took vanilla pods and cacao beans back to Spain. But Mexico retained a monopoly because the pods would only form when pollinated by native orchid bees. That is until the 1830s, when a Belgian botanist unravelled the mystery and devised a technique of hand pollination. In 1874, German chemists created a synthetic alternative to the natural flavour, and now 97 per cent of vanilla-flavoured foods are made with synthetic vanillin.

Region of cultivation
Vanilla is native to Mexico and Central America, where it is still cultivated. It is also grown in Madagascar, Réunion, India, Sri Lanka, Indonesia, and Tahiti.

Kitchen creativity }

Rich, mellow vanilla has historically been used in sweet cookery, but is an increasingly popular addition to savoury dishes, particularly fish and seafood. Tread carefully, though, as it can easily overwhelm a dish.

BLENDING SCIENCE

Vanillin is a phenol that makes up 85 per cent of vanilla's flavour and has a natural affinity with other sweetly fragrant spices. But more than 250 flavour compounds can be present, which encompass woody, spicy, floral, and fruity aromas. These lesser compounds distinguish vanilla pods from synthetic vanillin flavouring.

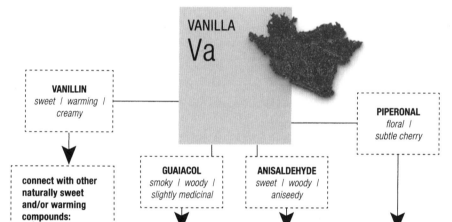

VANILLA
Va

VANILLIN
sweet | warming | creamy

PIPERONAL
floral | subtle cherry

GUAIACOL
smoky | woody | slightly medicinal

ANISALDEHYDE
sweet | woody | aniseedy

connect with other naturally sweet and/or warming compounds:

⊕ **cinnamon, cassia** intensify sweetness and bring in spicy heat and floral notes

⊕ **ginger, galangal** convey both heat and sweetness, and cherry hints from galangal

⊕ **liquorice** is an ideal partner due to intensely sweet glycyrrhizin and its aniseed flavour

draw out notes of wood and smoke:

⊕ **cacao**'s blend of smoky, earthy flavours have close synergy

⊕ **allspice** has a warming woodiness

⊕ **black pepper**'s warm, woody, and citrusy aspects make it an unexpected partner

boost aniseed with spices that share a similar compound:

⊕ **clove, nutmeg** are sweet, woody, and somewhat penetrating, which harmonizes with the aniseed flavour

⊕ **anise** also has anisaldehyde as a minor compound

pick out an unusual cherry connection:

⊕ **mahleb** has a nutty sweetness and lingering cherry taste

FOOD PARTNERS

⊕ **Vegetables** Add seeds to carrots, cauliflower, root vegetables, or potatoes. Put a split pod in a tomato chutney.

⊕ **Strawberries** Combine vanilla and black pepper in a caramelized sugar syrup for macerating strawberries.

⊕ **Fish, seafood** Stir into melted butter and brush over grilled lobster, scallops, or fish; put a sliver of pod in a pan of mussels before steaming.

⊕ **Desserts** Add to chocolate and cream puddings. Use vanilla-flavoured sugar in sponge and pancake batters.

RELEASE THE FLAVOUR

Many trace compounds in vanilla are quick to evaporate: use seeds immediately and cook on low heat to avoid losing subtle nuances.

Lightly pound pods to release flavour from the inner fibres.

Add whole pods early in cooking to allow flavours to diffuse out of the tough tissue.

Vanilla chooser

Depending on where they were grown and how they were dried and cured, vanilla pods will derive from one of three orchid species and have varying levels of vanillin and different flavour profiles.

Country	Plant	Flavour content	Description
Madagascar, Réunion	*Vanilla planifolia*	2% vanillin	Bourbon vanilla is esteemed as rich and balanced.
Mexico	*Vanilla pompona*	1.75% vanillin	Mexican vanilla carries wine-like and fruity flavour compounds.
Tahiti	*Vanilla tahitensis*	1.70% vanillin	The most expensive vanilla, with a deep flavour that includes cherry-chocolate, liquorice, and caramel.
India, Sri Lanka	*Vanilla planifolia*	1.50% vanillin	Vanilla grown in South Asia has lower levels of vanillin, resulting in a gentler flavour and a smokiness.

NUTMEG

Bittersweet | Woody | Warm

BOTANICAL NAME
Myristica fragrans

ALSO KNOWN AS
True nutmeg, fragrant nutmeg.

MAJOR FLAVOUR COMPOUND
Myristicin.

PARTS USED
Seed kernels.

METHOD OF CULTIVATION
The fruits are harvested several times a year; one tree yields 10,000 or more nutmegs a year.

COMMERCIAL PREPARATION
Fruit is split open, dried, and the lacy aril removed to make mace. Seeds shells are cracked open to remove nutmegs.

NON-CULINARY USES
In pharmaceuticals, including tooth paste and cough syrups. Mild pain-killing power is used to treat toothache and joint pain.

The plant
Nutmeg comes from a tropical evergreen tree that produces two distinct spices: the seed (nutmeg) and its lacy covering (mace).

Fleshy fruit casing *encloses the woody seed*

Bell-shaped flowers *have a lily-of-the-valley scent*

Grows *to at least 16m (40ft) high*

Powder
Nutmeg is available **pre-ground**, but its flavour oils are among the quickest of all spices to evaporate: far preferable to buy whole and grate fresh.

Kernels *are revealed after cracking open the seed casing*

Whole
Kernels keep for at least a year, in a sealed container in a cool, dark place. Discard if black spots develop.

Spice story

Native to the Banda Islands in the Moluccas (Maluku) archipelago of Indonesia, nutmeg has a complex, violent history. Its source was initially kept secret by traders who wanted to protect their valuable commodity, treasured for its rarity, flavour, and apparent aphrodisiac and healing properties. By the 16th century there was such huge demand for nutmeg in Europe that it was said to be more precious than gold, triggering a race to find and take control of its source. Portugal conquered the Moluccas in 1511, then the Dutch wrested control in 1599, and England seized two of the Banda Islands in 1603. The spice was so valued by the Dutch that they struck a deal with England to take back one of the islands in return for one of their settlements in the New World. The land they gave to England was known then as New Amsterdam – and today as New York City.

Region of cultivation
Nutmeg trees are grown throughout the Maluku (Moluccas) islands of Indonesia, and also in Sri Lanka, the Caribbean (notably Grenada), and South Africa.

Kitchen creativity }

Nutmeg's deep, sweet, woody flavour works in both sweet and savoury dishes. Somewhat penetrating and astringent with tannins, it can easily overpower a dish, but blends happily with other strong spices.

BLENDING SCIENCE

Nutmeg's woody aroma comes from myristicin, which is integral to its flavour profile, although it makes up only a small proportion of the oil. Nutmeg also contains peppery, fruity sabinene, floral geraniol and safrole, clove-like eugenol, eucalyptus-scented cineole, and conifer-like pinene.

NUTMEG
Nu

EUGENOL AND CINEOLE
clove-like | eucalyptus | penetrating

SABINENE
orangey | peppery | woody

GERANIOL AND SAFROLE
rosy | sweet

MYRISTICIN
woody | warm | balsamic

bolster with other penetrating spices:

⊕ **cardamom** shares both compounds and brings floral sweetness and hints of camphor

⊕ **grains of Selim** shares cineole and also pinene, bringing a medicinal camphorous flavour like rosemary

⊕ **clove**'s flavour is owed to cineole and it brings added depth and sweetness

⊕ **cassia** has cineole and its cinnamaldehyde can resist nutmeg

add depth to the sweetness:

⊕ **allspice** contains similarly floral linalool and shares eugenol and cineole

⊕ **curry leaf** has many flavour profile overlaps with nutmeg, sharing both these compounds, as well as pinene and cineole

complement with warming spices:

⊕ **ginger**'s zingerone adds zesty heat, with citrus-sweet crossover

⊕ **black pepper** also has a a shared floral and citrus background

⊕ **anise** has some myristicin and enhances nutmeg's sweet woodiness

bring out sabinene's fruity piquancy:

⊕ **garlic** shares sabinene, and its sulphurous pungency stands up well to powerful nutmeg

⊕ **juniper** shares nutmeg's pinene, and citrus notes from limonene work well with orangey sabinene

FOOD PARTNERS

⊕ **Spinach** Grate over buttered or creamed spinach or add to the filling for spinach and ricotta ravioli.

⊕ **Lamb** Add a generous grating to meatball mixture or use in moussaka.

⊕ **Sauces and drinks** Include nutmeg in béchamel, cheese fondue, soufflés, Indian golden latte (*haldi doodh*), eggnog, and Caribbean nutmeg ice cream.

⊕ **Sweet bakes** Use in a Sienese *panforte* or sprinkle over custard tarts.

RELEASE THE FLAVOUR

Nutmeg's flavour oils are so powerful they can easily overpower a dish, yet they are also short-lived.

Use sparingly: a grating literally means one stroke on a grater

Add towards the end of the cooking time for a stronger, more complex flavour, as the oils are very quick to evaporate.

BLENDS TO TRY

Use and adapt these classic blends featuring nutmeg:

Turkish baharat p23
Bumbu p52
Jamaican jerk rub p64
Mulling spice p73
Quatre épices p74

Neolignans' cooling effect

A group of chemicals called neolignans were recently discovered in nutmeg oil. These act on the temperature-sensing nerves on the tongue and in the mouth to give a numbing sense of lingering coolness.

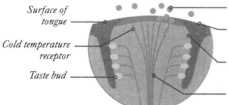

Surface of tongue

Cold temperature receptor

Taste bud

Neolignan molecules

Tongue turns slightly numb from the effect

Tongue papilla

False cold signals are sent to the brain

CHICKEN AND AUBERGINE BIRYANI WITH SEVEN-SPICE

The biryani is a true melting pot of a dish. Conceived in Persia, it was introduced to India by Arab merchants, and became popular in almost every region. Seven-spice, Lebanon's answer to garam masala, gives this version a rich, smoky, Middle Eastern flavour. For less of a chilli kick, simply halve the amount of chilli flakes.

SPICE IDEAS

Experiment with **your own seven-spice** mix: replace sweet spices with cumin and/or nigella for earthiness, or fenugreek for musty, bittersweet notes.

Highlight eucalyptus-like cineole found in several of the dry spices by **swapping fresh ginger** for cineole-rich galangal.

Preserve more of the pungent gingerols and zingiberene by **adding fresh ginger later** – at the same time as the peas – for a zestier hit of flavour.

Serves 4–6

Prep time 30 mins

Cooking time 1 hour 40–50 mins

For the seven-spice

1 tbsp black peppercorns

1 tbsp allspice berries

1 tsp cloves

1 tsp coriander seeds

1 tbsp ground cinnamon

1 tsp ground ginger

1 tsp grated nutmeg

For the biryani

75g (2½oz) butter

4 skinless, boneless chicken thighs

4 cloves

1 star anise

8 black peppercorns

250g (9oz) basmati rice

4–5 tbsp vegetable oil

6–8 garlic cloves, thinly sliced

sea salt flakes and freshly ground black pepper

7cm (3in) piece fresh root ginger, finely grated

1 tbsp seven-spice (see above)

1 tsp chilli flakes

2 aubergines, cut into 1cm (½in) cubes

100g (3½oz) frozen petits pois

1 Make the seven-spice by grinding the whole spices and mixing with the remaining spices. Reserve 1 tablespoon and store the rest.

2 Preheat the oven to 160°C (325°F/Gas 3). In a large, ovenproof pan, melt about 25g (1oz) of the butter and gently sauté the chicken thighs with the cloves, star anise, and peppercorns. When the chicken starts to turn opaque, cover with boiling water and bring to a simmer. Cook in the oven with the pan lid on for about an hour, until the meat is tender. Take out the chicken and set aside.

3 Remove the spices from the liquid, then add boiling water to fill the pan. Add the rice and a good pinch of salt. Boil for 7–8 minutes, until the rice starts to soften. While the rice is cooking, shred the chicken, then line a large, heavy-based saucepan with baking paper. Drain the rice and rinse under the cold tap.

4 Heat 2 tablespoons of the oil in a frying pan and fry the garlic for less than a minute over a medium heat. Then add the ginger, chilli flakes, 1 tablespoon of seven-spice, and a good pinch of sea salt. Add the chicken, followed by a little more oil and the diced aubergines. Stir fry for about 5 minutes, until the chicken and aubergine are coated in oil and spices. Season with salt and pepper.

5 Melt the remaining butter with a little oil, then pour into the paper-lined saucepan. Sprinkle with sea salt and add a thin layer of rice, then a layer of chicken and aubergine mix. Repeat, alternating the layers and finishing with rice. Poke a few holes in the mixture with a wooden-spoon handle, to allow steam to rise through the dish.

6 Wrap the pan lid in a tea towel and put it on the pan. Cook over the lowest heat possible for 35–45 minutes. With 15 minutes to go, add the peas to the pan. At the end of cooking, use a fork to check that the bottom layer of rice has formed a crust. If it has not, raise the heat and cook for up to 5 more minutes.

7 To serve, flip the biryani onto a dish, so that the golden, crispy rice base – known in Persian as the *tahdig* – is on top. For a crispier crust, omit the paper, but that ensure the rice does not burn while cooking.

MACE

Sweet | Warm | Aromatic

BOTANICAL NAME
Myristica fragrans

PARTS USED
Aril (seed covering) of the nutmeg seed.

MAJOR FLAVOUR COMPOUND
Sabinene.

METHOD OF CULTIVATION
Ripe fruits are often harvested from trees using a long pole with a basket attached, called a *gai-gai*.

COMMERCIAL PREPARATION
The split fruit reveals a nutmeg seed with a plasticky, scarlet-red covering called an aril. The leathery aril is peeled off, pressed and dried. Grenadian mace is traditionally "cured" in the dark for several months. Mace is then either ground or sold whole as "blades" after drying

NON-CULINARY USES
In perfumes, soaps, and shampoos; in traditional medicine to relieve bronchial disorders and rheumatism, aid digestion, and improve circulation.

Spice story

Native only to the tiny Banda Islands in the Moluccas (Maluku) archipelago of Indonesia, mace was being traded with the Byzantine empire by the 6th century CE, where it was widely valued as a cure-all, food preservative, fumigant, and aphrodisiac. By the Middle Ages, mace had become one of the most sought-after and expensive spices of European cuisine. The appetite for these spices prompted a centuries-long, bloody power struggle between the Portuguese, Dutch, and English to gain control of the growing regions. Eventually, the English managed to establish their own supply by successfully transplanting nutmeg trees, along with their soil, to several of their colonies, including Grenada and Sri Lanka. With greater availability, nutmeg and mace overtook saffron and mustard as the spices of choice in Western cuisine, with mace more common (and cheaper) than nutmeg.

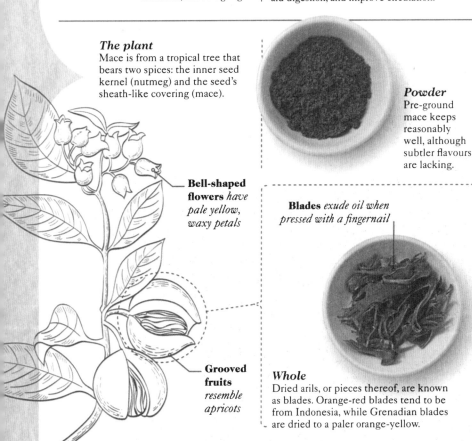

The plant
Mace is from a tropical tree that bears two spices: the inner seed kernel (nutmeg) and the seed's sheath-like covering (mace).

Bell-shaped flowers *have pale yellow, waxy petals*

Grooved fruits *resemble apricots*

Powder
Pre-ground mace keeps reasonably well, although subtler flavours are lacking.

Blades *exude oil when pressed with a fingernail*

Whole
Dried arils, or pieces thereof, are known as blades. Orange-red blades tend to be from Indonesia, while Grenadian blades are dried to a paler orange-yellow.

MALUKU ISLANDS

SRI LANKA

Region of cultivation
Mace is cultivated across the Maluku (Moluccas) archipelago of Indonesia, and also in Sri Lanka, South Africa, and the Caribbean – notably Grenada, which features an image of nutmeg and mace on its national flag.

Kitchen creativity }

Mace will substitute for nutmeg in most sweet dishes, but it is mostly used to flavour savoury sauces, meat, pickles, and chutneys. Use whole blades to infuse pale creams and clear broths where flecks of grated nutmeg are unwanted.

BLENDING SCIENCE

Peppery sabinene is less dominating in mace than in nutmeg and mace has more fragrant oils, with a wider diversity of perfumed compounds, including floral elemicin, which works in partnership with terpineol, and small amounts of eugenol and safrole. Mace lacks the mouth-puckering tannins of nutmeg, giving it a smoother mouthfeel.

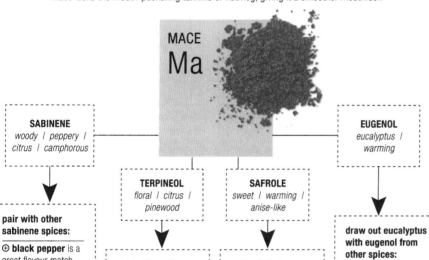

MACE
Ma

SABINENE
woody | peppery | citrus | camphorous

EUGENOL
eucalyptus | warming

TERPINEOL
floral | citrus | pinewood

SAFROLE
sweet | warming | anise-like

pair with other sabinene spices:

⊕ **black pepper** is a great flavour match, sharing many of sabinene's qualities

⊕ **black cardamom** also brings smokiness, and limonene traces to enhance the citrus

⊕ **curry leaf** also has extra woody notes, pine flavours, and hints of mint

pair with another spice that is smooth with hyacinth-like aromas:

⊕ **coriander** is powerfully floral, with distinct pine and citrus compounds, making a highly effective match

add safrole from elsewhere:

⊕ **star anise** carries this uncommon compound too and is strongly flavoured with anise-like anethole; it also brings penetrating pepperiness

draw out eucalyptus with eugenol from other spices:

⊕ **clove**'s sweet scent is from eugenol, which strengthens mace's eucalyptus, and also shares terpineol

⊕ **allspice** also has strong eugenol, and adds deep, sweet pepperiness with a floral background

FOOD PARTNERS

⊕ **Vegetables** Sprinkle ground mace over a creamy potato bake, spinach or carrot soup, or try it in a vegetable pilau.

⊕ **Shellfish** Add a blade of mace to a shellfish broth, or sprinkle ground mace over potted shrimp or crab before stirring it through warm pasta or serving it on toasted rye bread.

⊕ **Pork, chicken** Sprinkle a little ground mace into the mixture for pork, ricotta, and lemon-zest meatballs. Add a blade to a béchamel sauce for a creamy chicken pie.

⊕ **Cheese sauce** Infuse milk with a blade of mace, then make into a cheese sauce for lasagne or macaroni cheese.

⊕ **Desserts** Infuse into custard for a trifle, or whisk into sweetened whipped cream to serve with fruit.

⊕ **Baking** Add ground mace to spiced cake batters, or sprinkle sparingly over American pumpkin pie or milk puddings.

BLEND TO TRY

Use and adapt this spice blend recipe featuring mace:
Garam masala p40

RELEASE THE FLAVOUR

The oil-based compounds in mace dissolve poorly in water and its flavour can change with prolonged heating: some compounds evaporate and degrade while new terpene-like compounds are formed, producing tastes many people dislike.

Mace's more subtle terpene flavours can be lost through evaporation, so grind as needed and use immediately.

Include oil in the cooking liquor or gently fry, for example with an onion base, near the beginning of a dish.

Add whole mace early to give maximum time for oils to diffuse out of the blades, but be wary of lengthy cooking.

Add powder later as it diffuses and spreads more quickly, and this reduces evaporation of terpenes.

CARAWAY

Menthol | Warming | Earthy

BOTANICAL NAME
Carum carvi

ALSO KNOWN AS
Carvies, and (incorrectly) wild cumin,
Persian cumin, meridian fennel.

MAJOR FLAVOUR COMPOUND
S-carvone.

PARTS USED
Seed-like fruits.

METHOD OF CULTIVATION
Plants are grown for two years and harvested
in the second summer, when the seed-like
fruits darken.

COMMERCIAL PREPARATION
The cut flower heads are left for up to
10 days to dry and finish ripening, before
being cleaned and threshed.

NON-CULINARY USES
The essential oil flavours commercial
mouthwash and children's medicines;
as a traditional remedy to aid digestion.

Spice story

Archaeologists have discovered
caraway seeds in Stone Age refuse
pits and 5,000-year-old dwellings
in Switzerland, but the first written
reference dates to around 1,500 BCE,
in an Egyptian herbal encyclopedia.
The spice also held symbolic
significance for the Egyptians, who
placed the seeds in tombs to ward
off evil spirits. The Romans knew it
as *karo* or *careum*, and introduced the
spice to northern Europe. By the
Middle Ages, caraway had became a
common ingredient in game and meat
cookery, and bean and cabbage dishes,
as well as sweeter confections and as
a flavouring for alcohol; *Kümmel*, the
German for caraway, is also the name
of a still-popular liqueur. Folklore
abounds that placing caraway seeds
in your lover's pocket will keep
them faithful.

The plant
Caraway is a frost-hardy
biennial in the carrot family.
It thrives in rich clay soil, and
can grow up to 60cm (2ft) tall.

Fruits *develop
from umbels
of creamy
white flowers*

Feathery leaves *are
edible and taste quite
similar to dill*

*The "seeds"
are actually a
dry fruit*

Whole
Store the brown, crescent-shaped
"seeds" in a sealed container in a
cool, dark place for up to six months.
They benefit from gentle toasting.

Powder
Caraway can be
bought in powder
form, but the flavour
quickly diminishes,
and it is better to
buy whole and
grind as needed.

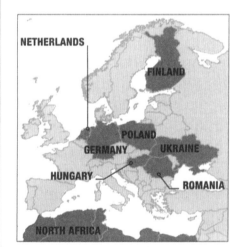

NETHERLANDS
FINLAND
POLAND
GERMANY
UKRAINE
HUNGARY
ROMANIA
NORTH AFRICA

Region of cultivation
Caraway is native to central Europe and Asia,
and its major producers are Finland, Poland, the
Netherlands, Germany, Ukraine, Hungary, and
Romania. Cultivation has also spread to North
Africa, Egypt, and North America.

Kitchen creativity }

Caraway has a complex, warming taste, and its flavour can be found in many central European dishes. It is a key component of the Algerian and Tunisian blend *tabil*, and may be used in harissa, the chilli-based paste from North Africa.

BLENDING SCIENCE

The most abundant flavour compound is the oil-loving terpene S-carvone, which, unlike most terpenes, confers a powerfully spicy flavour, with hints of menthol and rye, reminiscent of anise. The other major flavour compounds are citrusy limonene, with lesser amounts of woody sabinene.

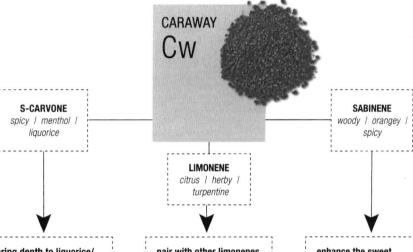

CARAWAY
Cw

S-CARVONE
spicy | menthol | liquorice

LIMONENE
citrus | herby | turpentine

SABINENE
woody | orangey | spicy

bring depth to liquorice/ anise notes through related compounds:

⊕ **anise** and **star anise** are also liquorice-like, due to medicinal anethole, and both bring woody warmth

⊕ **cinnamon** and **allspice** feature the very similar eugenol and will bring out the sweetness in caraway

pair with other limonenes to strengthen the zesty edge:

⊕ **cardamom** also brings sweetness and penetrating herbiness

⊕ **black pepper** adds gentle pungency and enhances the pepperiness

⊕ **ginger** has a complementary citrus background, and brings characteristic heat to a dish

enhance the sweet citrus notes with more sabinene:

⊕ **nutmeg** and **mace** are both partly dominated by sabinene and add a rich sweetness

FOOD PARTNERS

⊕ **Cabbage, beetroot** Add ground to buttered cabbage, and whole to beetroot slaw or soup.

⊕ **Red meats** Stir into sausage, beef, or lamb stews, or use to flavour dumplings and serve on the side.

⊕ **Duck, goose** Massage a mix of ground caraway, salt, and garlic over duck and goose, before roasting.

⊕ **Oily fish** Combine with pepper, fennel, and coriander in a cure.

⊕ **Swiss cheese** Drop a pinch of ground caraway into silky fondue.

⊕ **Biscuits** Sprinkle the seeds over just-baked shortbread.

RELEASE THE FLAVOUR

Cook with oil to allow flavour compounds to dissolve and add late in cooking if using ground caraway.

130°C (266°F) – 180°C (356°F)

Dry frying caraway increases the flavour intensity, but take care not to over-toast, which makes them bitter.

BLEND TO TRY

Try this recipe for a classic blend featuring caraway, and why not adapt it with some blending science?

Harissa p33

Mirror-image compounds

S-carvone, the main flavour compound in caraway, has exactly the same molecular structure as D-carvone, the cooling, minty flavour compound found in spearmint. However, they are mirror images, which means these twin chemicals produce completely different aromas, and caraway's flavour is spearmint turned inside out!

D-carvone (spearmint)

S-carvone (caraway)

DILL

Bitter | Citrus | Woody

BOTANICAL NAME
Anethum graveolens

ALSO KNOWN AS
False aniseed.

MAJOR FLAVOUR COMPOUND
D-carvone.

PARTS USED
"Seeds" (technically fruits).

METHOD OF CULTIVATION
Fruits are harvested after flowering. Seeds are left to ripen and dry on the stalk.

COMMERCIAL PREPARATION
Cut stalks are stacked and left for a week or so to dry. The fruits are then threshed from the flower heads by machine.

NON-CULINARY USES
In traditional medicine to treat stomach complaints – it's a common ingredient of gripe water – and as a gentle sedative.

The plant
Dill is a hardy annual plant in the parsley family.

"Seeds" *are the ripe fruits of the plant that have been allowed to dry on the stalk*

Fern-like *leaves are used as a herb*

Powder
Dill seed is available pre-ground, but don't get it confused with "dill weed", a name the dried herb is sometimes sold under.

Whole
The oval, brown-beige seeds look very similar to fennel seeds. They have little aroma until crushed and ground.

Spice story

Evidence suggests that the seeds and fronds of the dill plant were used for medicinal purposes in Egypt as early as 3000 BCE, and the ancient Greeks appreciated dill's digestive and sedative properties. The seeds were first used as a seasoning and flavouring for vinegars and pickles in Scandinavia and in central and eastern Europe. By the Middle Ages, dill was a common culinary herb, and was also used in witchcraft, love potions, and as an aphrodisiac. Kosher dill pickles later became a dietary staple for Jews living in eastern Europe and in Russia, and were introduced to the USA by eastern European Jewish immigrants in the late 1800s and early 1900s. Dill rapidly became an important commercial crop for the pickling industry in the USA, although today most of that industry's seed supply comes from India.

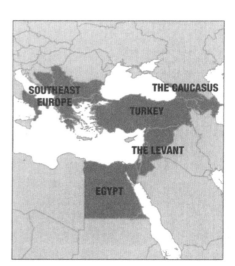

Region of cultivation
Dill is native to southern Europe, the Middle East, and the Caucasus. It is now mainly grown in India, Pakistan, the USA, and countries around the southeast Mediterranean.

Kitchen creativity }

The flavour of dill seeds resembles a cross between anise and a milder version of caraway, having the latter's herby flavour with lemony overtones and a gentle woodiness. There is also a hint of bitterness.

BLENDING SCIENCE

The flavour profile of dill seeds is dominated by D-carvone, a terpene flavour compound, which is spicy with hints of menthol, rye, and anise-like liquorice. The other significant flavour compound is citrus-scented limonene. There are also small amounts of bitter fenchone, and phellandrene, which has minty aromas.

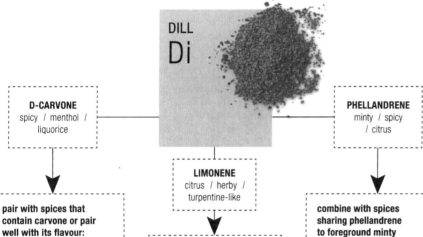

DILL
Di

D-CARVONE
spicy / menthol / liquorice

PHELLANDRENE
minty / spicy / citrus

LIMONENE
citrus / herby / turpentine-like

pair with spices that contain carvone or pair well with its flavour:

⊕ **caraway** echoes the herbiness of dill, introducing pine and woody qualities

⊕ **anise** enhances the liquorice notes of dill

⊕ **fennel** adds complexity to anise-like flavours and brings citrus notes through shared limonene

combine with other spices carrying limonene to boost citrus flavours:

⊕ **coriander** is a particularly effective pairing, adding warmth and floral notes

⊕ **cardamom** lends a sweet, penetrating mintiness

⊕ **ginger** is a good match for introducing pungent heat thanks to shared limonene, which also adds sweetness

combine with spices sharing phellandrene to foreground minty and lemony nuances:

⊕ **allspice** provides a sweet peppery warmth

⊕ **star anise** contributes earthy, floral notes, and an undercurrent of eucalyptus, as well as aniseed

⊕ **bay** adds fresh floral-herbal notes, penetrating eucalyptus, and slight bitterness

FOOD PARTNERS

⊕ **Apples** Caramelize apples in butter and sugar with dill seeds; good on its own or with roast pork.

⊕ **Carrots, onions** Sprinkle over baked onions or honey-roasted carrots.

⊕ **Fish** Lightly toast seeds with cumin and coriander, coarsely grind, and rub over fish skin before grilling or roasting.

⊕ **Goulash** Swap caraway seeds for dill seeds in a paprika-spiced beef or pork goulash, served with lashings of sour cream.

⊕ **Flatbreads** Heat the seeds in melted butter or ghee and brush over flatbread before serving.

Dill pickles

Although dill's flavour compounds do not dissolve well in water, the ample pickling time and fermentation process help the compounds to escape.

Compounds such as carvone and limonene dissolve in alcohol

Fermentation in low-temperature pickling produces alcohol to help disperse flavours.

RELEASE THE FLAVOUR

Dill benefits from toasting to create new flavour compounds from the interaction of sugars and amino acids. Both new and existing compounds dissolve poorly in water, however.

Dry fry seeds to create nutty and roasted flavour compounds, particularly pyrazines.

Cook in oil or fats to allow flavour compounds to escape.

EJJEH WITH COURGETTE, FETA, AND DILL AND BLACK LIME HARISSA

Ejjeh is a Lebanese omelette of fresh herbs and courgettes, normally spiced with a regional *baharat* (see pp23 and 26), but enlivened here with North African harissa paste. In a twist on the paste's usual recipe, dill seeds replace caraway, black lime supplants preserved lemon, and the rich smokiness comes from chipotle instead of smoked paprika.

(see pp23 and 26)

SPICE IDEAS

Try swapping dill for other spices on the **aniseed spectrum**, such as anise, star anise, allspice, or liquorice.

Experiment with different **sweet–sour substitutes** for black lime, such as sumac, barberry, amchoor, anardana, tamarind, or lemon myrtle.

Draw on the **wide range of chillies** available, fresh and dried, to vary the degrees of heat, smokiness, and flavour complexity.

Serves 2–3

Prep time 10 mins

Cooking time 30 mins

For the harissa
5 large red chillies

1 red pepper

1 tbsp chipotle chilli paste

½ tsp dried chilli flakes

½ tsp cumin seeds, toasted and ground

½ tsp dill seeds, toasted and ground

2 large garlic cloves, crushed

1½ tsp red wine vinegar

3 tbsp olive oil

pinch of sea salt

½ tsp black lime powder

For the omelette
1 tbsp olive oil, plus extra for dressing

1 courgette, grated

large handful of parsley leaves, chopped

large handful of mint leaves, chopped

1 tbsp harissa (use extra for more heat)

200g (7oz) feta cheese, drained and roughly chopped

4 large eggs, lightly beaten and seasoned with sea salt and black pepper

sea salt and black pepper

To serve
pitta breads and a radish and green leaf salad, dressed in olive oil and *za'atar* (see recipe p22)

1 First make the harissa paste. Preheat the oven to 200°C (400°F/ Gas 6). Place the chillies and pepper on a lightly oiled baking sheet and roast in the oven – 15–20 minutes for the chillies, and around 30 minutes for the pepper – turning a few times until tender and lightly charred.

2 Remove from the oven and place in a sealed plastic bag for a few minutes to help to loosen the skin. Once they are cool enough to handle, pat them dry and peel. Deseed the pepper and roughly chop, along with the chillies.

3 Blend the chillies and pepper in a food processor, then add the rest of the harissa ingredients and blitz until smooth. Loosen with a little water if the mixture is too thick. Transfer to a small, clean glass jar, seal, and store in the fridge. You will have enough harissa for 15 tablespoons, and it will keep for about a week in the fridge.

4 Now make the omelette. Set the grill to a high heat. Place a medium-sized frying pan over a medium heat, add the olive oil, and cook the grated courgette for 4–5 minutes, stirring, until it starts to soften and turns slightly golden.

5 Sprinkle over the herbs, dot the harissa around, and then add the chopped feta and a grind or two of black pepper. After 30 seconds, pour in the eggs and cook for 3–4 minutes, until the base is firm but the top is still liquid. Transfer to the grill and cook for 1–2 minutes, until the omelette is risen but still slightly gooey.

6 Serve stuffed into pitta bread with a *za'atar*-dressed radish and green leaf salad.

ANNATTO

Peppery | Earthy | Sweet

BOTANICAL NAME
Bixa orellana

ALSO KNOWN AS
Achiote, bijol, lipstick tree, *roucou, urucu.*

MAIN FLAVOUR COMPOUND
Germacrene.

PARTS USED
Seeds.

METHOD OF CULTIVATION
Seed pods are harvested when ripe pods have split to reveal the triangular seeds.

COMMERCIAL PREPARATION
The ripe pods are dried, then beaten with sticks to remove the seeds, and finally carefully winnowed by hand or machine.

NON-CULINARY USES
Fabric dye; colouring agent in cosmetics and medications; in traditional South American and Ayurvedic medicine.

Spice story

This New World spice, sometimes called "poor man's saffron", has been used as a natural dye for centuries. The Mayan Indians of Central America made a red paste from the brightly coloured seeds to paint on their bodies in preparation for battle. Annatto was also used by early Aztec civilizations as a ceremonial pigment, and apparently as a means of protecting the skin from sunburn. The Aztecs added annatto to hot drinks to colour their mouths red – hence the common name "lipstick tree". By the 17th century, this spice had arrived in Europe and was being used as a food colouring agent. It subsequently became a popular means of giving cheese and smoked fish products an attractive golden-orange colour – a practice that continues to this day.

The plant
Annatto is a tropical evergreen shrub or small tree in the achiote family.

Each *prickly red fruit capsule contains about 50 seeds, covered in red waxy pulp*

Heart-shaped *glossy leaves with reddish veins*

Seeds *are bright red in colour and yield a vivid orange-yellow dye*

Whole
The angular seeds are too hard to grind without a very powerful blender, and should be removed before serving. Store for up to three years.

Powder
Ground annatto has a fainter aroma and milder flavour, but is easier to use and yields colour faster than whole seeds. The powder has a shelf-life of one year.

Region of cultivation
Annatto is native to the Caribbean and tropical South America. It is also cultivated in the Philippines, Sri Lanka, India, Africa, and Asia.

Kitchen creativity }

Often employed solely for its staining ability, annatto is not just about colour, and can bring a peppery, slightly citrus, almost smoked-earth flavour to dishes.

BLENDING SCIENCE

The gently flavoured terpene family of compounds provide much of annatto's taste, in the form of germacrene, elemene, and copaene, all of which possess an underlying sweetness. The contrasting peppery, bitter edge to annatto comes from caryophyllene.

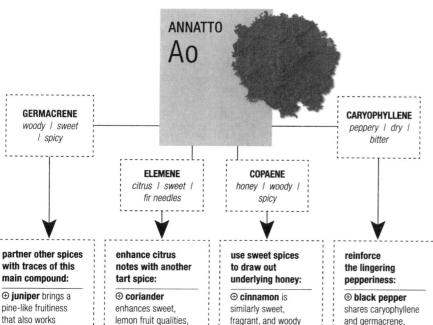

ANNATTO
Ao

GERMACRENE
woody | sweet | spicy

ELEMENE
citrus | sweet | fir needles

COPAENE
honey | woody | spicy

CARYOPHYLLENE
peppery | dry | bitter

partner other spices with traces of this main compound:

⊕ **juniper** brings a pine-like fruitiness that also works with elemene

⊕ **asafoetida**'s onion flavours are rounded off by germacrene's sweet notes

enhance citrus notes with another tart spice:

⊕ **coriander** enhances sweet, lemon fruit qualities, bringing in floral notes

⊕ **sumac** will reinforce the citrus quality of elemene

use sweet spices to draw out underlying honey:

⊕ **cinnamon** is similarly sweet, fragrant, and woody

⊕ **allspice** lends warmth and spice to the mix

⊕ **clove** has notes of camphor that also suit the fir-tree flavours of elemene

reinforce the lingering pepperiness:

⊕ **black pepper** shares caryophyllene and germacrene, and has a flavour profile that includes citrus and pine

⊕ **grains of Selim** have a peppery smokiness and share germacrene

RELEASE THE FLAVOUR AND COLOUR

Whole annatto gives the best flavour, but the hard, dense seeds need time for the flavour molecules to escape, and must be removed before serving. For these reasons, it is best to cook with oil or water flavoured by the seeds.

Cook *seeds slowly in light oil over a low heat*

Infusing in oil

Annatto oil has a stronger taste because most flavour compounds dissolve best in oil. The oil-loving bixin pigment is plentiful, so cooking with fat will give the strongest colouring.

Steep *the seeds for at least an hour*

Steeping in water

Use more seeds than for infusing oil, as flavour compounds dissolve less readily in water, and the water-solvent norbixin pigment is four times less abundant than bixin.

FOOD PARTNERS

⊕ **Sweetcorn** Drizzle annatto-infused oil over hot corn on the cob.

⊕ **Fish** Steep the seeds in hot oil and then use the oil to fry fishcakes or fritters.

⊕ **Meat** Use achiote paste in a marinade for chicken, pork, or beef before slow cooking and serving the meat "pulled" in tacos or tostadas.

⊕ **Rice** Use annatto-steeped water instead of saffron in Spanish rice with chicken.

⊕ **Chocolate** Add a pinch of ground annatto, cinnamon, and chilli to chocolate mousse.

MASTIC

Pine-like | Resinous | Woody

BOTANICAL NAME
Pistacia lentiscus

ALSO KNOWN AS
Arabic gum (not to be confused with gum arabic), *mastiha*, lentisk.

MAJOR FLAVOUR COMPOUND
Pinene.

PARTS USED
Resin.

METHOD OF CULTIVATION
The tree's bark is scored in late summer to exude resin. Trees produce resin at 5 years and can continue for 60 years.

COMMERCIAL PREPARATION
Resin gradually hardens at the base of the tree into pear-shaped "tears", which are collected, cleaned, and dried.

NON-CULINARY USES
In cosmetics and perfumery; in traditional medicine for treating wounds.

Spice story

The tree that produces mastic grows only on the Greek island of Chios, where this unique product has been cultivated for more than 2,500 years. The Ancient Greeks and Romans chewed it as a breath freshener – it is the origin of the word "masticate". When the Genoese took Chios from the Venetians in 1346 CE, they provided the islanders with protection from pirates in return for a monopoly over the lucrative mastic trade, which was by then a highly sought-after spice. In 1566, the Ottoman Turks seized control of the island and controlled mastic trade until Chios became part of the Greek state in 1913. Today, the 24 remaining mastic-producing villages – known as *mastichoria* – harvest and process the resin in the same time-honoured way. Chios mastic is now a product of Protected Designation of Origin (PDO) and most of it is exported to Turkey and the Middle East.

The plant
Mastic is harvested from small evergreen trees in the sumac family, closely related to pistachios.

Colour is light ivory at first, darkening to golden-yellow due to reaction with sunlight and air

Inedible berries turn from red to black

Grows *to 2–6m (6½–20ft) high*

Resin "tears"
Hard, translucent pieces are used in cooking and called *dahtilidopetres* (flintstones). Lower-grade, softer, larger tears are called *kantiles* (blisters) and are mainly used for chewing.

Region of cultivation
Mastic trees are native to the Mediterranean and the resin is harvested exclusively on the Greek island of Chios.

Kitchen creativity }

In Turkey, mastic is added to Turkish delight; in Lebanon, it flavours a slightly chewy, eggless ice cream, scented with rosewater. In Egypt, it is added to red meat and poultry dishes, often along with cardamom.

BLENDING SCIENCE

Mastic's subtle aroma is mostly due to the flavour compound pinene, which comprises up to 80 per cent of its chemical make up. Lesser amounts of myrcene and other terpene compounds give opportunities to partner mastic with a wide variety of savoury, sweet, or woody spices.

MASTIC
Mc

PINENE
pine-like / penetrating

CARYOPHYLLENE
woody / bitter

MYRCENE
peppery / light balsam

LINALOOL
floral / lilac

add complexity to the dominant pine:

⊕ **nutmeg** brings a complex profile of orange, floral, and woody notes alongside shared pinene and the equally harmonizing camphene

boost pepperiness with myrcene-carrying spices:

⊕ **coriander** adds a refreshing citrus quality and shares many other compounds, making it a top match

⊕ **allspice** has a peppery sweetness and also shares floral aromas of linalool

draw out floral aromas:

⊕ **rose** brings a sweet-smelling raft of floral compounds

⊕ **cardamom**'s sweet mintiness and penetrating eucalyptus, alongside linalool, also help balance out mastic's dominant pine flavour

use caryophyllene-carrying spices for more woodiness:

⊕ **cinnamon** also brings warming sweetness and floral fragrance

⊕ **clove**'s powerful eucalyptus-like eugenol also holds its own against mastic's pinene

FOOD PARTNERS

⊕ **Fruit preserves** Add a little mastic to apple jelly or fig jam.

⊕ **Roast lamb** Rub a joint of lamb with mastic, crushed onion and garlic, and some cardamom before roasting.

⊕ **Bread** Add a teaspoon of ground mastic and some fennel seeds to a savoury bread dough

⊕ **Sweet bakes** Add mastic to macaroons – mastic pairs happily with almonds – or to rosewater-scented sponge cake.

⊕ **Rice pudding** Make a mastic-scented rice pudding and drizzle with an orange-blossom-flavoured syrup.

RELEASE THE FLAVOUR

Mastic is best ground before use and mixed with another powdery-like ingredient so that it is dispersed throughout the dish.

Grind with sugar for a sweet recipe, or salt for savoury dishes, or flour for either. This also stops the mastic sticking to the grinder.

Try adding mastic to dishes via a sauce made from a roux of flour, mastic, and butter or other fats.

Plastic mastic

Adding whole mastic to a cooking broth runs the risk of creating a gluey plastic paste stuck to the bottom of the pan.

Mixed with water, myrcene flavour molecules in mastic clasp on to one another very rapidly to form long chains, or polymers, which tangle together into a sticky mass.

Microscopically thin cables are similar to those found in natural and man-made plastics and rubbers

JUNIPER

Resinous | Sharp | Floral

BOTANICAL NAME
Juniperus communis

ALSO KNOWN AS
Common juniper.

MAJOR FLAVOUR COMPOUND
Pinene.

PARTS USED
Berries (actually cones, like those on pine trees, but with fleshy scales).

METHOD OF CULTIVATION
Shrubs are grown on chalky soils. Berries are harvested in late summer or autumn.

COMMERCIAL PREPARATION
Berries are often partially dehydrated at a temperature below 35°C (95°F) to limit the evaporation of essential oils, which contain the flavour compounds.

NON-CULINARY USES
In perfumes; as a fabric dye; as an insecticide. In traditional medicine, as a diuretic and anti-inflammatory.

The plant
Juniper is a dense, prickly, evergreen shrub. Female seed cones produce the "berries", which take several years to ripen.

"Berry" flesh *contains several sacs of flavourful oils*

Ground
Berries are available roughly pre-ground, but the flavour-containing oils soon degrade and the spice needs to be used quickly.

Oiliness *of the berry indicates good quality*

Each berry *contains 6 black seeds*

Whole
The berries are available fresh, but more commonly bought semi-dried. Store in a sealed container as the oils evaporate easily; whole spice is best used within six months.

Spice story

In folklore, juniper is associated with healing and magical powers, and the dense shrub is known as a place of safe refuge; in one legend the infant Jesus is concealed in a juniper hedge to hide him from King Herod's soldiers. Since ancient times, branches of the bush have been burned to smoke meat and fish, and in the Middle Ages the wood was burned to purify the air in times of plague. Italy has been exporting home-grown juniper for more than 500 years. Most of the country's crop goes straight to distilleries for making gin, and it is still a legal requirement for juniper to be the dominant aromatic in all gins. The Dutch in the 13th century appear to have been the first to flavour spirits with juniper, using the green, unripe berries to produce a strongly alcoholic drink they named *jenever*.

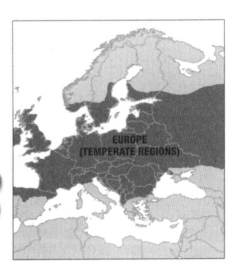

EUROPE
(TEMPERATE REGIONS)

Region of cultivation
Juniper is native to temperate regions of Europe, Russia, and the Caucasus, North America, and Japan. The strongest-tasting berries are grown in warm, sunny southern Europe.

Kitchen creativity }

Juniper has a sweet taste with a strong aroma of pine and hints of turpentine. Its clean, citrus qualities make it particularly well suited to meat, on which its acids have a mild tenderizing effect.

BLENDING SCIENCE

Juniper's principal flavour – light, woody pine – reflects the coniferous tree from which it originates; fragrant terpene compounds make up 80 per cent of juniper's flavour oils, with the pinewood aroma of pinene foremost. This range of pleasantly fragrant terpenes, combined with juniper's high sugar content (up to 33 per cent), provide ample blending opportunities.

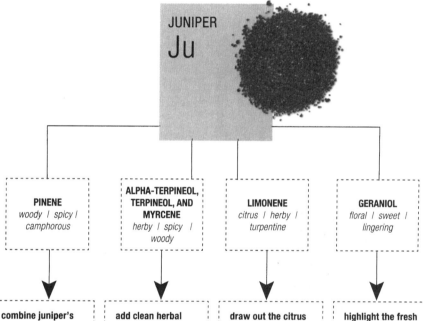

JUNIPER
Ju

PINENE
woody | spicy | camphorous

ALPHA-TERPINEOL, TERPINEOL, AND MYRCENE
herby | spicy | woody

LIMONENE
citrus | herby | turpentine

GERANIOL
floral | sweet | lingering

combine juniper's dominant pine with other complex spices featuring pinene:

⊕ **cumin** has a rich, heady aroma but with a strong pinewood background from pinene

⊕ **grains of Selim** have high levels of pinene, and contribute distinctive eucalyptus notes

⊕ **black pepper** highlights the pine aroma, while adding a peppery heat

add clean herbal notes to strongly flavoured terpenes:

⊕ **bay** contributes woody-tasting terpineol, alongside pinene and geraniol, making for a strong match

⊕ **cardamom**'s terpene compounds carry woody spice base notes, in addition to sharing limonene and geraniol

draw out the citrus notes with another limonene:

⊕ **lemon myrtle**, which also has floral hints of linalool, will bring an intensely sweet citrus taste

highlight the fresh floral notes with geraniols:

⊕ **nutmeg** also contains terpineol and pinene for a woody and earthy depth

⊕ **coriander** also contains pinene and myrcene, making it a great fit

⊕ **ginger** has both sweet and lemon flavours, which can both be brought out

FOOD PARTNERS

⊕ **Cabbage, beetroot** Add crushed berries to coleslaw, along with slivers of tart apple; mix with salt and sprinkle over beetroots before roasting.

⊕ **Citrus fruits** Flavour citrus preserves with a couple of crushed berries, or top lemon sorbet with a small pinch.

⊕ **Meat** Use in marinades, rubs, and stuffing for most meats, particularly game. Drop crushed berries into casseroles and stews, with a strip of orange peel.

⊕ **Salmon** Juniper's resinous qualities work well with oily fish: include it in a homemade cure for salmon gravlax.

⊕ **Chocolate** Stir crushed berries into a truffle or mousse cake mixture.

RELEASE THE FLAVOUR

Juniper berries don't need roasting, but do benefit from crushing or grinding to speed the rate at which the terpene-rich oils spread through a dish.

Crush berries just before using them; compounds soon evaporate when the oil sacs are broken.

Terpenes from the oil dissolve poorly in water but spread easily through oil and alcohol.

Meat rubs of crushed juniper give a strong taste as the surface fats disperse the flavours.

ROSE

Floral | Musky | Sweet

BOTANICAL NAME
Rosa x *damascena*
(most commonly used species)

ALSO KNOWN AS
Damask rose.

MAJOR FLAVOUR COMPOUND
Geraniol.

PARTS USED
Dried buds or petals.

METHOD OF CULTIVATION
Buds and flower heads are harvested by hand. For petals, they are picked before or at sunrise on the first day in full bloom.

COMMERCIAL PREPARATION
Buds and petals are dried to sell as a spice, or distilled to produce rose oil.

NON-CULINARY USES
In perfumery and cosmetics; in traditional herbal medicine as an antidepressant and antiseptic, and to treat anxiety.

Spice story

The rose was first cultivated about 5,000 years ago by the ancient civilizations of China, who prized the flower for its beauty, perfume, and healing properties. The Romans grew roses extensively and documented their medicinal uses, including (when worn as a floral crown) protection from hangovers. In the 7th century CE cultivation of roses spread throughout the Middle East. Around this time the Persians discovered how to extract oil from the flower, and its culinary use became more widespread. By the Middle Ages, roses were used at medieval banquets to perfume water for hand washing, and to flavour savoury and sweet dishes. During the Crusades, the highly scented damask rose, the main source of rose oil, reached northern Europe. In Victorian England, rose-petal sandwiches were considered a refined teatime treat.

The plant
The damask rose is a hardy flowering shrub and the main source of rose flavouring used in cooking, although *Rosa rugosa* is popular in China, Japan, and Korea.

A bush *can be productive for up to 40 years*

Petals ➤

◄ *Buds*

Petals and buds
These are available dry for use as a spice, or crystallized for decorating cakes and desserts.

BULGARIA

TURKEY

IRAN

INDIA

Region of cultivation
The rose is native to temperate regions of the northern hemisphere, probably originating in China; the damask rose is native to the Middle East. It is cultivated in Turkey, India, Iran, Bulgaria, and Morocco.

Kitchen creativity }

Rose petals add sweet floral aromas to both sweet and savoury dishes. The petals of any unsprayed scented rose can be used, but those cultivated specifically for consumption have a more potent flavour than garden roses.

BLENDING SCIENCE

Rose's flavour profile is dominated by terpene flavour compounds that have a sweet, floral character, including geraniol, nerol, eugenol, and linalool. The unique rose aroma is produced by potent flavour compounds called "rose ketones", which provide fresh green notes, herby spiciness, woody sweetness, and berry-like notes.

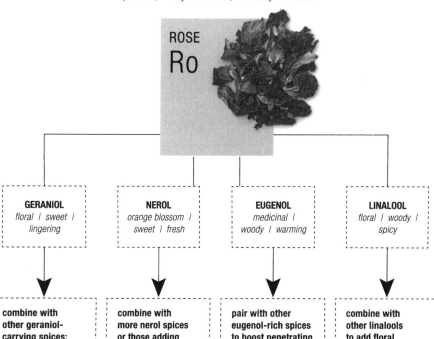

ROSE
Ro

GERANIOL
floral | sweet | lingering

NEROL
orange blossom | sweet | fresh

EUGENOL
medicinal | woody | warming

LINALOOL
floral | woody | spicy

combine with other geraniol-carrying spices:

⊕ **ginger** adds pungent warmth and citrus notes, and also shares linalool

⊕ **nutmeg** used sparingly brings a warm, earthy spiciness, and also shares eugenol

combine with more nerol spices or those adding complex sweetness:

⊕ **lemongrass** lends citrus notes, mild pepperiness, and slight spiciness, also shares linalool

⊕ **vanilla** has rich, mellow creaminess and complex flavours that including subtle cherry notes

pair with other eugenol-rich spices to boost penetrating menthol nuances:

⊕ **allspice** provides sweet peppery flavours

⊕ **clove** adds sweet, astringent, eucalyptus-like notes

combine with other linalools to add floral complexity:

⊕ **cinnamon, cassia** contributes warming sweetness, with a touch of bitterness from cassia

⊕ **coriander** provides a powerful citrus spiciness alongside floral qualities

FOOD PARTNERS

⊕ **Cherries** Add to stewed cherries and use instead of jam in a tart.

⊕ **Vegetables** Add dried petals to harissa and serve with grilled vegetables.

⊕ **Chicken** Sprinkle crushed petals into a Moroccan-style chicken stew.

⊕ **Mackerel** Serve grilled mackerel with couscous scented with ground rose petals.

⊕ **Shortbread** Add a few crushed dried rose petals to the dough for shortbread biscuit.

⊕ **Ice cream** Use ground petals or rosewater to make rose ice cream.

RELEASE THE FLAVOUR

Rose's most potent flavour compounds are oil-soluble, but can easily overpower a dish: this is one spice that benefits from being used in a water-based way. Even so, rosewater contains several hundred flavour compounds, which give it a complex subtle flavour.

Make your own rosewater by steeping rose petals in water. Allow several days for the flavour compounds to slowly dissolve into the liquid.

BLEND TO TRY

Use and adapt this classic blend, suitable for sweet or savoury dishes:

Advieh p27

CORIANDER
Citrus | Floral | Warming

BOTANICAL NAME
Coriandrum sativum

ALSO KNOWN AS
Cilantro; sometimes mistakenly called
Indian, Chinese, or Japanese parsley.

MAJOR FLAVOUR COMPOUND
Linalool.

PARTS USED
"Seeds" (in fact fruits), leaves, and roots.

METHOD OF CULTIVATION
Grown in fields as an annual crop; the
fruits form on the plant about three
months after sowing.

COMMERCIAL PREPARATION
Stalks are cut before the fruits are fully ripe.
Fruits are threshed, cleaned and dried.

NON-CULINARY USES
Essential oil in perfumes and cosmetics.
Also used as traditional remedy for ulcers
and stomach problems.

Spice story

The discovery of an 8,000-year-old
stockpile of the spice in the Nahal
Hemar cave in Israel, together
with evidence from Egyptian tombs,
suggests coriander has its origins as
a commercial crop in the Near East.
The Greeks and Romans used it as
a medicine and a meat preservative,
as well as a spice in dishes such as
lentils with chestnuts. The spice
travelled to India via Persia around
2,000 years ago, and four centuries
later evidence points to its widespread
use from China to Anglo-Saxon Britain.
Early European settlers took the spice
to North America, where it became
naturalized and widely cultivated.
By the 18th century, the spice had
fallen out of favour in Europe, and
its use became largely limited to gin
distilling and beer brewing; it is still
a popular flavouring in Belgian beers.

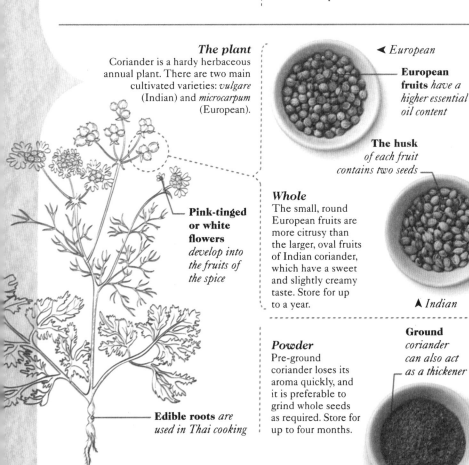

The plant
Coriander is a hardy herbaceous
annual plant. There are two main
cultivated varieties: *vulgare*
(Indian) and *microcarpum*
(European).

◄ *European*

**European
fruits** *have a
higher essential
oil content*

The husk
*of each fruit
contains two seeds*

**Pink-tinged
or white
flowers**
*develop into
the fruits of
the spice*

Whole
The small, round
European fruits are
more citrusy than
the larger, oval fruits
of Indian coriander,
which have a sweet
and slightly creamy
taste. Store for up
to a year.

▲ *Indian*

Edible roots *are
used in Thai cooking*

Powder
Pre-ground
coriander loses its
aroma quickly, and
it is preferable to
grind whole seeds
as required. Store for
up to four months.

Ground
*coriander
can also act
as a thickener*

Region of cultivation
Native to the Mediterranean and southern
Europe, coriander is now cultivated extensively
throughout the world for both seed and leaves.
The main centres of production are in India
and Russia, with large exports from Morocco,
Romania, Iran, China, Turkey and Egypt.

Kitchen creativity }

Coriander is a versatile spice with a bittersweet taste reminiscent of dried orange peel. While it can be used on its own, the spice is more frequently partnered with earthy cumin to form the backbone of savoury blends the world over.

BLENDING SCIENCE

Lilac-scented linalool dominates the flavour profile of coriander, followed by a variety of mildly flavoured terpenes, including pinene, cymene, and limonene, making it a versatile spice for pairing.

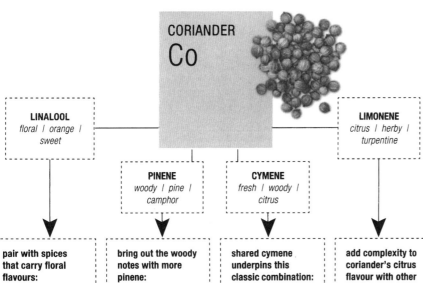

CORIANDER
Co

LINALOOL
floral | orange | sweet

LIMONENE
citrus | herby | turpentine

PINENE
woody | pine | camphor

CYMENE
fresh | woody | citrus

pair with spices that carry floral flavours:

⊕ **cardamom** also contributes an herbal sweetness

⊕ **nutmeg, mace** bring warming sweetness with a strong floral element

bring out the woody notes with more pinene:

⊕ **black pepper**'s woody pinene and limonene mean pepper's gentle pungency blends well

⊕ **anise, allspice** contribute woody, warming flavours and add sweetness

shared cymene underpins this classic combination:

⊕ **cumin**'s slightly bitter earthiness is a great foil for the floral citrus nature of coriander

add complexity to coriander's citrus flavour with other fruity nuances:

⊕ **ginger** provides harmonious zesty notes

⊕ **lemongrass** powerfully enhances floral citrus

⊕ **caraway** brings subtle anise-like peppery flavours

FOOD PARTNERS

⊕ **Celery, fennel, cabbage** Toss a few crushed seeds into coleslaw or when braising.

⊕ **Citrus, apples, pears** Add toasted and ground to citrus sorbets and to crumble topping or pastry dough for apples and pears.

⊕ **Pork, game, chicken** Use as a dry marinade or rub, or in stuffing mixtures.

⊕ **Tuna and shellfish** Rub ground over tuna steaks before searing, or add whole to a court-bouillon for poaching shellfish.

⊕ **Preserves** Works well as a pickling spice, and in tomato relish and marmalade.

⊕ **Sponge cake** Add a pinch to plain sponge; it also works beautifully with citrus, blueberries, or blackberries.

BLENDS TO TRY

Try these recipes for classic blends featuring coriander, or why not adapt them with some blending science?

Zhug p24
Dukkah p28
Durban curry masala p37
Malaysian fish curry paste p51
Chimichurri p66

RELEASE THE FLAVOUR

Coriander's most flavoursome oils are deep inside the seeds, and its taste profile changes greatly when the seeds are toasted.

Leave untoasted to allow the green, floral flavours to dominate.

130°C (266°F) – 180°C (356°F)

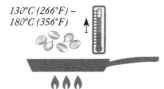

Dry fry to a deep brown colour to develop nutty, earthy pyrazines.

Crack open or grind seeds to release the oils, especially for quick-cooking dishes.

WEST AFRICAN PEANUT CURRY WITH DURBAN MASALA

Inspired by the peanut soups and stews of West Africa, this recipe foregos the usual fiery Scotch bonnet chillies for a twist from South Africa's Eastern Cape – a Durban curry masala spice blend. The heat comes mainly from the cayenne pepper, so use less for a milder kick. For a hearty soup, simply add more water at the end of cooking.

SPICE IDEAS

Blend your own masala: swap in black cardamom or grains of Selim, for smokiness, or replace ginger or coriander with woody, balsamic mace.

Dry fry the whole spices to **create new toasted pyrazine flavours**, but take care, as they can dominate.

Add fresh spices to the frying vegetables for a **deeper base flavour**: the pungency of garlic and ginger will mellow and sweeten with prolonged cooking.

Serves 6–8

Prep time 20 mins

Cooking time 25–35 mins

For the Durban masala blend
2 tsp cumin seeds
1 tsp coriander seeds
½ tsp fenugreek seeds
seeds of 5 cardamom pods
1 cinnamon stick
5 cloves
1 tsp cayenne pepper
½ tsp ground ginger

For the curry
4 tbsp unsweetened peanut butter
500ml (16fl oz) water
2 tbsp oil
3 large carrots, peeled
2 parsnips, peeled
1 swede or turnip, about 500g (1lb 2oz)
4 baby aubergines or white garden egg aubergines (optional)
1 medium onion, diced
400g (14oz) mushrooms, wild, cultivated, or mixed
1 tbsp tomato purée
2 ripe tomatoes, finely diced
500ml (16fl oz) vegetable stock
salt and pepper to taste

1 For the Durban masala, grind the whole spices and combine with the cayenne pepper and ginger. Set aside.

2 Prepare the peanut butter by blending it with a cup of water in a food processer. Once it is smooth, pour into a pan and stir in the remaining water. Simmer on a low heat for about 15 minutes, until oil starts to gather on the surface.

3 Chop the carrots and parsnips into 2–3cm (1in) chunks. Heat 1 tablespoon of the oil in a large pan. Add the vegetables and fry over a medium–high heat for 10–15 minutes, only stirring occasionally, until the sides brown and caramelize. Remove from the pan and set aside.

4 Heat the remaining oil in the pan and add the onions and spices. Sauté over a medium heat for a few minutes, then add the tomato purée and chopped tomatoes. Increase the heat to the maximum, add the mushrooms, and fry for 3 minutes.

5 Add the vegetable stock, peanut sauce, and vegetables to the pan. Chop the aubergines (if using) into 2–3cm (1in) chunks and add. Bring to the boil, then simmer for 15–20 minutes, until the vegetables are tender.

6 Check for seasoning and add salt or pepper. Remove any large whole spices and serve the dish with sticky rice. Alternatively, to serve as a soup, add water and bring back to the boil.

CUMIN

Earthy | Herby | Woody

BOTANICAL NAME
Cuminum cyminum

ALSO KNOWN AS
Roman caraway, *jeera*.

MAJOR FLAVOUR COMPOUND
Cuminaldehyde.

PARTS USED
"Seeds", which are technically fruits

METHOD OF CULTIVATION
Grown as an annual crop, plants are cut around four months after planting, when the fruits turn yellow-brown.

COMMERCIAL PREPARATION
Stalks are dried then threshed to separate fruits, which are then further dried.

NON-CULINARY USES
Essential oil in perfumes and veterinary medicines. In traditional medicine, taken to aid indigestion and relieve flatulence.

Spice story

Evidence of cumin in Egypt's pyramids suggests that it was in use more than 5,000 years ago. The Ancient Greeks and Romans used cumin as a table seasoning alongside salt. Roman naturalist Pliny the Elder regarded it as the king of condiments, and in modern-day Georgia and Africa salt combined with cumin is still a popular seasoning. From the 7th century CE, Arab traders transported cumin on their spice caravans to North Africa and east to Iran, India, Indonesia, and China, and it became a key component of many regional spice mixes, including *baharat* (Middle East), *garam masala* and *panch phoran* (India), and *ras el hanout* (Morocco). Spanish conquistadors introduced cumin to the Americas in the 16th century, notably to Mexico, where the spice became deeply embedded in the cuisine.

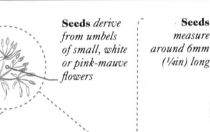

Seeds *derive from umbels of small, white or pink-mauve flowers*

Seeds *measure around 6mm (¼in) long*

Multi-stemmed *plant grows to 30–60cm (1–2ft) tall*

Whole
The boat-shaped, light brown seeds will keep their flavour for up to a year if stored in a sealed container somewhere cool and dark.

The plant
Cumin is a drought-tolerant, annual herbaceous plant in the parsley family.

Powder
Buy ground cumin in small quantities, as it quickly loses its potency; use within a couple of months.

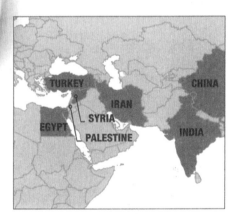

Region of cultivation
Thought to be native to Egypt's Nile Valley and the Eastern Mediterranean, cumin is cultivated in India (the largest producer and consumer), China, Syria, Turkey, and Iran. Palestine and USA are other producers.

Kitchen creativity }

Cumin is an essential component of Indian, North African, Levantine, and Mexican cuisine. Used alone or in combination with other spices, it imbues a diverse range of savoury dishes with its distinctive, highly aromatic, and pungent flavour.

BLENDING SCIENCE

Cumin's uniquely musky, spicy flavour derives from cuminaldehyde, a compound found in roast beef and cinnamon but sparingly in other spices. Other important compounds include pinene, which gives the spice its dry, pinewood nuance, and cymene, which has a fresh, turpentine-like aroma.

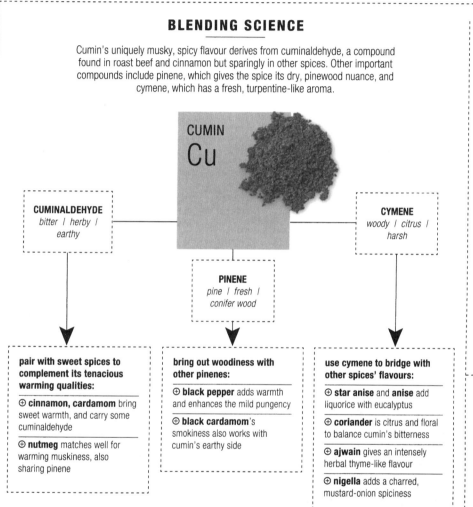

CUMIN
Cu

CUMINALDEHYDE
bitter | herby | earthy

PINENE
pine | fresh | conifer wood

CYMENE
woody | citrus | harsh

pair with sweet spices to complement its tenacious warming qualities:

⊕ **cinnamon, cardamom** bring sweet warmth, and carry some cuminaldehyde

⊕ **nutmeg** matches well for warming muskiness, also sharing pinene

bring out woodiness with other pinenes:

⊕ **black pepper** adds warmth and enhances the mild pungency

⊕ **black cardamom**'s smokiness also works with cumin's earthy side

use cymene to bridge with other spices' flavours:

⊕ **star anise** and **anise** add liquorice with eucalyptus

⊕ **coriander** is citrus and floral to balance cumin's bitterness

⊕ **ajwain** gives an intensely herbal thyme-like flavour

⊕ **nigella** adds a charred, mustard-onion spiciness

FOOD PARTNERS

⊕ **Aubergine and root vegetables** Toast and crush seeds for sprinkling over roasted aubergine, a beetroot dip, or puréed roots.

⊕ **Pulses** Use as a flavouring for dhal and other lentil stews, in falafel mix, and scattered over hummus.

⊕ **Beef and lamb** Add a pinch of ground cumin to minced lamb for Moorish-style kebabs, or to beef rendang, Mexican mole, and chilli con carne.

⊕ **Salt** Toast seeds and then grind with an equal quantity of sea salt, for sprinkling over roast chicken, tomato salad, avocado toast, tacos, or roast potatoes.

⊕ **Yogurt** Combine cumin seeds, yogurt, and lemon to make a dressing for roasted vegetables or a salad of bitter leaves, such as mustard greens or kale.

BLENDS TO TRY

Try these recipes for classic blends featuring cumin, or why not adapt them with some blending science?

RELEASE THE FLAVOUR

Cumin is particularly responsive to toasting: bruise and dry fry the seeds to produce roasted-tasting pyrazines. Some new toasted compounds also contain sulphur.

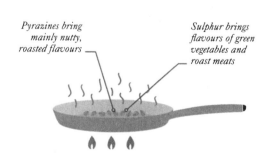

Pyrazines bring mainly nutty, roasted flavours

Sulphur brings flavours of green vegetables and roast meats

NIGELLA

Mild | Peppery | Herbaceous

BOTANICAL NAME
Nigella sativa

ALSO KNOWN AS
Love-in-a-mist, black onion seeds, black cumin, black caraway.

MAJOR FLAVOUR COMPOUND
Nigellone.

PARTS USED
Seeds.

METHOD OF CULTIVATION
An annual plant, it produces large seed capsules that are harvested as they ripen.

COMMERCIAL PREPARATION
The capsules are dried then crushed to release the seeds, which are either sold whole or have their oil extracted.

NON-CULINARY USES
In natural remedies the seeds are used to alleviate cold symptoms, treat digestive ailments, and encourage lactation.

Plants *reach a height of about 60cm (2ft)*

Tear-drop shaped seeds *are beige until dried in air*

The plant
Nigella is a small, herbaceous annual plant from the buttercup family. It produces pale-blue, five-petalled flowers and feathery grey-green foliage.

Whole
Seeds will keep for up to two years. They are very hard, so grind them in a spice or coffee grinder rather than by hand with a pestle and mortar.

Spice story

Reputedly found in King Tutankhamun's tomb in ancient Egypt, nigella has been cultivated for its seeds for more than 3,000 years. Its name derives from the Latin *nigellus* or *niger* (black). Ancient Greeks and Arabs appreciated the seed's curative and preservative properties; according to an Arab proverb, nigella is "a remedy for all diseases except death". An ancient Arab text describes it as *habbatul barakah*, "seed of blessing", while in the Old Testament it is called *ketzah*. The Roman physician and philosopher Galen prescribed nigella seeds to treat colds, and they are still used in this way: a spoonful of seeds is wrapped in muslin, held to the nostril, and inhaled to clear a blocked nose. Nigella has been used as a herbal remedy across southern Europe, western Asia, and the Middle East.

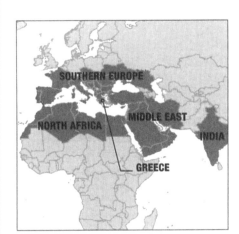

Region of cultivation
Native to southern Europe, Turkey, the Caucasus, and the Middle East, nigella is now cultivated in India – the largest modern-day producer – and Egypt, North Africa, and southern Asia.

Kitchen creativity }

Nigella is a punchy spice that releases a mild heat on the tongue and has a slightly bitter, herby, charred onion-like flavour. It is widely used in Indian cooking and its preservative properties make it a fine pickling spice for fruit and vegetables.

BLENDING SCIENCE

Look to the secondary flavour compounds of nigella for effective spice pairings: significant concentrations of cymene give the spice its earthy, fresh aroma, and smaller amounts of the mild terpenes pinene and limonene are also present.

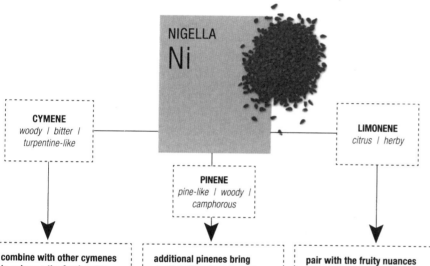

NIGELLA
Ni

CYMENE
woody | bitter | turpentine-like

PINENE
pine-like | woody | camphorous

LIMONENE
citrus | herby

combine with other cymenes to enhance the fresh notes:

⊕ **ajwain**'s thymol tastes like oregano and links to nigella's herbiness, adding bitterness and menthol-like cooling

⊕ **cumin** brings musky warmth

⊕ **nutmeg** used sparingly adds woody, warming spicy notes

additional pinenes bring depth to the pine elements:

⊕ **black pepper** contributes mild pungency and bitterness

⊕ **cinnamon** enhances the woody qualities, drawing out sweetness

pair with the fruity nuances of other limonenes:

⊕ **coriander**'s dominant floral citrus counterbalances nigella's onion-like bitterness

⊕ **caraway** brings anise-like, peppery pungency

FOOD PARTNERS

⊕ **Vegetables** Add to vegetarian curries made with root vegetables, squash, or aubergine.

⊕ **Grains and pulses** Flavour rice and bulgur wheat with lightly toasted seeds; fry briefly in oil or ghee and stir into just cooked dhal.

⊕ **Eggs** Sprinkle over scrambled or fried eggs.

⊕ **Breads** Combine with white sesame seeds and stir into flatbread dough or sprinkle on top. Also works well with rye breads.

⊕ **Goat's cheese** Work the seeds into a cheese dip made with whipped feta or other goat's cheese.

⊕ **Lamb** Use in a slow-braised Indian korma or Moroccan tagine.

RELEASE THE FLAVOUR

Nigella seeds are hard to break, and their flavoursome oils are locked away in minute capsules. One way to help the oils escape is by grinding seeds, then toasting in a dry frying pan, which also generates additional pyrazine flavour compounds.

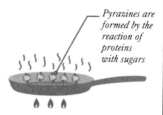

Pyrazines are formed by the reaction of proteins with sugars

BLEND TO TRY

Try this recipe for a classic blend featuring nigella, or why not adapt it with some blending science?

Panch phoran p43

The oregano connection

Nigella's main flavour compound – nigellone – is almost unique in nature, yet many people detect a similarity with oregano. The explanation is that nigellone forms from the sticking together of molecules of thymoquinone, a medicinal-tasting compound that is also found in oregano.

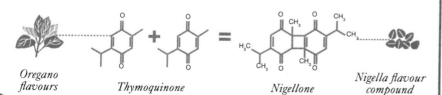

Oregano flavours   *Thymoquinone*   *Nigellone*   *Nigella flavour compound*

GRAINS OF SELIM

Musky | Resinous | Bitter

BOTANICAL NAME
Xylopia aethiopica

ALSO KNOWN AS
Uda pod, Ethiopian pepper, *habzeli*, kimba pepper, *Selem kili*, Guinea pepper.

MAJOR FLAVOUR COMPOUND
Fenchone.

PARTS USED
Pods (fruits) and seeds.

METHOD OF CULTIVATION
Trees are harvested for their pods, which are picked at various stages of maturity.

COMMERCIAL PREPARATION
In Senegal, immature fruits are smoked and then pounded; elsewhere, the sun-dried pods are ground or used whole.

NON-CULINARY USES
In traditional African medicine: fruit and/or roots are used to treat a variety of complaints. Bark extract is used in skin ointments.

The plant
Grains of Selim come from an evergreen tree, which grows in humid tropical regions of Africa. Trees can grow to a height of 30m (98ft).

Seed pods *form in dense clusters*

Pods *contain five to eight seeds*

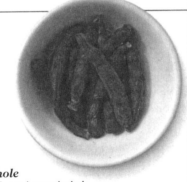

Whole
Pods can be used whole and removed from the dish before serving.

Powder
Grind or pound pods and use immediately, since the flavour compounds evaporate quickly. For this reason pre-ground powder is rarely available.

Spice story

Grains of Selim are a popular spice across Africa, from Ethiopia to Ghana. Like grains of paradise, during the Middle Ages the spice was exported north to Europe and sold as a substitute for scarce and expensive black pepper. However, its popularity in Europe waned from the 16th century; by then, Portuguese sailors and merchants had established sea trade routes from Asia to Europe, and this vastly improved the availability of black pepper and other exotic spices. Outside its indigenous regions, the spice is often called Ethiopian pepper, but it is no relation to *Piper nigrum*. It is valued as both a culinary spice and a medicine in Africa, particularly southern Nigeria, and deserves to be better known outside the continent.

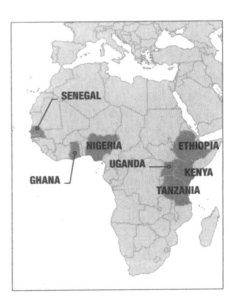

Region of cultivation
The spice is native to Ethiopia and is cultivated there, as well as in Kenya, Uganda, Tanzania, Nigeria, Ghana, and Senegal.

Kitchen creativity }

Whole pods add a raw pepperiness to soups, porridges, stews, and sauces, while the ground pods make excellent dry rubs for meat and fish. The whole pods are sometimes tied in a muslin pouch so that they can be removed easily before serving.

BLENDING SCIENCE

The unique flavour of grains of Selim is due to a powerful and unusual compound called fenchone. You can also make interesting matches with its less dominating flavour compounds, such as vanillin, germacrene, linalool, geraniol, and pinene.

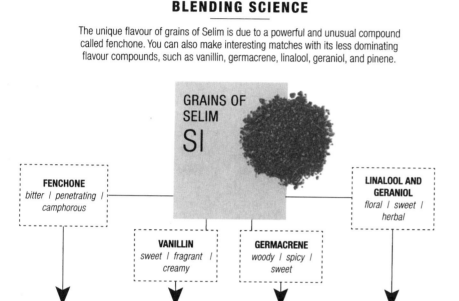

GRAINS OF SELIM
SI

FENCHONE
bitter | penetrating | camphorous

VANILLIN
sweet | fragrant | creamy

GERMACRENE
woody | spicy | sweet

LINALOOL AND GERANIOL
floral | sweet | herbal

team with other spices that carry this compound:

⊕ **fennel** brings a strong liquorice taste and accentuates pine flavour

⊕ **dill** carries subtler, anise-like flavours and adds hints of citrus

complement sweet hints with fruity, tangy spices:

⊕ **juniper** is an excellent sweet match, sharing pinene and geraniol

⊕ **sumac** brings mouth-puckering sweet-sour notes

⊕ **liquorice** contains intensely sweet glycyrrhizin and shares cineole

enhance woody notes with similar compounds

⊕ **nutmeg** and **mace** contain a woody compound called myristicin

add a fragrant floral spice to the mix:

⊕ **coriander**'s floral flavours are sweet and citrus infused

⊕ **cardamom** shares linalool while penetrating cineole complements the lingering camphor notes

FOOD PARTNERS

⊕ **Drinks** Use the ground spice to make the Senegalese coffee drink *café touba*.

⊕ **Vegetables** Add the ground spice to a vegetable curry of beans, tomatoes, and courgettes; sprinkle the ground spice over a spiced squash soup.

⊕ **Fish** Use the ground spice as a rub for fish, such as cod, before grilling, baking, or adding to a richly spiced gumbo.

⊕ **Meat** Make peppersoup, a West African soup containing grains of Selim, nutmeg, chilli, and assorted meats.

⊕ **Rice** Add a whole pod to pilaf or biryani, or to Nigerian "one-pot" jollof rice.

MAXIMIZE THE SMOKINESS

Dried pods are smoked during drying to give a musky, wood-smoke aroma. Most of the smokiness is in the pods, so for the fullest smoky flavour grind the whole pods just before use.

Aroma-laden fragments embed in the skin of the pods

Pleasantly fragrant molecules (particularly phenolics) are deposited by the rising smoke particles as they wash over the dry fruit.

RELEASE THE FLAVOUR

The main flavour compounds of grains of Selim dissolve and mix well in fats and alcohol, but less so in water-based liquids.

Cook briefly in fat before adding to a dish, or add towards the end of the frying time.

Add early when cooking in watery dishes, to allow time for flavours to infuse the dish.

BLEND TO TRY

Use and adapt this classic blend featuring grains of Selim.
Yaji p36

BLACK CARDAMOM

Smoky | Camphorous | Resinous

BOTANICAL NAME
Amomum subulatum

ALSO KNOWN AS
Winged cardamom, brown or greater cardamom, large cardamom, black gold.

MAJOR FLAVOUR COMPOUND
Cineole.

PARTS USED
Seeds and whole fruit ("pod").

METHOD OF CULTIVATION
Grown in forest shade; the seed pods of three-year-old plants are handpicked from near the base, before they fully ripen.

COMMERCIAL PREPARATION
Pods are dried for 24–72 hours over an open fire in a curing kiln, which gives them their dark colour and smoky taste.

NON-CULINARY USES
In perfumes and dental products; in traditional medicine for treating sore throats, stomach disorders, and malaria.

Spice story

Black cardamom has suffered from an unwarranted reputation as an inferior substitute for its green cousin, and until the 20th century was mainly used for perfumes in the West. The spice has traditionally been cultivated by the Lepcha community of Sikkim, a state in Northeast India. The Sikkimese themselves use black cardamom for medicinal purposes and rarely cook with it, but in China its culinary value has been appreciated for centuries. The spice has only been cultivated outside Sikkim since the 1960s, when it was introduced to Nepal and Bhutan, then later still to Darjeeling in West Bengal. Now both areas cultivate it for domestic use, notably as a key constituent of garam masala spice blends, and, increasingly, for export to the Middle East, Japan, and Russia.

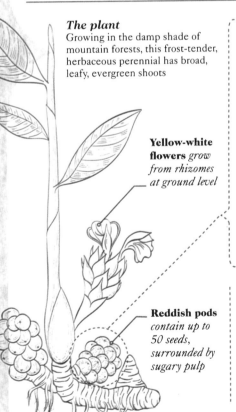

The plant
Growing in the damp shade of mountain forests, this frost-tender, herbaceous perennial has broad, leafy, evergreen shoots

Yellow-white flowers *grow from rhizomes at ground level*

Reddish pods *contain up to 50 seeds, surrounded by sugary pulp*

Seeds *are held in clusters inside the husk*

Pods *are about three times the size of green cardamom pods*

Black cardamom
Buy whole black cardamom pods (not ground seeds) and store in an airtight container for up to 1 year. Seeds begin to lose their flavour when pods are broken open: use immediately.

Chinese black cardamom
Also known as *cao guo*, these are the much larger pods of a different species of *Amomum*, but they have a very similar taste and can be used interchangeably.

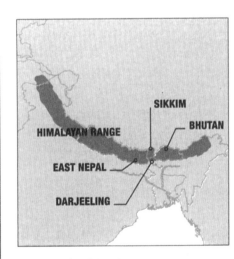

SIKKIM
BHUTAN
HIMALAYAN RANGE
EAST NEPAL
DARJEELING

Region of cultivation
Native to the damp, hilly forest areas of the eastern Himalayas, from Nepal into China; up to 90 per cent of black cardamom is still grown in the state of Sikkim in Northeast India.

Kitchen creativity }

Black cardamom is best suited to slow-cooked, savoury dishes. It is typically used in the braised meat dishes of Sichuan cuisine, in pho and other Vietnamese broths and soups, and in garam masala and pilafs of India and Nepal.

BLENDING SCIENCE

Black cardamom is dominated by the same penetrating cineole compound that gives green cardamom its flavour, but here the similarity ends. Varied smoky phenols, significant amounts of clove-like eugenol, pine-like pinene, and citrusy limonene, offer a wide range of pairing opportunities.

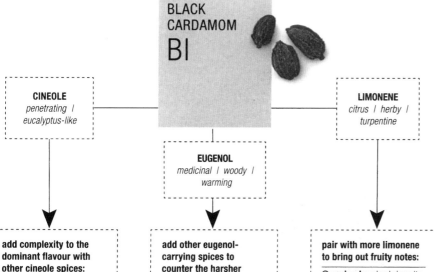

BLACK CARDAMOM BI

CINEOLE
penetrating | eucalyptus-like

EUGENOL
medicinal | woody | warming

LIMONENE
citrus | herby | turpentine

add complexity to the dominant flavour with other cineole spices:

⊕ **allspice** provides a sweet, peppery warmth

⊕ **cardamom** gives a sweeter, more floral edge

⊕ **galangal** enhances the camphorous flavours

add other eugenol-carrying spices to counter the harsher notes of cineole:

⊕ **nutmeg** used sparingly adds warm, spicy notes

⊕ **cinnamon** contributes sweet, fragrant qualities

pair with more limonene to bring out fruity notes:

⊕ **coriander** also brings its strong floral flavour

⊕ **caraway** brings an additional anise-like taste that goes well with cardamom's smokiness

FOOD PARTNERS

⊕ **Bitter greens** Stir in a pinch of ground seeds when slow cooking bitter leafy vegetables, such as collard greens.

⊕ **Pickled vegetables** Whole pods work well in sweet or savoury brines when pickling carrots, cucumbers, marrows, or tomatoes.

⊕ **Vegetarian stews** The char-grilled taste makes black cardamom a useful substitute for smoked bacon in stews and hotpots.

⊕ **Red meat** Add the bashed seeds to dry barbecue rubs for red meat.

⊕ **Chocolate** Sprinkle crushed seeds sparingly over dark chocolate mousse or over partially set chocolate when making chocolate bark or truffles.

BLENDS TO TRY

Try these recipes for classic blends featuring black cardamom, or why not adapt them with some blending science?

Garam masala p40

Shandong spice bag p58

Advieh p27

Vindaloo paste p44

RELEASE THE FLAVOUR

Most of the smoky flavours are in the husk, so use whole pods if you want to retain the meaty smokiness.

Dry fry whole pods or ground seeds to create nutty and roasted flavour compounds that interact with the smoky compounds.

Lightly crush whole pods before adding them early in cooking so that the full flavour can be infused into the dish.

Grind the seeds to release their flavoursome oils for a more intense taste, but use immediately, as the oils quickly evaporate.

CARDAMOM

Eucalyptus | Citrusy | Floral

BOTANICAL NAME
Elettaria cardamomum

ALSO KNOWN AS
Small cardamom, green cardamom, true cardamom, queen of spices.

MAJOR FLAVOUR COMPOUND
Cineole.

PARTS USED
Whole "pods" (fruits) containing seeds.

METHOD OF CULTIVATION
Almost ripe seed pods are harvested by hand five or six times a year.

COMMERCIAL PREPARATION
Seed pods are washed and then dried in the sun or in heated "curing" rooms.

NON-CULINARY USES
Perfumery; cosmetics; in some cough sweets; in Ayurvedic medicine to treat depression, skin conditions, urinary conditions, and jaundice.

The plant
Cardamom is a tropical perennial in the ginger family. Its tall shoots develop from rhizomes (underground stems).

Sword-shaped leaves *are very mildly aromatic.*

Fruits *contain 15–20 seeds that ripen from white to reddish-brown or black*

Flowers *are green with a violet-streaked white petal*

Seeds
The seeds in good-quality cardamom pods should be black and slightly sticky. Avoid using seeds that are dry and pale.

Whole pods
The papery pods are normally yellowish green; white pods are bleached for aesthetic reasons, and have a weakened aroma.

Pods *are graded by width, with the fattest ones containing the most seeds*

Spice story

Cardamom has been used for culinary and medicinal purposes in India for more than 2,000 years. The spice was known by the ancient Greeks and Romans, who valued its qualities as a perfume and digestive aid. Vikings from northern Europe are reported to have encountered the spice during their raids on Constantinople in the 9th century CE, and to have taken it back to Scandinavia, where it remains a popular flavouring for breads and pastries. Cardamom began to be grown as a secondary crop in the coffee plantations of British India in the 19th century, and in 1914 the spice was introduced to Guatemala, which is now the world's largest producer. Around 60 per cent of all cardamom is consumed in Arab countries, where it is a key ingredient of *gahwa*, a fragrant coffee served as a symbol of hospitality.

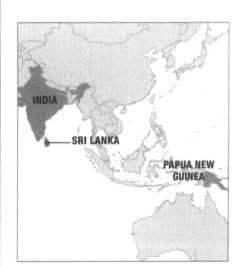

Region of cultivation
Cardamom is native to southern India and Sri Lanka, but Guatemala is now the world's largest producer, followed by India, Papua New Guinea, Sri Lanka, and Tanzania.

Kitchen creativity }

This highly aromatic spice is sweet, somewhat minty, and penetrating, making it suitable for both sweet and savoury dishes, and more versatile than black cardamom, which lacks sweetness and has a smoky aroma that may not work in desserts.

BLENDING SCIENCE

Cardamom's flavour profile is dominated by a powerfully penetrating eucalyptus-like flavour compound called cineole. It also contains a less common flavour compound, alpha-fenchyl acetate, which is sweet, minty, and herbal. In addition, there are significant amounts of several pleasant terpene compounds, including lemony limonene and delicately floral linalool.

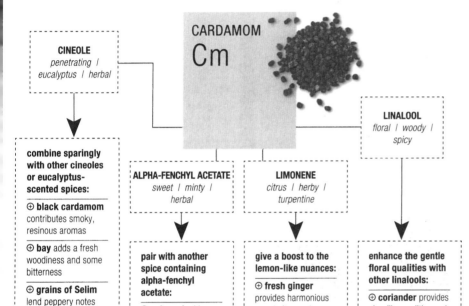

CARDAMOM
Cm

CINEOLE
penetrating | eucalyptus | herbal

LINALOOL
floral | woody | spicy

ALPHA-FENCHYL ACETATE
sweet | minty | herbal

LIMONENE
citrus | herby | turpentine

combine sparingly with other cineoles or eucalyptus-scented spices:

⊕ **black cardamom** contributes smoky, resinous aromas

⊕ **bay** adds a fresh woodiness and some bitterness

⊕ **grains of Selim** lend peppery notes

⊕ **allspice** and **nutmeg** offer a slightly subtler match with their eucalyptus scent and sweetness

pair with another spice containing alpha-fenchyl acetate:

⊕ **galangal** adds powerfully aromatic flavours and enhances the eucalyptus quality through shared cineole

give a boost to the lemon-like nuances:

⊕ **fresh ginger** provides harmonious sweet citrus notes

enhance the gentle floral qualities with other linalools:

⊕ **coriander** provides pine-like qualities and shares citrus flavours

⊕ **lemongrass** adds a variety of floral flavours alongside fresh lemon

FOOD PARTNERS

⊕ **Apples** Add a small pinch of freshly ground cardamom to oven-baked apples.

⊕ **Rice** Toast a couple of bruised pods lightly in oil, ghee, or butter before adding rice for a pilaf or biryani.

⊕ **Meat** Add a bruised pod to a creamy korma chicken curry or a lamb hotpot, to assuage the richness.

⊕ **Drinks** Steep a couple of bruised pods in black tea, coffee, liqueurs, or mulled wine.

⊕ **Baking** Sprinkle a pinch of freshly ground cardamom into a gingerbread mixture before baking.

BLENDS TO TRY

Use and adapt these recipes for classic blends featuring cardamom:

Turkish baharat p23

Advieh p27

Hawaij p29

Durban curry masala p37

Vindaloo paste p44

Shandong spice bag p58

Finnish gingerbread spice p72

RELEASE THE FLAVOUR

Whole pods give a subtle flavour and are suited to slow cooking, but always crush them before use. For a fresher, more intense flavour, and for quick-cooking dishes, remove the seeds and grind them.

Crushing also helps cooking oils and liquid to reach the seeds

Toast pods or seeds to add a bouquet of smoky, nutty, and roasted flavour compounds not previously present.

Lightly crush pods to open the husk and bruise the seeds, allowing flavourful oils to seep out from their storage cells.

Cook with fat in the dish, as most of the flavour compounds are almost insoluble in water.

BAY

Resinous | Herbal | Floral

BOTANICAL NAME
Laurus nobilis

ALSO KNOWN AS
Sweet bay, bay laurel.

MAJOR FLAVOUR COMPOUND
Cineole.

PARTS USED
Leaves, and less commonly the berries.

METHOD OF CULTIVATION
Leaves can be harvested at any time of year. Two- to three-year-old leafy shoots are cut off the main plant by hand.

COMMERCIAL PREPARATION
Shoots are dried in the shade. Leaves are then collected, graded, and packaged.

NON-CULINARY USES
Perfumery and cosmetics; in traditional medicine as a cough medicine and antiseptic, and to treat skin and joint problems.

The plant
Bay is a fairly hardy evergreen shrub in the laurel family. It grows up to 7.5m (23ft) tall.

Clusters of yellow-white flowers *develop in warm regions*

Shiny, deep green leaves *are aromatic, particularly when crushed or bruised*

Fresh
Fresh leaves are quite edible, but can be leathery, and have a slight bitterness that gradually dissipates.

Dried
Good-quality leaves remain pale green in colour. They have less bitterness and little aroma, but the fragrance is released upon cooking.

Spice story

The ancient Greeks and Romans both regarded bay as symbolic of victory and high status. The Romans used bay leaves to flavour roast meats, and added ground bay berries to stews and sauces. They also used bay leaves medicinally, and believed that garlands of the leaves would dispel evil spirits. The bay laurel was introduced from Asia Minor to all parts of the Mediterranean region in ancient times. By the Middle Ages it had reached right across Europe and continued to be ascribed spiritual significance. In the 17th century, the English herbalist Nicholas Culpeper wrote that a bay tree would provide protection from harm, and branches of the plant were burned in public spaces in times of plague.

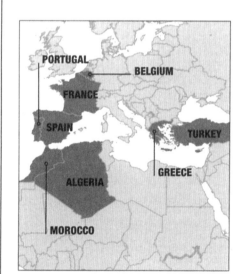

Region of cultivation
Bay is native to the eastern Mediterranean region (Asia Minor). It is cultivated mainly in Turkey, which supplies more than 90 per cent of the world market, but also across Europe, North Africa, Mexico, Central America, and southern USA.

Kitchen creativity }

Added at the beginning of cooking, fresh or dried bay leaves yield their fragrant, warm flavours gradually. Traditionally, bay is an indispensable part of a bouquet garni, tied in a bundle with thyme and parsley, and removed before serving.

BLENDING SCIENCE

The flavour profile of bay leaf is dominated by a terpene compound called cineole, which has an unusually penetrating, powerful eucalyptus scent. The next most abundant flavour compound is a spicy, sweet, warming phenol called eugenol. There are also small amounts of peppermint-like and slightly citrusy phellandrene, pine-like pinene and terpineol, and floral geraniol and linalool.

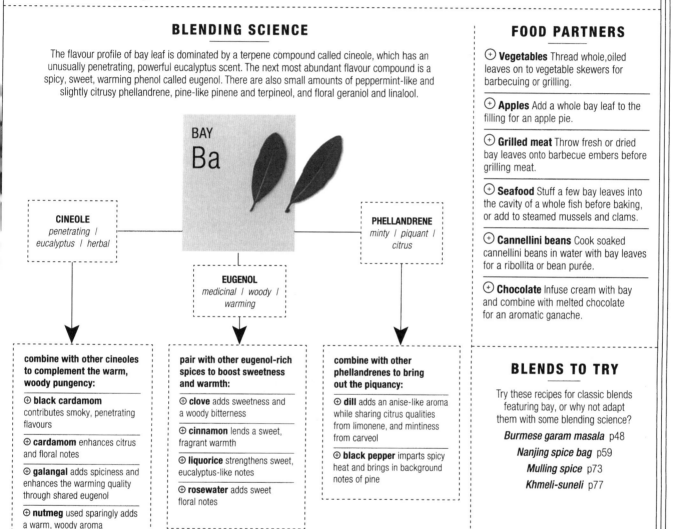

BAY
Ba

CINEOLE
penetrating | eucalyptus | herbal

EUGENOL
medicinal | woody | warming

PHELLANDRENE
minty | piquant | citrus

combine with other cineoles to complement the warm, woody pungency:

⊕ **black cardamom** contributes smoky, penetrating flavours

⊕ **cardamom** enhances citrus and floral notes

⊕ **galangal** adds spiciness and enhances the warming quality through shared eugenol

⊕ **nutmeg** used sparingly adds a warm, woody aroma

pair with other eugenol-rich spices to boost sweetness and warmth:

⊕ **clove** adds sweetness and a woody bitterness

⊕ **cinnamon** lends a sweet, fragrant warmth

⊕ **liquorice** strengthens sweet, eucalyptus-like notes

⊕ **rosewater** adds sweet floral notes

combine with other phellandrenes to bring out the piquancy:

⊕ **dill** adds an anise-like aroma while sharing citrus qualities from limonene, and mintiness from carveol

⊕ **black pepper** imparts spicy heat and brings in background notes of pine

FOOD PARTNERS

⊕ **Vegetables** Thread whole, oiled leaves on to vegetable skewers for barbecuing or grilling.

⊕ **Apples** Add a whole bay leaf to the filling for an apple pie.

⊕ **Grilled meat** Throw fresh or dried bay leaves onto barbecue embers before grilling meat.

⊕ **Seafood** Stuff a few bay leaves into the cavity of a whole fish before baking, or add to steamed mussels and clams.

⊕ **Cannellini beans** Cook soaked cannellini beans in water with bay leaves for a ribollita or bean purée.

⊕ **Chocolate** Infuse cream with bay and combine with melted chocolate for an aromatic ganache.

BLENDS TO TRY

Try these recipes for classic blends featuring bay, or why not adapt them with some blending science?

Burmese garam masala p48

Nanjing spice bag p59

Mulling spice p73

Khmeli-suneli p77

RELEASE THE FLAVOUR

Bay's flavour oils are deep within the leaf, which explains why dried leaves are still effective. Flavour compounds dissolve well in oil, fat, and alcohol, but poorly in water.

Use in water-based cooking liquids for a delicate flavour, and allow time for flavour compounds to spread into the dish.

One small bay leaf to 3 tbsp oil is a good ratio for most dishes

Bay leaf   *3 tbsp oil*

Extract maximum flavour by adding to oil and heating gently before mixing with other ingredients.

GALANGAL

Warming | Pungent | Peppery

BOTANICAL NAME
Alpinia galanga

ALSO KNOWN AS
Greater galangal, Laos root,
Thai ginger, Siamese ginger.

MAJOR FLAVOUR COMPOUND
Cineole.

PARTS USED
Rhizomes (underground stems).

METHOD OF CULTIVATION
Grown as an annual crop, rhizomes
develop clumps of green stalks and are
harvested 3–4 months after planting.

COMMERCIAL PREPARATION
Rhizomes are washed, then cut up and
scraped to be sold fresh, dried, or ground.

NON-CULINARY USES
Essential oil in perfumery; in traditional
Ayurvedic medicine to boost appetite
and treat heart and lung diseases.

Spice story

The Greek philosopher Plutarch
noted that the ancient Egyptians
burnt galangal as a fumigant, to
perfume and disinfect the air. It was
also used as a medicine by ancient
civilizations from the Mediterranean to
China. Greek and Roman physicians
included the spice, brought from Asia
on early trade routes, in their
expensive concoctions for wealthy
patients. In the Middle Ages, the
German herbalist Hildegard of Bingen
(1098–1179) described galangal as "the
spice of life", but evidence suggests it
was a different variety, known today as
lesser galangal, that became popular in
European cooking. It appears in a
sauce recipe in *The Forme of Cury*, a
14th-century English cookery book,
and in many other medieval and Tudor
recipes. Today it is an important spice
in Southeast Asian cuisine.

The plant
Galangal is a tropical
herbaceous perennial
in the ginger family,
growing to 2.5m (8ft)
tall in large clumps.

Flowers *and
buds are edible*

Leaves *are
long and
blade-shaped*

Rhizomes
*resemble
those of
ginger, but
are darker*

Dried
Galangal can be
dried and either
sliced or ground
into a powder.

Dried slices *are
best softened
in water before use*

Rhizomes *look
yellow-orange
after scraping*

Fresh
The flesh is
tougher and more
fibrous than that of
ginger. Peel it, and
then grate, slice, or
pound to a paste.

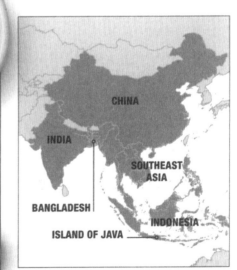

CHINA
INDIA
SOUTHEAST
ASIA
BANGLADESH
INDONESIA
ISLAND OF JAVA

Region of cultivation
Galangal is native to Java, in Indonesia, but is
now cultivated throughout Southeast Asia,
India, Bangladesh, China, and Suriname.

Kitchen creativity }

Galangal's flavour is an intriguing mix of cardamom, ginger, and saffron, with mustard and citrus notes. It has a reputation for heightening other flavours while retaining its own distinctive character.

BLENDING SCIENCE

Galangal's trademark lingering pungency comes from penetrating cineole and medicinal camphor, and unusual galangal acetate is responsible for its wasabi-like tang. Similarly uncommon methyl cinnamate and fenchyl acetate are often found in fruits, lending subtle notes of balsamic vinegar and fir tree, respectively.

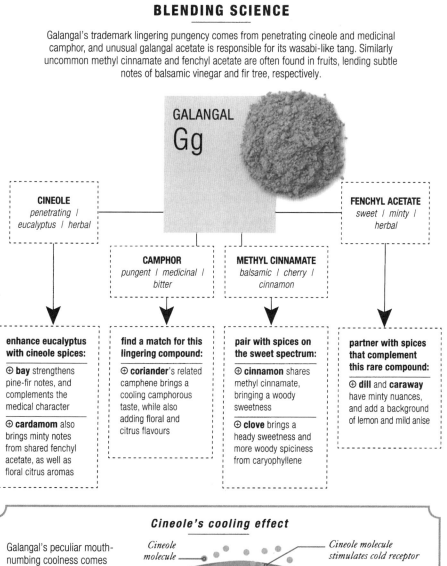

GALANGAL
Gg

CINEOLE
penetrating | eucalyptus | herbal

FENCHYL ACETATE
sweet | minty | herbal

CAMPHOR
pungent | medicinal | bitter

METHYL CINNAMATE
balsamic | cherry | cinnamon

enhance eucalyptus with cineole spices:

⊕ **bay** strengthens pine-fir notes, and complements the medical character

⊕ **cardamom** also brings minty notes from shared fenchyl acetate, as well as floral citrus aromas

find a match for this lingering compound:

⊕ **coriander**'s related camphene brings a cooling camphorous taste, while also adding floral and citrus flavours

pair with spices on the sweet spectrum:

⊕ **cinnamon** shares methyl cinnamate, bringing a woody sweetness

⊕ **clove** brings a heady sweetness and more woody spiciness from caryophyllene

partner with spices that complement this rare compound:

⊕ **dill** and **caraway** have minty nuances, and add a background of lemon and mild anise

FOOD PARTNERS

⊕ **Meat** Add galangal paste to your base for a beef rendang, slow-cooked beef ribs, or chicken marinade. Simmer slices in beef or chicken stock to form a base for *pho*, the Vietnamese noodle soup.

⊕ **Smoothies** Swap ginger for a smaller amount of galangal in your favourite fruit or vegetable smoothie.

⊕ **Fish and shellfish** Combine galangal and lemongrass with shallots, garlic, chilli, and fish sauce to make a paste for Thai fish curry.

⊕ **Fruit** Grated galangal with lime juice, fish sauce, sugar, chilli, and garlic makes a zingy dressing for green papaya or other fruit salads.

RELEASE THE FLAVOUR

Fresh galangal is best grated or pounded to a paste; slices release flavour more slowly. Oils are essential for fullness of flavour. Powder is harsher and less complex than fresh because subtler flavour compounds evaporate with processing.

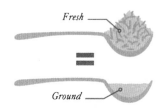

Fresh

=

Ground

If substituting ground galangal, use half as much as fresh.

BLENDS TO TRY

Use and adapt these classic blends featuring galangal:

Khao kua p49

Bumbu p52

Galangal's peculiar mouth-numbing coolness comes from cineole. This flavour compound has a molecular shape that directly stimulates a cold thermoreceptor, called TRPM8, which normally senses cold temperatures.

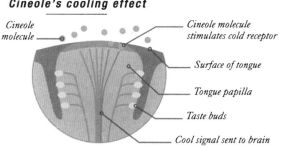

Cineole's cooling effect

Cineole molecule

Cineole molecule stimulates cold receptor

Surface of tongue

Tongue papilla

Taste buds

Cool signal sent to brain

ASIAN LARB SALAD WITH CURRIED DUCK AND KHAO KUA

Popular in both Laos and Thailand, larb is a fiery salad most often made with finely minced meat or fish, which is flavoured with fresh spices and herbs and topped with roasted rice powder. This version mixes things up by adding in garam masala – the warm, aromatic spice mix at the heart of much Indian cooking.

SPICE IDEAS

Reinvent the citrus sour in *khao kua* by replacing or enhancing lemongrass and lime leaves with lemon myrtle, sumac, or dried lime powder.

Instead of lime juice, **use tamarind water** in the dressing for a more lusciously fruity sweet–sour flavour.

Personalize the garam masala: create a more floral character with coriander and green cardamom; add fennel, dill, or caraway for underlying aniseed.

Serves 2–3

Prep time 10 mins

Cooking time 2–3½ mins

1 tbsp vegetable oil

2 tsp garam masala (see recipe p40)

1 tsp Thai chilli flakes, or any crushed dried chillies

2 duck fillets, skin removed, then minced

juice of 2 limes

2 tbsp Thai fish sauce (*nam pla*)

1 tbsp palm sugar or muscovado sugar

4 shallots, finely sliced

2 lemongrass stalks

handful of fresh mint leaves, chopped

handful of fresh coriander leaves, chopped

1 tbsp *khao kua* roasted rice powder (see recipe p49)

1 Heat the oil in a frying pan over a medium heat. Add the garam masala and chilli flakes and stir-fry for 1–2 minutes, until fragrant.

2 Turn the heat to high and add the duck mince. Fry for 1–2 minutes, until the meat is browned on the outside but still pink in the middle. Transfer to a plate and set aside.

3 To make the dressing, mix the lime juice and fish sauce with the sugar in a large bowl. Stir until the sugar has dissolved.

4 Prepare the lemongrass stalks by trimming the tops and bases and peeling off the woody outer layers. Crush the pale green, tender inner stalks, using the back of a heavy knife, to release the aromatic oils. Chop the stalks finely.

5 Add the warm duck, shallots, chopped lemongrass, mint, and coriander to the bowl of dressing. Stir until all the ingredients are well combined.

6 Sprinkle the *khao kua* over the salad and serve immediately. If you are preparing the salad ahead of time, only add the rice powder when you are ready to serve, so that it stays crunchy.

DRIED LIME

Tangy | Sour | Musky

BOTANICAL NAMES
Citrus x *latifolia* or *C. aurantifolia*

ALSO KNOWN AS
Persian lime, noomi (*C.* x *latifolia*); Omani lime, loomi (*C. aurantifolia*).

MAJOR FLAVOUR COMPOUND
Citral.

PARTS USED
Dried fruits.

METHOD OF CULTIVATION
Trees are grown in orchards and the fruits picked when under-ripe and hard.

COMMERCIAL PREPARATION
Fruits are boiled in brine to sterilize, reduce bitterness, and trigger browning enzymes. They are then dried in the sun until hard, dark, and brittle, and beginning to ferment.

NON-CULINARY USES
Used by Arabian Bedouins as black fabric dye; as a traditional digestion stimulant.

The plant
Limes grow on small, evergreen trees in the citrus family, native to tropical and sub-tropical regions.

Fruits *are picked when full size, but still pale green*

Leaves *are aromatic and sometimes used in cooking*

Powder
Lime powder is made from grinding dried black limes and has a sharp, tangy flavour.

▲ *White lime*

Black lime ➤

Peel *is leathery*

Whole
Black limes have had longer to ferment and develop stronger, musky flavours. The paler types are dried for less time.

Spice story

Limes are native to Southeast Asia and were brought to the Middle East by Arab traders, though exactly how and when is unclear, since lemons and limes were often referred to by the same name in Arabic texts. By the 10th century CE, Arab traders had introduced the fruits to Egypt and North Africa, and from there they spread across southern Europe during era of the Crusades. Limes first made it to the Americas in the 16th century, planted in the West Indies by European explorers. The practice of drying limes first developed in Oman. Some believe the idea suggested itself after unharvested fruits dried on the trees and began to ferment. Used in cooking throughout the Middle East and the Indian subcontinent, dried limes are most closely associated with Persian cuisine.

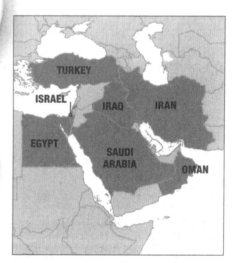

Region of cultivation
The most important lime producers for the Middle Eastern market are Egypt, Turkey, and Israel. The preparation of dried limes is carried out in Oman, Saudi Arabia, Iraq, and Iran.

Kitchen creativity }

Limes are the most acidic of all citrus fruits, but they carry a fragrant, floral quality that is unique in the citrus family. The process of drying limes develops vinegary, earthy qualities, a hint of smoke, alongside mild fermented flavour.

BLENDING SCIENCE

Some acids break down into sugar, meaning dried lime is less powerfully sour than fresh lime, allowing its other flavours to shine. Pair with spices that also highlight its subtle woody, camphorous, floral, and sweet notes.

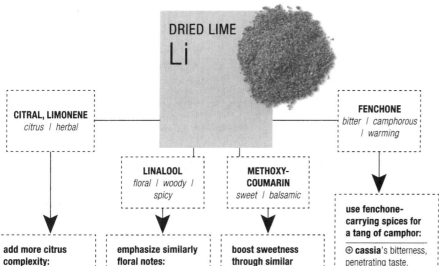

DRIED LIME
Li

CITRAL, LIMONENE
citrus / herbal

LINALOOL
floral / woody / spicy

METHOXY-COUMARIN
sweet / balsamic

FENCHONE
bitter / camphorous / warming

add more citrus complexity:

⊕ **ginger**'s lemony qualities from shared citral synergize with lime, while gingerol adds zesty heat

⊕ **cardamom** has a eucalyptus flavour and shares citrus limonene, sweetness from herby a-fenchyl acetate, and floral linalool

emphasize similarly floral notes:

⊕ **nutmeg** adds the floral aromas of safrole and geraniol

⊕ **allspice**'s main compound, eugenol, has an intensely perfumed presence

⊕ **coriander** shares both limonene and linalool, echoing lime's citrus/floral balance

boost sweetness through similar coumarin:

⊕ **vanilla**'s aromatic sweetness resembles coumarin, bringing indulgent flavours to sweet dishes if balanced well

⊕ **mahleb** intensifies sweetness with almond, creamy, cherry-pie nuances

use fenchone-carrying spices for a tang of camphor:

⊕ **cassia**'s bitterness, penetrating taste, tannins, and sweet coumarin balance the acidity of dried lime

⊕ **grains of Selim** also add floral and pine flavours with linalool and pinene

⊕ **fennel**'s subtle aniseed works well with the bittersweet qualities of dried lime

RELEASE THE FLAVOUR

Unlike the eye-watering hit of fresh limes, the complex flavours of whole dried limes need coaxing out, although powder can offer an imperfect shortcut.

Pierce whole limes with a skewer before adding to a dish: the flesh gradually rehydrates to release flavours.

Fats and alcohol release fragrant terpenes in the peel. Methoxycoumarin, acids, and sugar dissolve in water, hence low-fat dishes are sweet and tart, but lacking in aroma.

Lime powder is best for quick-cook dishes. If using in slower dishes, add later so the terpenes have less time to evaporate.

Grind in an electric grinder, first cutting in half and removing the seeds.

FOOD PARTNERS

⊕ **Fruit salad** Swap lemon juice for ground dried lime in a syrup for a fruit salad.

⊕ **Vegetables** Add a whole dried lime to the base of an Iranian chickpea and vegetable stew, after softening onions, carrots, and garlic.

⊕ **Fish** Introduce powdered dried lime to a fish curry, or over grilled shellfish or sea bass.

⊕ **Chicken** Pierce a dried lime and place it in the cavity of a chicken before roasting, or add to the poaching broth for chicken, along with turmeric, saffron, and onion.

⊕ **Grains** Use ground dried lime to flavour rice dishes and pilafs, or sprinkle over a quinoa or bulgur wheat tabbouleh salad.

LEMON MYRTLE

Citrusy | Warm | Bitter

BOTANICAL NAME
Backhousia citriodora

ALSO KNOWN AS
Sweet verbena tree, lemon ironwood.

MAJOR FLAVOUR COMPOUND
Citral.

PARTS USED
Leaves (fresh or dried).

METHOD OF CULTIVATION
Leaves are harvested all year round, by mechanical harvesters or by hand.

COMMERCIAL PREPARATION
The leaves are separated from their stems and then dried using drying machines. They are packaged whole or ground.

NON-CULINARY USES
Cosmetics and perfumery; in herbal medicine for its antibacterial and antioxidant properties; topical antiseptic.

Spice story

The potent aromatic foliage of the lemon myrtle tree has long been prized – possibly for millennia – by aboriginal Australians, who use it in cooking and to treat cuts. The leaves were first distilled for essential oil in 1888, and during World War II an extract from the lemony leaves was used as a substitute for commercial lemon essence, supplies of which had become scarce. However, it was not until the early 1990s that lemon myrtle, by then a potentially lucrative crop for the food and drink industry, began to be cultivated as a spice. Demand is now outstripping supply, and plantations have been established outside Australia. Since 2010, lemon myrtle has been under attack from myrtle rust, a fungal infection, which could threaten this species in the long term.

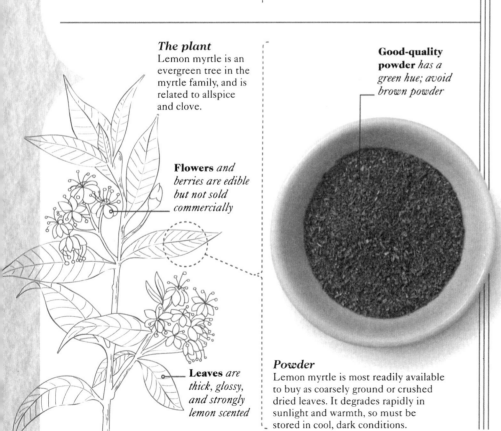

The plant
Lemon myrtle is an evergreen tree in the myrtle family, and is related to allspice and clove.

Flowers *and berries are edible but not sold commercially*

Leaves *are thick, glossy, and strongly lemon scented*

Good-quality powder *has a green hue; avoid brown powder*

Powder
Lemon myrtle is most readily available to buy as coarsely ground or crushed dried leaves. It degrades rapidly in sunlight and warmth, so must be stored in cool, dark conditions.

Region of cultivation
Lemon myrtle is native to coastal subtropical rainforests of Queensland, Australia. It is grown in some subtropical areas of Australia (mainly in Queensland and northern New South Wales), Malaysia, and China.

Kitchen creativity }

Lemon myrtle has a bright citrus flavour – more lemony than lemon, but without the acidity of that fruit's juice – with green, herbal notes and a subtle scent of eucalyptus. Add sparingly to both sweet and savoury dishes.

BLENDING SCIENCE

The leaf oil of lemon myrtle consists almost entirely of citral – a lemon-scented flavour compound that is up to 30 times more concentrated in this spice than in lemon rind. Alongside are small amounts of floral linalool, peppery myrcene, and the green-tasting ketone sulcatone.

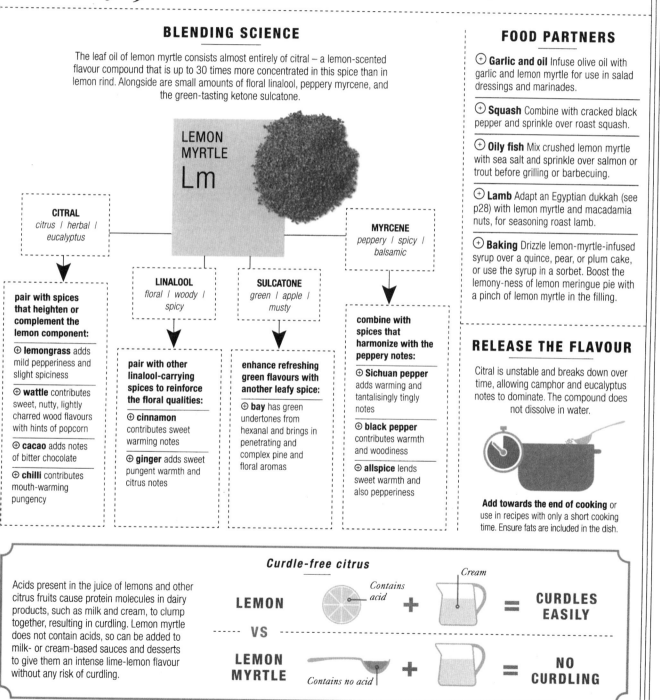

LEMON MYRTLE Lm

CITRAL
citrus | herbal | eucalyptus

pair with spices that heighten or complement the lemon component:

⊕ **lemongrass** adds mild pepperiness and slight spiciness

⊕ **wattle** contributes sweet, nutty, lightly charred wood flavours with hints of popcorn

⊕ **cacao** adds notes of bitter chocolate

⊕ **chilli** contributes mouth-warming pungency

LINALOOL
floral | woody | spicy

pair with other linalool-carrying spices to reinforce the floral qualities:

⊕ **cinnamon** contributes sweet warming notes

⊕ **ginger** adds sweet pungent warmth and citrus notes

SULCATONE
green | apple | musty

enhance refreshing green flavours with another leafy spice:

⊕ **bay** has green undertones from hexanal and brings in penetrating and complex pine and floral aromas

MYRCENE
peppery | spicy | balsamic

combine with spices that harmonize with the peppery notes:

⊕ **Sichuan pepper** adds warming and tantalisingly tingly notes

⊕ **black pepper** contributes warmth and woodiness

⊕ **allspice** lends sweet warmth and also pepperiness

FOOD PARTNERS

⊕ **Garlic and oil** Infuse olive oil with garlic and lemon myrtle for use in salad dressings and marinades.

⊕ **Squash** Combine with cracked black pepper and sprinkle over roast squash.

⊕ **Oily fish** Mix crushed lemon myrtle with sea salt and sprinkle over salmon or trout before grilling or barbecuing.

⊕ **Lamb** Adapt an Egyptian dukkah (see p28) with lemon myrtle and macadamia nuts, for seasoning roast lamb.

⊕ **Baking** Drizzle lemon-myrtle-infused syrup over a quince, pear, or plum cake, or use the syrup in a sorbet. Boost the lemony-ness of lemon meringue pie with a pinch of lemon myrtle in the filling.

RELEASE THE FLAVOUR

Citral is unstable and breaks down over time, allowing camphor and eucalyptus notes to dominate. The compound does not dissolve in water.

Add towards the end of cooking or use in recipes with only a short cooking time. Ensure fats are included in the dish.

Curdle-free citrus

Acids present in the juice of lemons and other citrus fruits cause protein molecules in dairy products, such as milk and cream, to clump together, resulting in curdling. Lemon myrtle does not contain acids, so can be added to milk- or cream-based sauces and desserts to give them an intense lime-lemon flavour without any risk of curdling.

LEMON *Contains acid* + *Cream* = **CURDLES EASILY**

----- VS -----

LEMON MYRTLE *Contains no acid* + = **NO CURDLING**

LEMONGRASS

Citrusy | Peppery | Refreshing

BOTANICAL NAME
Cymbopogon citratus

ALSO KNOWN AS
Serai, oil grass,
West Indian lemongrass.

MAJOR FLAVOUR COMPOUND
Citral.

PARTS USED
Stalks, leaves.

METHOD OF CULTIVATION
Around five times a year, the whole clump
of leaf bases and young stems are hand-cut
near the base of the plant.

COMMERCIAL PREPARATION
Stems are separated, cleaned, and trimmed
to lengths of 20cm (8in), and then bundled
for drying or using fresh.

NON-CULINARY USES
In perfumes, soaps, and toiletries; in insect
repellents; anti-inflammatory medication;
as a fungicide, and to relieve joint pain.

The plant
Lemongrass is a member
of the grasses family and
grows in many different
soil types in warm,
tropical climates.

Powder
Dried, ground
lemongrass (also
called *sereh*)
imparts only a
fraction of the
spice's complex
character.

One teaspoon *is
roughly equivalent to
a stalk of lemongrass*

Narrow leaves
*grow from the
bulbous base
to a height of
1.5–2m (5–7ft)*

Aromatic oils
*are concentrated
in the stems*

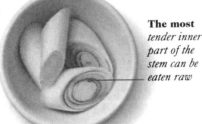

The most
*tender inner
part of the
stem can be
eaten raw*

Fresh
Store well wrapped in the refrigerator for
up to 2 weeks. Leaf blades can also flavour
dishes: tie in a knot and gently bruise.

Spice story

The Latin name for lemongrass,
Cymbopogon, derives from the Greek
words *kymbe* (boat) and *pogon* (beard),
referring to the shape of its flowers,
now rarely present in cultivated
varieties. The spice has been used
both medicinally and as a flavouring
agent in its native Asia for thousands
of years. In 10th-century China it was
used as an insect repellent, the fragrant
leaves being placed on beds to ward
off fleas. By the Middle Ages,
lemongrass had made its way to
Europe from Asia via caravan spice
routes – the spice appears in several
brewing and spiced wine recipes of
the time. In the 19th century, India
began cultivating lemongrass, mainly
to export the aromatic oil for scenting
soaps and cosmetics. However, it was
Southeast Asian rather than Indian
cuisine that adopted lemongrass as
a staple spice.

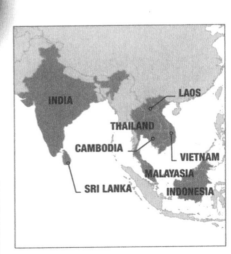

Region of cultivation
Lemongrass is cultivated throughout the tropics,
in India, Sri Lanka, Thailand, Laos, Cambodia,
Vietnam, Malaysia, Indonesia, Australia, the
Americas, and West Africa.

Kitchen creativity }

Delicate lemongrass enlivens curries, stir-fries, pickles, salads, and soups. Use the tender inner stalk in curry pastes, marinades, and spice rubs, or bruise the whole fibrous stalk and use in stocks or soups, removing it before serving.

BLENDING SCIENCE

Lemon-scented citral makes up 70 per cent of the spice's flavour compounds, but the key to spice pairing is to avoid intensifying this dominant citrus with another lemony spice. Instead, bring out lemongrass's mild pepperiness from myrcene, and/or its sweet and floral elements from linalool and geraniol.

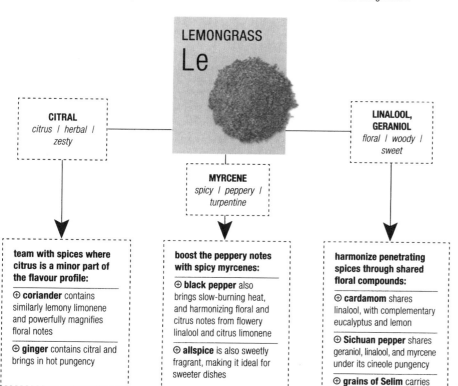

LEMONGRASS
Le

CITRAL
citrus | herbal | zesty

LINALOOL, GERANIOL
floral | woody | sweet

MYRCENE
spicy | peppery | turpentine

team with spices where citrus is a minor part of the flavour profile:

⊕ **coriander** contains similarly lemony limonene and powerfully magnifies floral notes

⊕ **ginger** contains citral and brings in hot pungency

boost the peppery notes with spicy myrcenes:

⊕ **black pepper** also brings slow-burning heat, and harmonizing floral and citrus notes from flowery linalool and citrus limonene

⊕ **allspice** is also sweetly fragrant, making it ideal for sweeter dishes

harmonize penetrating spices through shared floral compounds:

⊕ **cardamom** shares linalool, with complementary eucalyptus and lemon

⊕ **Sichuan pepper** shares geraniol, linalool, and myrcene under its cineole pungency

⊕ **grains of Selim** carries both compounds, plus eucalyptus and bitterness

RELEASE THE FLAVOUR

Most of lemongrass's flavour comes from oil glands deep inside the grass. The stems must be crushed to burst open the glands and release the oils.

Slice, grate, or pound for quicker cooking: the greater the damage, the faster the oils will leak out. Add powder late in cooking.

Gently bruise or bend leaf blades for lengthy cooking, to prevent too many of the flavour compounds evaporating.

Cook with fats, such as coconut milk, to ensure oil-based citrus and floral flavour compounds spread throughout the dish.

FOOD PARTNERS

⊕ **Fishcakes** Make Thai fishcakes by adding lemongrass, chilli, ginger, garlic, and lime leaves to fish and potato before frying.

⊕ **Pork** Marinade pork in a paste of finely chopped lemongrass, ginger, coconut, and turmeric before grilling or barbecuing.

⊕ **Granita** Infuse a sugar syrup with lemongrass and lime zest. Strain to make granitas or ice lollies.

⊕ **Salad** Add finely chopped lemongrass to a dressing for a Thai noodle salad with slivers wof carrot, chilli, cucumber, and a handful of toasted nuts and herbs.

⊕ **Fruit** Instead of adding pared lemon peel to the poaching liquid for pears, rhubarb, quince, or peaches, add a bruised stick of lemongrass for a hint of pepperines.

BLEND TO TRY

Try this recipe for a classic blend featuring lemongrass, or why not adapt it with some blending science?

Khao kua p49

AMCHOOR

Citrus | *Herbaceous* | *Bittersweet*

BOTANICAL NAME
Mangifera indica

ALSO KNOWN AS
Mango powder, amchur.

MAIN FLAVOUR COMPOUND
Ocimene.

PARTS USED
Flesh of unripe fruits.

METHOD OF CULTIVATION
Unripe mangoes are harvested
mechanically or by hand.

COMMERCIAL PREPARATION
Fruits are peeled, sliced, and oven- or
sun-dried to remove 90 per cent of their
moisture, then packed as slices or ground.

NON-CULINARY USES
In Ayurvedic medicine to treat respiratory
diseases and digestive complaints.

The plant
Mango is a large
tropical evergreen tree
in the cashew family.

**Cream or
pink flowers**
*develop into
fruits*

**Green,
unripe fruits**
*have sour,
astringent flesh*

Powder
Amchoor powder has a coarse texture
and is light beige in colour. It can be
stored for up to a year in a sealed container
away from sunlight.

Whole
Dried slices are light brown and resemble
rough-textured wood. Store in a sealed
container in a cool, dark place for up to
4 months, and grind as needed.

Spice story

Mangoes have been cultivated in
India for more than 4,000 years, and
are strongly linked to the Ayurvedic
system of traditional Indian medicine.
According to Hindu folklore they also
have sacred properties, and Ganesh,
the Hindi elephant-headed god, is
often shown holding a ripe mango as a
symbol of attainment. Buddhist monks
took mangoes to East Asia in the 4th
and 5th centuries CE, and the fruit was
subsequently transported west along
trade routes, reaching Africa in around
1000 CE and northern Europe by the
early 14th centuy. The fruit was
introduced to Brazil by Portuguese
explorers in the 17th century, and also
reached Mexico via the Philippines.
In the mid- to late 18th century,
mangoes reached the West Indies,
probably via Brazil.

Region of cultivation
Mangoes are native to India and Myanmar,
and over 40 per cent of the total world crop is
cultivated in India. Other major producers
include Pakistan, Bangladesh, China, Thailand,
Indonesia, the Philippines, and Mexico.

Kitchen creativity }

Amchoor has a fruity, very tart but slightly resinous taste, with a citrus tang. It is often used as a souring agent, much like lemon but with the benefit of not adding moisture. Use it judiciously, as the bittersweet flavour can be overpowering.

BLENDING SCIENCE

As well as partnering with the following spices that share the same or similar fruity, herbal, and vegetable-like flavour compounds, take advantage of the sweet and puckering qualities of amchoor by pairing with galangal and ginger, or the sweetly aromatic nutmeg and cinnamon.

AMCHOOR
Am

OCIMENE
floral | vegetal | tropical

CADINENE
herbal | woody | spicy

CUBEBENE
lemony | fruity | radish-like

pair with other spices that share this main compound:

⊕ **nigella** lends an onion-like savouriness

⊕ **grains of Selim** add a camphor-like sweetness

⊕ **annatto** brings a peppery edge

⊕ **bay** has penetrating fruit-floral aromas

combine with other sharply fruity spices:

⊕ **sumac** has a similarly sweet but tart citrus profile

⊕ **coriander** also contributes floral and bitter notes

enhance woody notes with spices that share this gentle terpene:

⊕ **juniper** brings a sweet pine-like woodiness

⊕ **carob**'s sweet vanilla notes will foreground amchoor's fruitiness

⊕ **asafoetida** pairs well despite its very different, predominantly sulphurous and musky taste

FOOD PARTNERS

⊕ **Fish and prawns** Add to a crumb or batter coating for fried fish or prawns.

⊕ **Lamb** Use amchoor to make a marinade for lamb chops, shoulder, or shanks. Rub it over the meat and leave it overnight before grilling or slow roasting; the acidity works as a tenderizer.

⊕ **Lentils** Stir into a soothing dhal to add a touch of piquancy.

⊕ **Vegetables** Sprinkle over roasted cauliflower, or add a pinch to stir-fried aubergine or okra.

⊕ **Tropical fruit** Add a pinch to a sweet tropical fruit sorbet or salad.

RELEASE THE FLAVOUR

Many of amchoor's terpene flavours quickly evaporate, but the fruit sugars do not. Citric acid also boils less easily than water, which means its sweet–tart effect will increase with prolonged cooking.

Add late for a fragrant effect   *Add early for acidity and sweetness*

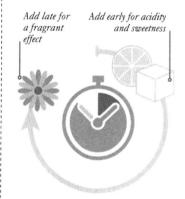

Concentrated sweet-and-sour taste

Drying the mango evaporates most of its water, reducing its moisture content from over 80% to less than 10%. In the process, the acids, sugars, and flavour compounds become highly concentrated, resulting in a distinctly sweet-and-sour taste profile.

One teaspoon of amchoor powder has the acidity of three tablespoons of lemon juice.

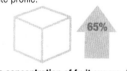

65%

The concentration of fruit sugars rises to around 65 per cent during drying.

BLENDS TO TRY

Use and adapt this recipe for a classic blend featuring amchoor:

Chaat masala p42

ANARDANA

Sweet | Sour | Fruity

BOTANICAL NAME
Punica granatum

ALSO KNOWN AS
Pomegranate.

MAJOR FLAVOUR COMPOUNDS
Citric acid and malic acid.

PARTS USED
Fruitlets (incorrectly called seeds).

METHOD OF CULTIVATION
The fruit is cut off the tree when fully ripe, but before it splits open.

COMMERCIAL PREPARATION
The seeds and pulp are separated from the bitter white membrane and dried in the sun.

NON-CULINARY USES
The seeds and rind are widely used in Indian, traditional European, and Middle Eastern medicine to reduce fever, aid digestion, and as an anti-inflammatory.

Spice story

Pomegranate has been grown for at least 5,000 years, making it one of the oldest cultivated fruits, probably originating in and around Persia (now Iran). By the early Bronze Age, cultivation had spread throughout the southern Mediterranean and eastwards to India and China. Its abundant seeds made the pomegranate an enduring symbol of fertility in many ancient cultures, notably Egypt, where pomegranate motifs can be found in temples and tombs. In the Graeco-Roman period, physicians prescribed it to treat tapeworm, and the Roman recipe book *Apicius* contains a recipe for a digestive pomegranate drink supposedly enjoyed by Emperor Nero. The culinary home of the dried spice in particular remains, as it has for millennia, in Indian and Persian cuisine.

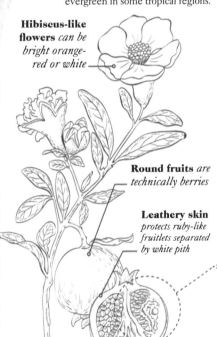

The plant
Anardana comes from the fruits of a large flowering shrub in the loosestrife family. It is deciduous in temperate climates but evergreen in some tropical regions.

Hibiscus-like flowers *can be bright orange-red or white*

Round fruits *are technically berries*

Leathery skin *protects ruby-like fruitlets separated by white pith*

Slow-dried fruitlets *are reddish-brown to black in colour*

Dried fruitlets
Consisting of seeds surrounded by fleshy aril (pulp), these are slightly soft, sticky, and semi-moist.

Powder
Dried fruitlets are also available ground into powdered form.

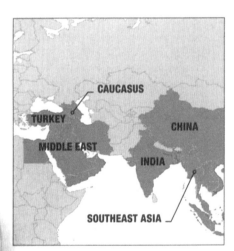

Region of cultivation
Pomegranate is native to and mainly cultivated in the Middle East, Turkey, the Caucasus, and India; it is also cultivated in Southeast Asia and in China.

Kitchen creativity }

Anardana is popular in northern India, where it is used as a souring agent in curries, pakoras, and chutneys. Many Iranian dishes – such as *fesenjan*, a chicken and walnut stew – combine the spice with pomegranate molasses for a richer flavour.

BLENDING SCIENCE

Pomegranate's tangy fruitiness primarily comes from its mix of acids, sugars, and tannins. The compounds giving its appetizing aromas range from "green" hexanal and citrusy limonene to peppery myrcene and sweet, turpentine-like carene. These compounds are pivotal when looking for suitable spice partners.

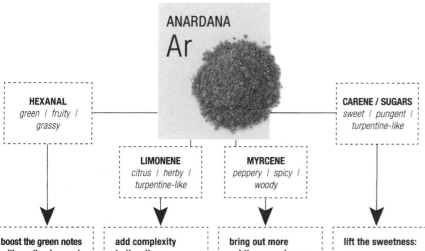

ANARDANA
Ar

HEXANAL
green | fruity | grassy

LIMONENE
citrus | herby | turpentine-like

MYRCENE
peppery | spicy | woody

CARENE / SUGARS
sweet | pungent | turpentine-like

boost the green notes with another hexanal:

⊕ **barberry**, like pomegranate, has a high acid content that produces a sour fruitiness

add complexity to the citrus flavours:

⊕ **ginger** contains lemony citral, adding a pungent heat dimension

⊕ **tamarind** is an ideal partner, sharing lemony notes and adding bready and floral ones

bring out more subtle pepperiness:

⊕ **black pepper** shares myrcene and deepens spicy flavours with pungent piperine

⊕ **cumin** is an ideal partner, bringing warming, savoury earthiness

lift the sweetness:

⊕ **vanilla** adds a creaminess and complex character

⊕ **mahleb** has cherry and almond notes

⊕ **cinnamon** brings warmth and sweetness

FOOD PARTNERS

⊕ **Tropical fruit** Sprinkle ground anardana over a mango and lime salad.

⊕ **Vegetables** Add dried seeds to braised vegetables; sprinkle whole or ground over curried carrot or parsnip soup, or potato and cauliflower curry.

⊕ **Meatballs** Make *ash-e anar*, an Iranian soup containing meatballs, pomegranate (fresh and dried), yellow split peas, rice, and herbs.

⊕ **Chicken** Add dried seeds to a spiced yogurt marinade for chicken, before grilling or barbecuing.

⊕ **Rice, chickpeas** Pair with dried fruits in a fragrant pilaf, or scatter over fried cooked chickpeas along with cumin and salt.

⊕ **Sweet bakes** Stir dried seeds into a mix for granola bars or cookie dough.

RELEASE THE FLAVOUR

Anardana's main flavour profile comes from sugars, acids, and tannins, all of which dissolve in water.

Add directly to a watery sauce (no need for oil) to infuse a dish with the spice's pleasant tang.

Pound dried seeds for a more intense flavour, but use a pestle and mortar as the seeds will stick to a grinder.

Sweet-and-sour

The decidedly tart yet fruity flavour profile of anardana is due to a relatively high acid content balancing out the fruit sugars, while large amounts of tannins provide a mouth-drying finish.

Exact proportions vary depending on the region of cultivation; seeds from North India are known for their sourness.

 Anardana = *23% sugar content* + *11% acid content* + *5% tannin content*

SUMAC

Sour | Fruity | Woody

BOTANICAL NAME
Rhus coriaria

ALSO KNOWN AS
Elm-leaved sumac.

MAJOR FLAVOUR COMPOUND
Malic acid.

PARTS USED
Dried berries (in fact drupes, not true berries).

METHOD OF CULTIVATION
In late summer, just before the fruits fully ripen, the branches are dried in the sun. The berries are then rubbed off.

COMMERCIAL PREPARATION
Berries are cleaned and may be brined for several days before grinding. Further drying may be needed after grinding.

NON-CULINARY USES
Fabric dye; leather tanning; in traditional Middle Eastern medicine to treat fever.

Spice story

The name "sumac" is derived from the Aramaic word *summaq*, meaning "red". Long before lemons reached Europe, the Romans imported sumac from Syria to use as a souring agent and also as a dye. The Roman naturalist Pliny the Elder celebrated its astringent and cooling properties. Sumac has been used in Middle Eastern cooking since at least the 13th century CE in the *za'atar* spice blend, alongside sesame seeds and dried herbs. The spice is mainly used in Lebanese, Syrian, Turkish, and Iranian cuisine. Until the 1980s, sumac was almost impossible to obtain outside of the Middle East. However, a number of food writers have championed Middle Eastern cuisine in the last couple of decades, and as a result this spice is now experiencing a renaissance among cooks in the West.

The plant
Sumac is a deciduous shrub in the cashew family. It grows in uplands and on rocky mountains in temperate and subtropical regions.

Green leaves
turn red in autumn

Rust-coloured berries *are borne in conical clusters*

Coarse powder
is brick-red and slightly moist

Powder
Sumac is not highly scented, so lack of aroma need not be a sign of poor quality. Salt may be mixed in to prevent clumping; avoid buying sumac with this additive. Whole dried berries may also be available.

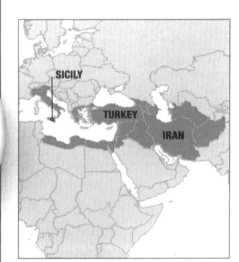

Region of cultivation
Sumac grows wild and is cultivated across the Mediterranean and the Middle East, particularly in Sicily, Turkey, and Iran, and in some parts of Central Asia.

Kitchen creativity }

Sumac has a sharp, acidic taste, reminiscent of lemon balm, and a spicy, earthy, woody aroma. It can be used in any dish that calls for lemon zest or lemon juice, or as a seasoning added like salt.

BLENDING SCIENCE

Sumac owes its sharp, mouth-puckering tartness to high levels of organic acids (mainly citric, tartaric, and malic acids) and astringent tannins. Fragrance comes from the terpenes caryophyllene, which has a musty, woody aroma, and pinene, which carries a fresh, pine-like aroma. "Green" aldehydes, such as earthy decenal and fruity, floral nonanal, complement the freshness.

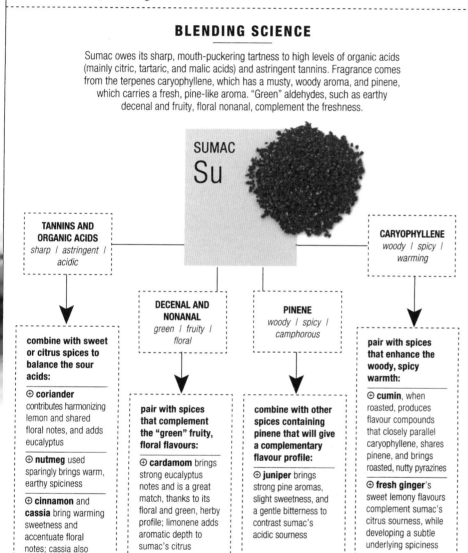

SUMAC
Su

TANNINS AND ORGANIC ACIDS
sharp | astringent | acidic

DECENAL AND NONANAL
green | fruity | floral

PINENE
woody | spicy | camphorous

CARYOPHYLLENE
woody | spicy | warming

combine with sweet or citrus spices to balance the sour acids:

⊕ **coriander** contributes harmonizing lemon and shared floral notes, and adds eucalyptus

⊕ **nutmeg** used sparingly brings warm, earthy spiciness

⊕ **cinnamon** and **cassia** bring warming sweetness and accentuate floral notes; cassia also adds bitterness

⊕ **anise** balances with sweet liquorice and adds nuances of cherry, creamy vanilla, and cocoa

⊕ **allspice** adds sweet peppery warmth

pair with spices that complement the "green" fruity, floral flavours:

⊕ **cardamom** brings strong eucalyptus notes and is a great match, thanks to its floral and green, herby profile; limonene adds aromatic depth to sumac's citrus sourness

⊕ **vanilla** adds rich, mellow creaminess and subtle cherry notes

combine with other spices containing pinene that will give a complementary flavour profile:

⊕ **juniper** brings strong pine aromas, slight sweetness, and a gentle bitterness to contrast sumac's acidic sourness

pair with spices that enhance the woody, spicy warmth:

⊕ **cumin**, when roasted, produces flavour compounds that closely parallel caryophyllene, shares pinene, and brings roasted, nutty pyrazines

⊕ **fresh ginger**'s sweet lemony flavours complement sumac's citrus sourness, while developing a subtle underlying spiciness

FOOD PARTNERS

⊕ **Root vegetables** Sprinkle ground sumac over roasted root vegetables.

⊕ **Tomatoes** Garnish sliced ripe tomatoes with sumac and a drizzle of pomegranate molasses.

⊕ **Chickpeas** Sprinkle over hummus or fried chickpeas, or use in falafels.

⊕ **Meat** Use sumac to garnish grilled or roast chicken or quail, with oil as a marinade for meat, or in lamb kofte.

⊕ **Fish** Sprinkle sumac over Lebanese-style spicy baked fish.

⊕ **Yogurt and cheeses** Scatter sumac over a whipped feta and tahini dip, baked feta, or fresh labneh with herbs, or over grilled halloumi.

RELEASE THE FLAVOUR

Much like salt, sumac enhances the flavours of foods to which it is added. Use powder to experience the full intensity of sumac's dry tartness and aroma.

The strained juice has a milder flavour that works well in jellies and sweet, summery drinks.

Sprinkle sumac as a garnish over a finished dish for maximum impact, rather than at the start of cooking.

BLEND TO TRY

Use and adapt this recipe for a classic Syrian seasoning:

Za'atar p22

TAMARIND

Sour | Fruity | Sweet

BOTANICAL NAME
Tamarindus indica

ALSO KNOWN AS
Indian date.

MAJOR FLAVOUR COMPOUNDS
Furfural, 2-phenyl acetaldehyde.

PARTS USED
Pulp of ripe pods.

METHOD OF CULTIVATION
Pods are harvested when fully ripe, and are either picked by hand, or fall to the ground when the tree is shaken.

COMMERCIAL PREPARATION
Pod shells are removed and the pulp is compressed into blocks of paste.

NON-CULINARY USES
In traditional medicine to treat bowel disorders, jaundice, and nausea. All parts have laxative and antiseptic properties.

The plant
The tamarind tree is a large tropical evergreen tree in the bean family. It can grow to a height of 30m (98ft).

Flowers *are yellow and grow in clusters*

Leaves *and flowers are edible*

Pods *contain up to 10 seeds surrounded by a sticky pulp*

Block
The semi-dried fibrous mass of pulp is soaked in hot water, then mashed to a paste and passed through a sieve.

Soak *in hot water to obtain a flavoured liquid*

Paste
Pre-prepared pastes are available for convenience. To use, thin the paste by mixing with warm water.

Spice story

Tamarind is a well-travelled spice: it has been used and traded widely for thousands of years. The Ancient Greek botanist Theophrastus described the plant in his writings on herbal medicine. Its English name comes from the Arabic "*tamr hindi*", meaning "date of India", because it reminded Arab sea traders of their native date palm; however, tamarind is actually in the pea family, and is native to East Africa. It probably arrived in India more than 2,000 years ago, and became established throughout the subcontinent both as an essential cooking spice and as a medicine. Traders brought it to Europe during the Middle Ages, by which time India had become the main supplier. During the 17th century, Spanish explorers carried it to the New World, including the West Indies, where it became important both in cooking and as an ornamental plant.

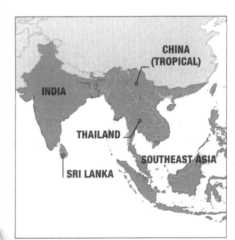

Region of cultivation
Tamarind is native to eastern Africa, possibly Madagascar. It is cultivated in most tropical regions, with India, Thailand, and Sri Lanka being among the main producers.

Kitchen creativity }

In Africa, Asia, the Middle East, and India, tamarind plays an essential role in chutneys, sauces, curries, soups, and drinks. Its fruity-sour taste helps to temper fiery dishes. It is often used as a fruitier-tasting alternative to lemon juice.

BLENDING SCIENCE

The principal flavour compounds of tamarind are the fruity aldehydes furfural and phenyl acetaldehyde. Having scant supply of oil, there are relatively small amounts of rapidly evaporating flavour molecules, so tamarind has only a mild aroma, but citrusy limonene is present in sufficient amounts for its fragrance to be detected.

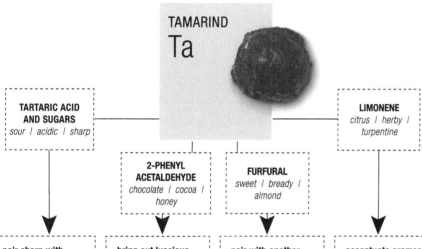

TAMARIND
Ta

TARTARIC ACID AND SUGARS
sour | acidic | sharp

2-PHENYL ACETALDEHYDE
chocolate | cocoa | honey

FURFURAL
sweet | bready | almond

LIMONENE
citrus | herby | turpentine

pair sharp with sweet for spice harmony:

⊕ **cinnamon** contains sweet cinnamaldehyde, which complements tamarind's high sugar content

⊕ **licorice**'s intensely sweet glycyrrhizin makes a perfect sweet-sour match

bring out luscious aromas with similar compounds:

⊕ **vanilla** is a good match with its honeyed flavour compounds and heady mix of sweet aromas

pair with another furfural:

⊕ **sesame**'s shared furfural makes it an unusual but effective partner, balancing richness with tamarind's sour fruitiness

accentuate aromas with other citrusy compounds:

⊕ **ginger** shares limonene and adds flowery notes, especially when fresh

⊕ **lime** shares limonene and adds a green citrus tang

⊕ **black pepper** carries limonene, making it an excellent partner in spicy blends

FOOD PARTNERS

⊕ **Vegetables** Drizzle a little tamarind juice into a yogurt dip for cauliflower or onion pakoras.

⊕ **Fish** Combine with raw sugar and chillies for a dipping sauce with fish.

⊕ **Pork and lamb** Mix paste or juice with soy sauce and ginger as a marinade for pork or lamb.

⊕ **Bulgar wheat** Make a dressing with liquid or diluted paste, pomegranate molasses, olive oil, and Middle Eastern herbs and spices, then drizzle over a bulgur wheat salad.

⊕ **Drinks** Make your own "tamarind-ade", combining strained liquid with sparkling water or soda, adding sugar to taste, and serving over ice.

RELEASE THE FLAVOUR

Derived from fruit pulp, the distinctive chemical components of tamarind make it an effective flavouring for water-based dishes, and give it a long shelf life.

The principal flavour compounds of tamarind readily dissolve in water – unusual among spices – so there is no need to fry in oil to release the flavours.

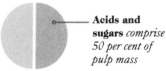

Acids and sugars *comprise 50 per cent of pulp mass*

High acid and sugar content prevents the growth of bacteria, so a block can be stored for a year or more.

Don't ditch the seeds!

Tough tamarind seeds can in fact be made palatable, and need not be discarded after extracting the "juice" from a block. They have a pleasant peanut-like taste.

Remove traces of pulp and roast in a dry frying pan.

Soak the seeds in water and peel off the protective coat.

Boil the seed kernels, or fry them in oil.

DATE <u>AND</u> TAMARIND GRANITA <u>WITH</u> CARAMELIZED PINEAPPLE

In this innovative ice, warming notes of cumin and garam masala contrast with astringent tamarind, zesty ginger, and the herbal pungency of fresh green chillies. It is a combination inspired by South Asian street food, in which these spices work together as thirst quenchers in the intense heat of high summer.

SPICE IDEAS

Replace amchoor with ground anardana in the chaat masala to **bring a slightly bitter tang** to the fruity sourness.

Fans of liquorice-like flavours could **add two whole star anise** and a teaspoon of toasted fennel seeds to the date palm syrup.

Strengthen the ginger by replacing fresh root with a teaspoon of ground; the nutty warmth of cumin will soften any rough aftertaste.

Serves 6 as a starter

Prep time 2 hours

Cooking time 30–35 mins

For the granita
¾ tsp cumin seeds

125g (4½oz) jaggery or palm sugar, chopped

50g (1¾oz) liquid glucose

750ml (1¼ pints) water

75g (2½oz) fresh root ginger, peeled and roughly chopped

1 large lime

150g (5½oz) seedless tamarind block, broken into pieces

100g (3½oz) pitted dates, roughly chopped

2–3 green chillies, chopped, with seeds

large bunch of fresh mint

½ tsp garam masala (see recipe p40)

½ tsp black salt

For the caramelized pineapple
4 tbsp icing sugar

2 tsp *chaat masala* (see recipe p42)

1 tsp Kashmiri chilli powder or hot paprika

300g (10oz) fresh pineapple, peeled, cored, and diced

handful of fresh mint leaves

1 To make the granita, heat a small, heavy-based frying pan over a medium heat and toast the cumin seeds for about 1 minute, until fragrant. Cool, then pound to a powder using a pestle and mortar.

2 Put the jaggery or palm sugar, liquid glucose, and water in a saucepan and cook over a moderate heat, stirring occasionally, until the sugar has dissolved. Simmer for 3–4 minutes.

3 Remove the rind from the lime with a vegetable peeler, taking care not to include any bitter white pith. Add the lime rind, chopped ginger, tamarind, dates, and chillies to the pan. Simmer, uncovered, over a medium–low heat for 20 minutes, until softened. Remove the pan from the heat.

4 Reserve a few small mint leaves for a garnish, then roughly chop the remaining leaves and stalks and add to the pan. Cover and leave to infuse for 30 minutes.

5 Push the pulp through a sieve set over a bowl, discarding anything left in the sieve. Whisk the garam masala, black salt, and ground cumin into the syrup in the bowl. Taste for sweetness and add more sugar if it is too sharp; aim for a balance of sweet and sour flavours.

6 Transfer the syrup to a freezerproof container. Leave to cool completely, and then place in the freezer for at least 1 hour, until ice crystals form and it has set.

7 Now make the caramelized pineapple. Sieve the icing sugar into a bowl with the *chaat masala* and chilli powder. Add the diced pineapple and stir to coat with the spice mix.

8 Heat a large, dry frying pan. Shake off any excess spice mix from the pineapple pieces and add the fruit to the pan. Cook over a medium heat, stirring frequently, for 5–8 minutes, until the pineapple caramelizes. Transfer the fruit to baking parchment and leave to cool.

9 Remove the granita from the freezer and rake it roughly with a fork. Spoon into small glasses and scatter each glass with the caramelized pineapple and mint leaves.

CAROB

Sweet | Astringent | Chocolatey

BOTANICAL NAME
Ceratonia siliqua

ALSO KNOWN AS
St John's bread, locust bean, locust seed.

MAJOR FLAVOUR COMPOUNDS
Pentanoic, hexanoic, and pyruvic acids.

PARTS USED
Dred ripened pods (technically fruits).

METHOD OF CULTIVATION
Trees grow in orchards and ripe pods are harvested by hand or by shaking them on to nets.

COMMERCIAL PREPARATION
Pods are partially dried and either left whole or crushed to remove the seeds.

NON-CULINARY USES
Animal feed; cigarette flavouring; seeds are used to make a gelling agent (locust bean gum) employed in food and cosmetics.

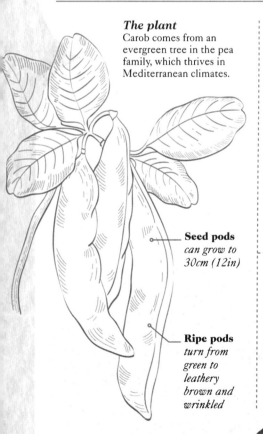

The plant
Carob comes from an evergreen tree in the pea family, which thrives in Mediterranean climates.

Seed pods
can grow to 30cm (12in)

Ripe pods
turn from green to leathery brown and wrinkled

Powder
Carob powder is usually made with roasted pod and pulp, but is also available raw. The powder will keep almost indefinitely in a sealed container in a cool, dark place.

Whole
Dried pods can be roasted and/or eaten whole, avoiding the rock-hard seeds; or use to make a syrupy liquid by boiling in water or milk. Broken pieces are also available as "kibble".

Spice story

The fruit of the carob tree has nourished humans and animals since ancient times. The tree's ability to fruit in poor-quality soil made it important when famine struck, and the Bible mentions its use as livestock fodder. The common names St John's bread and locust bean derive from the "locusts" that St John the Baptist was said to have eaten in the desert, which scholars believed were in fact carob pods (though most now think he was eating grasshoppers). The word "carat" originates from the Greek for the carob tree, *keration*: Arab jewellers used the seeds as a unit of weight for gold. The pods were easy to transport, and the Greeks and Arabs took carob west with them. Arabs brought it north to Spain and Portugal, where it was cultivated from the 17th century, and from there it spread to the New World.

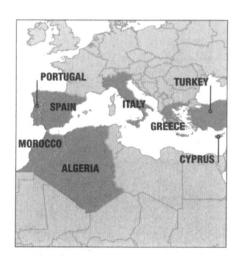

Region of cultivation
Carob is probably native to the eastern Mediterranean and the Levant. It is now cultivated mainly in Spain, but also in Italy (especially Sicily), Portugal, Morocco, Greece, Cyprus, Turkey, and Algeria.

Kitchen creativity }

Sweet and slightly acidic tasting, carob has a rich, warm, almost vanilla-like flavour that vaguely resembles milk chocolate, but it lacks cacao's bitterness, and has an unusual, slightly sour aroma. This spice is a rich source of sugar.

BLENDING SCIENCE

Pentanoic and hexanoic acids dominate, giving sour milk flavour and "sweaty cheese" aroma, respectively, while pyruvic acid has a brown sugar nuance. Sweet, fruity ketones are also present, including pineapple ketone, as well as warming, spicy cinnamaldehyde, and a terpene called farnesene, which has woody and sweet citrus notes. When roasted, pyrazines give chocolatey, nutty aromas, but cinnamaldehyde is degraded.

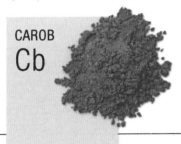

CAROB
Cb

PINEAPPLE KETONE AND PYRUVIC ACID
sweet | fruity | brown sugar | caramel

PENTANOIC ACID AND HEXANOIC ACID
sour milk | sweaty cheese

CINNAMALDEHYDE
warm | sweet | fragrant

PYRAZINES AND FARNESENE
nutty | roasted | bready | woody

combine with sweet spices that enhance the background of sugary fruit:

⊕ **fenugreek** shares brown sugar flavour, with a hint of maple syrup, while bringing savoury tastes reminiscent of clove

⊕ **fennel** seeds carry sweetness and a liquorice-like aroma, bringing floral and citrus elements

⊕ **cardamom** brings eucalyptus and is a surprisingly good match thanks to its sweet minty notes

⊕ **liquorice** is intensely sweet with potent aniseed notes

pair with acidic or sour spices to bring tangy tartness:

⊕ **tamarind** is strongly sour with underlying honey-caramel

⊕ **sumac** is tangy and earthy with plum nuances

⊕ **barberry** is fresh, green, invigoratingly sour and subtly floral

⊕ **amchoor** brings tropical fruit flavours and astringency

found in unroasted carob, highlight it with cinnamon flavour:

⊕ **cinnamon** lends sweet, fragrant, spicy, and warming qualities

⊕ **cassia** is similarly sweet and warming, but its bitterness is harsher and it has some astringency

pair with nutty, woody spices that enhance the deep, roasted flavours:

⊕ **roasted sesame** brings harmonizing nutty flavours

⊕ **cacao** has close harmony due to its backbone of roasted flavour compounds

⊕ **wattle** adds strong smoky overtones with earthiness

⊕ **grains of Selim** shares farnesene and carries sweet vanilla notes; its penetrating smokiness blends with roasted carob

⊕ **nutmeg** is sweetly aromatic and has woodiness, thanks in part to farnesene

FOOD PARTNERS

⊕ **Vegetables** Drizzle carob syrup over grilled or roast aubergine.

⊕ **Meat** Use carob syrup in a barbecue glaze for chicken or lamb, or mix the powder into a rub or marinade.

⊕ **Baking** Add carob powder to coffee cake batter and spiced vanilla biscuit dough or stir into a flapjack mixture (remember it is sweeter than cocoa).

⊕ **Desserts** Blitz frozen bananas with vanilla extract and a spoonful or two of the powder or syrup to make carob banana ice cream.

⊕ **Drinks** Blitz carob powder with cold milk and ice to make a refreshing alternative to an iced latte.

RELEASE THE FLAVOUR

Whole pods offer most flavour, but should be used according to the nature of the dish. Roasting causes amino acids and sugars to react with each other, creating new nutty, coffee-and-chocolate-like compounds, but reducing sweetness.

For quick-cook dishes, grind pods or soak until soft and mash or blitz.

For slow-cook, liquidy dishes whole pods can be added directly.

Roast raw pods for 40 minutes at 150°C (302°F). Reduce the time for kibble and check to prevent burning.

BARBERRY

Sour | Sharp | Tangy

BOTANICAL NAME
Berberis vulgaris

ALSO KNOWN AS
Piperidge, jaundice berry, *zereshk*.

MAJOR FLAVOUR COMPOUND
Hexanal.

PARTS USED
Dried berries.

METHOD OF CULTIVATION
Fruits are harvested manually, most commonly by hitting the branches with a stick until the berries fall off.

COMMERCIAL PREPARATION
Berries are dried in the sun, in the shade, or in industrial driers; research shows that driers yield the best-quality spice.

NON-CULINARY USES
In Iranian traditional medicine to treat jaundice, inflammation, and toothache.

The plant
This dense and prickly deciduous shrub grows in scrubland and belongs to the berberis family.

Orange-yellow *flowers are produced from late spring to early summer*

Oblong red berries *grow in dense clusters on spiked branches and ripen in autumn*

Grows *up to 2–3 m (6½–10ft) tall*

Use berries *whole or chopped, as they are as or soaked first*

Dried berries
Only choose berries that are bright red in colour, indicating they have been dried carefully and are not overly old. Store them in a sealed container in the freezer for up to 6 months, and defrost as needed.

Spice story
The earliest record of the use of barberry fruits dates back to 650 BCE, when a description of their blood-purifying properties was inscribed on clay tablets in the library of the Assyrian king Ashurbanipal. The plant's use in Chinese medicine dates back over 3,000 years, and evidence of its medicinal use in Europe has nearly as long a history; for example, the bark from the root and the stem was used as a purgative and tonic. Throughout the Middle Ages, barberry was widely used in preserves, syrups, and wines in western Europe. Later, the herbalist John Gerard (1545–1612) suggested that the berry could be used to season meat – a flavouring idea that has stood the test of time! Barberry was first cultivated in Iran over 200 years ago, and the berries have since become an important part of cooking in the Middle East and the Caucasus.

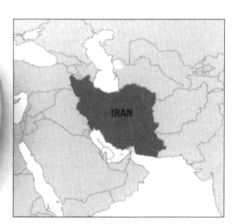

Region of cultivation
Barberry is native to central and southern Europe, northwest Africa, and western Asia. It is now cultivated mainly in Iran (which produces more than 10,000 tonnes of barberry fruits every year), but also in northern Europe and North America.

Kitchen creativity }

Barberries tolerate being combined with other strong flavours very well, and add zing to all kinds of savoury and sweet dishes. Their jewel-like appearance also makes them an attractive decoration.

BLENDING SCIENCE

Containing high levels of acids and sugars, dried barberries are a versatile flavouring that straddle the sweet–sour spectrum. The ability of sugars to reduce tastebud sensitivity to bitterness and sourness, alongside a bouquet of flavour compounds, including herby hexanal and floral linalool, offer a wide variety of spice-pairing options.

BARBERRY
Ba

MALIC, TARTARIC, AND CITRIC ACIDS
sharp | sour | lemony

SUGARS (EG. DEXTROSE, FRUCTOSE)
sweet

ALDEHYDES: HEXANAL AND NONANAL
green | grassy | fruity

pair with other acid-tasting spices for a potent, sour hit:

⊕ **sumac** shares all three acids

⊕ **tamarind** shares tartaric acid and like barberry has a sweet-and-tart profile

⊕ **galangal**'s penetrating spiciness works well with the acidity of citric acid

⊕ **coriander** brings complex floral and citrus notes through shared linalool

add more "green" spices to enhance the aldehydes:

⊕ **bay** adds fresh and floral notes that complement barberry's hexanal and linalool

⊕ **ajwain** lends a "green" quality that blends well with the aldehydes

enhance the sweetness of other sweetly fragranced spices, and dampen the sourness and bitterness:

⊕ **cacao**'s bitterness can be tempered, and its sweet aromas enhanced

⊕ **cinnamon** adds floral notes from shared linalool

⊕ **vanilla** brings a creamy quality that helps to balance barberry's sharp acidity

⊕ **annatto** is sweetly aromatic with an edge of bitterness from caryophyllene

FOOD PARTNERS

⊕ **Salad** Crush the dried berries and sprinkle them over salads.

⊕ **Red meats** Crush barberries with salt and use as a rub for lamb, beef, or game.

⊕ **Pilaf** Soak the dried berries and then fry them in butter before adding to rice to make a pilaf.

⊕ **Preserves** Use fresh berries to make a fruit "leather" by boiling down the fruit, straining it, and spreading it out on a tray to dehydrate.

⊕ **Drinks** Add a syrup made with the dried berries to refreshing cool drinks.

RELEASE THE FLAVOUR

Berries can be rehydrated before cooking to dilute their sharpness and speed up the release of flavour compounds. Soak in cold water for 10 minutes or simmer briefly in a little boiling water.

Add half the fruits' volume in water

Pectin powerhouse

Pectin is the chemical glue that holds plant cells together, and it is present in all fruits in varying amounts. When fruits are cooked in sugar and water, pectin seeps out and reforms into a gluey gel when cooled – the basis for a jam. Barberries are high in pectin, and their acidity causes it to be quickly released. Flavouring jams and jellies with barberries thus helps to achieve a quick, strong set, particularly for medium- to low-pectin fruits.

Low

Strawberries
0.4%

Medium

Apricots
1%

Apples (unripe)
1.5%

High

Barberries
2.2%

COMPARATIVE PECTIN LEVELS

CACAO

Earthy | Floral | Bittersweet

BOTANICAL NAME
Theobroma cacao

ALSO KNOWN AS
Cocoa.

MAJOR FLAVOUR COMPOUND
Isovaleraldehyde.

PARTS USED
Seeds (also known as "beans").

METHOD OF CULTIVATION
Ripe fruits are picked with a pole-mounted cutting hook, then broken open by hand.

COMMERCIAL PREPARATION
The bitter raw seeds are fermented to develop palatable flavours, then dried, often next to open wood fires, roasted, and cracked to release the inner kernel.

NON-CULINARY USES
In cosmetics; in traditional medicine as a stimulant; in modern medicine purported to protect against heart disease.

The plant
Cacao is a broad-leaved, tropical evergreen tree in the mallow family. It grows up to 7m (23ft) tall in plantations, and up to 15m (50ft) tall in the wild.

Clusters of pinkish-white flowers *are produced on the main trunk and branches*

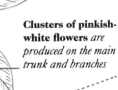

Fruit *is a green, yellow, or brown pod containing large seeds embedded in a white pulp*

Use nibs *whole, chop roughly, or grind to a coarse powder in a pestle and mortar*

Nibs
Cacao nibs are broken pieces of the unsweetened inner kernel of the cacao seed. They are available pre-roasted or, less commonly, raw (see Release the flavour).

Spice story

There is evidence that cacao was being used by the Olmec people of southern Mexico as early as 1500 BCE. By 600 BCE, the Olmec had introduced cacao to the Maya of Yucatan, who used it as a source of nourishment. They traded cacao to the Aztecs, who turned the beans into a thick, unsweetened drink. When the Spanish invaded Yucatan in the early 16th century they recognized that cacao was a precious commodity, and began sweetening it with cane sugar. The first recorded shipment of cacao beans to Europe reached Spain in 1585. Within a century, chocolate beverages were being consumed across Europe, long before coffee and tea. The first ever solid chocolate bar was manufactured by Fry's of Bristol in England in 1847.

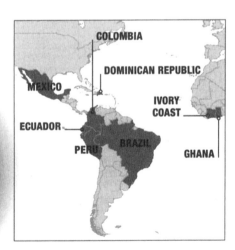

Region of cultivation
Cacao is native to tropical Central and South America. More than 50 per cent of the world's total crop is now produced in the Ivory Coast and Ghana, but many other tropical countries cultivate cacao, including Ecuador, Brazil, Peru, Colombia, Mexico, the Dominican Republic, and Indonesia.

Kitchen creativity }

One of the most complexly flavoured foods, cacao nibs are earthy, bitter, and fragrant, but unlike chocolate they do not melt without grinding to a paste. They have a nut-like crunchy texture and can be used whole, chopped, or ground to a coarse powder.

BLENDING SCIENCE

Cacao contains about 600 flavour compounds, and their relative amounts vary by region, tree variety, and processing method. Bitterness is partly produced by two stimulant compounds, caffeine and theobromine, which turn into bitter pyrazines on roasting. Cacao also contains sweet-tasting aldehydes and ketones, as well as fruity alcohols and phenols. Pyrazines also give the spice its roasted, nutty flavours.

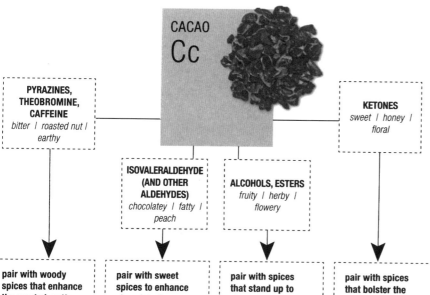

CACAO
Cc

PYRAZINES, THEOBROMINE, CAFFEINE
bitter | roasted nut | earthy

ISOVALERALDEHYDE (AND OTHER ALDEHYDES)
chocolatey | fatty | peach

ALCOHOLS, ESTERS
fruity | herby | flowery

KETONES
sweet | honey | floral

pair with woody spices that enhance the roasted, nutty flavours:

⊕ **wattle** adds roasted-coffee-like taste with powerful smoke aroma

⊕ **black pepper** lends a woody, slightly bitter, warm pungency

⊕ **sesame** brings harmonizing nutty flavours after roasting

⊕ **cumin** adds an earthy, smoky woodiness and introduces an aroma of pinewood

pair with sweet spices to enhance chocolate flavours:

⊕ **vanilla** is sweet, unmistakeably creamy rich and aromatic

⊕ **mahleb** contributes bittersweet cherry and almond aroma

⊕ **mace** brings sweet musky and orangey flavours (less so with nutmeg)

pair with spices that stand up to bitterness while enhancing fruity and floral notes:

⊕ **coriander** amplifies floral and enhances fruit with lemon notes

⊕ **chilli** brings fruity and green nuances, adding a mouth-warming dimension

⊕ **bay** brings a penetrating, fresh, slightly floral herbiness

⊕ **ginger** brings pungent warmth, sweet citrus, and floral linalool

pair with spices that bolster the sweet honey aroma of cacao:

⊕ **liquorice** carries an intense sweetness, bringing clove taste and strong eucalyptus

⊕ **cinnamon** contributes sweet warming qualities

⊕ **allspice** provides a sweet peppery warmth

⊕ **sweet paprika** enhances sweetness, introducing earthiness

FOOD PARTNERS

⊕ **Fennel, pumpkin** Sprinkle nibs over a fennel and blood orange salad, or grate over pumpkin and sage ravioli.

⊕ **Squid** Add roughly ground nibs to a tempura batter for squid.

⊕ **Meat** Rub ground toasted nibs onto steak before grilling; add to Italian *agrodolce* sauce for duck or pork; mix into a fruity, spicy lamb tagine.

⊕ **Sweet bakes** Add nibs to banana bread, flapjack, or cookies.

⊕ **Cheesecake** Add nibs to the biscuit base ingredients for a savoury or sweet cheesecake.

RELEASE THE FLAVOUR

Unroasted ("raw") cacao nibs are not sweet and much more bitter than chocolate. Roasting them before use helps to remove some of the bitterness.

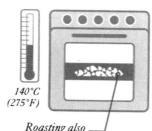

140°C (275°F)

Roasting also creates nutty pyrazine flavours

Roast nibs in an oven at 140°C (275°F) for 10–15 minutes.

BLEND TO TRY

Use and adapt this classic blend featuring cacao:

Mole mix p65

PAPRIKA

Bittersweet | Earthy | Fruity

BOTANICAL NAME
Capsicum annuum

ALSO KNOWN AS
Hungarian pepper, *pimentón*.

MAJOR FLAVOUR COMPOUNDS
Pyrazine combinations.

PARTS USED
Fruits.

METHOD OF CULTIVATION
The fruits of chilli peppers are harvested in summer when they are red and ripe.

COMMERCIAL PREPARATION
Fruits are dried then ground. Peppers for smoked paprika are hung in smoke houses before processing.

NON-CULINARY USES
In cosmetics and pharmaceuticals for its pigment and the inflammation-reducing properties of capsaicin.

The plant
Paprika comes from chilli pepper plants, which are frost tender, herbaceous perennials in the nightshade family, and grow well in warm, dry climates.

Plants *reach a height of around 80cm (2½ft)*

Fruits *are fleshy and hollow*

Varieties *differ; some have small, round fruits*

◄ *Hungarian*

Grades *range from erós, the spiciest, to különleges, the mildest*

Three main varieties *are picante (hot), dulce (sweet), and agridulce (bittersweet)*

Spanish ►

Powder
There are two main types of paprika: Hungarian, which is bright- or rust-red and with pronounced fruitiness, and Spanish – known as *pimentón* – which is darker and sweeter. Both are available smoked.

Spice story

Capsicum peppers probably originated in Mexico, where recent cave findings suggest they were being eaten as far back as 7000 BCE. In the late 15th century CE, explorer Christopher Columbus shipped peppers back to Europe from the Caribbean. Spanish monks started drying and grinding the fruits, and one of the world's best smoked paprikas is still made in La Vera valley in Extremadura, where ripe peppers are hung in smokehouses in the fields and ground in ancient stone mills. The Ottoman Turks introduced peppers to Hungary and by the mid-1800s Hungarians had adopted paprika as their national spice and made it a key ingredient of goulash, a rustic meat soup. French chef Georges Escoffier is credited with introducing paprika to the wider culinary world: he had it shipped from Hungary to his Monte Carlo restaurant in 1879 and put *poulet au paprika* on the menu.

Region of cultivation
Peppers are native to South and Central America, but peppers for paprika are grown and processed chiefly in Hungary, Spain, the Netherlands, and Turkey.

Kitchen creativity }

The various varieties of paprika are appreciated for their earthy and smoky flavours, spicy heat, and the sweet taste of the fruit's sugars. Choose very mild paprika to harness the rust-red pigment without changing the flavour of a dish.

BLENDING SCIENCE

Paprika's tang derives from sour-tasting citric acid, its sweetness from sugars and the rum-like flavour compound ethyl acetate, and its rich earthiness from pyrazines, many of which develop during the drying and/or smoking. From sweet and fruity, to bitter and smoky, the range of different types of paprika gives a wealth of pairing opportunities.

PAPRIKA
Pa

PYRAZINE COMBINATIONS
earthy | smoky

CITRIC ACID
tart | citrusy

pair with other pyrazines and related compounds:

⊕ **wattle**'s pyrazines and other smoke compounds bring notes of wood smoke and chocolate

⊕ **black cardamom** has an earthy flavour and smoked aroma

⊕ **sesame** brings rich, nutty, caramel flavours when toasted

⊕ **ajwain** in toasted form has a herbal earthiness and slight citrus notes

SUGARS AND ETHYL ACETATE
sweet | fruity

enhance the sweet side of paprika:

⊕ **cinnamon** lifts the sweetness and adds fragrant warmth

⊕ **allspice** brings clove-like sweetness and floral nuances

⊕ **caraway** has well-matched citrus and bittersweet flavours, alongside subtle aniseed

ISOVALERALDEHYDE AND ACETOINE
fatty | buttery

give prominence to the rich flavours:

⊕ **cacao** shares a raft of flavour compounds, including pyrazines, ketones, esters, and isovaleraldehyde

⊕ **saffron** when combined with milder paprika brings in a distinctive hay-like richness while gently enhancing earthiness

boost paprika's tanginess with other acidic or citrus spices:

⊕ **tamarind**'s tartaric acid, fruity aldehydes, and limonene bring a sweet-sour hit

⊕ **coriander** makes a good match through limonene, its cymene enhancing earthiness

⊕ **ginger**'s citrus notes, sweetness, and hot pungent elements can be drawn out by mild, sweet, and hot paprika respectively

FOOD PARTNERS

⊕ **Plums** Add smoked paprika to a sweet-sour plum sauce.

⊕ **Roasted roots** Serve roasted Jerusalem artichokes with a smoked paprika *aïoli*, or salt-baked new potatoes with a *mojo picón* sauce, which includes paprika, cumin, chillies, and garlic.

⊕ **Squid, octopus** Sprinkle hot paprika into the batter for fried squid or add to a Moroccan *chermoula* (herby marinade) for grilled octopus.

⊕ **Meat** Sprinkle smoked paprika and chopped herbs on to roast marrow bones; add to pork or duck rillettes; rub into beef brisket before slow-cooking; make an offal *paprikash*.

RELEASE THE FLAVOUR

Paprika is high in carotenoids (similar to carrots' orange pigment), which, along with its most fragrant flavour compounds, dissolve well in oil. Hence frying with oil at the start of cooking helps spread colour and flavour through a dish.

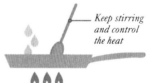

Keep stirring and control the heat

The powder's small particle size means it burns easily. Smoked varieties are already slightly bitter and prone to develop acrid bitterness from scorching.

BLENDS TO TRY

Use and adapt these classic recipes:

Jamaican jerk rub p64
Chimchurri p66
BBQ rub p68

Mild or hot?

Chilli heat comes from capsaicin molecules, most of which reside in the whitish pith. The degree of heat or mildness in paprika depends on capsaicin levels in the chilli variety used and how thoroughly the pith has been removed in processing. Poor quality hot paprika is often made from whole dried fruits, including stems, pith, and bitter seeds.

Capsaicin-containing oil glands run along the inner boundary between pith and flesh

WATTLE

Roasted | Woody | Musty

BOTANICAL NAME
Acacia victoriae
(most commonly used species)

ALSO KNOWN AS
Gundablue wattle.

MAJOR FLAVOUR COMPOUNDS
Pyrazine compounds.

PARTS USED
Seeds.

METHOD OF CULTIVATION
Ripe pods are dislodged using a mechanical tree shaker or beating by hand with a stick.

COMMERCIAL PREPARATION
Seeds are separated from pods by threshing and sieving, then dried and roasted.

NON-CULINARY USES
Has been used as animal feed; fruits, seeds, and gum from wattle trees used in traditional Aboriginal medicine for many ailments.

Spice story

Wattle has been used as a staple food by the aborigines of Australia for at least 4,000 years. Only a few of the hundreds of acacia species that grow in Australia have edible seeds, and some others are toxic. Over a period of thousands of years, the indigenous population identified the edible species. They either ate the seeds fresh, straight from the pod, or dried and roasted or baked them, crushing them between grinding stones to produce flour. Increasing commercial interest in the seeds has led to the development of small-scale plantations in Australia, although a significant proportion of the crop is still harvested from wild trees. As "bush food" increasingly features on Antipodean restaurant menus, wattle's importance as a culinary spice has grown.

The plant
Edible wattle seeds are produced by a small number of evergreen shrubs or small trees in the bean family.

Cream-coloured flowers *are edible and sometimes used as a culinary decoration*

Wattle *is both flavoursome and high in protein (about 20 per cent)*

Green pea-like pods *turn brown or yellow and become papery and brittle as they ripen*

Powder
This robust spice is usually bought pre-ground as a coarse dark brown powder that resembles ground coffee. It can be stored in a sealed container in a cool, dark place for up to two years.

AUSTRALIA
(SEMI-ARID AND ARID REGIONS)

Region of cultivation
Acacia victoriae and other edible species of wattle are native to arid and semi-arid regions of Australia. They are cultivated in South and Western Australia, Victoria, and New South Wales.

Kitchen creativity }

Wattle has a unique nutty, roasted coffee-like taste with a lightly charred woody and smoky aroma, plus notes of popcorn and sweet citrus. The complex flavours of this spice work well with both sweet and savoury recipes.

BLENDING SCIENCE

The flavour profile of wattle is dominated by a water-soluble pyrazine with a bitter, musty, earthy, roasted-coffee flavour with hints of cocoa, and an oil-soluble pyrazine with a sweet, nutty, charred wood taste with hints of popcorn. Some intensely lemon-flavoured citral and bitter-tasting phenols are also present.

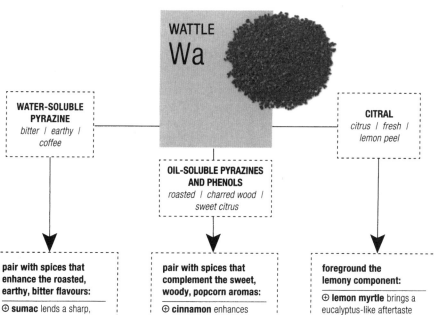

WATTLE
Wa

WATER-SOLUBLE PYRAZINE
bitter | earthy | coffee

OIL-SOLUBLE PYRAZINES AND PHENOLS
roasted | charred wood | sweet citrus

CITRAL
citrus | fresh | lemon peel

pair with spices that enhance the roasted, earthy, bitter flavours:

⊕ **sumac** lends a sharp, sweet acid tang

⊕ **tamarind** contributes caramel notes and cheese-like aroma

⊕ **juniper** adds herbal pine notes and citrus spiciness

⊕ **carob** enhances the coffee and cocoa notes, particularly when roasted

pair with spices that complement the sweet, woody, popcorn aromas:

⊕ **cinnamon** enhances sweet woody warmth, without bitterness

⊕ **paprika** contributes a sweet, woody pungency and smokiness

⊕ **cacao** adds bitter chocolate notes

⊕ **cumin** has a musky, earthy, almost burnt flavour

foreground the lemony component:

⊕ **lemon myrtle** brings a eucalyptus-like aftertaste

⊕ **lemongrass** adds mild floral pepperiness and slight spiciness

⊕ **dill** gives herbal, minty notes and mild woodiness

⊕ **caraway** lends anise-like, spicy notes

RELEASE THE FLAVOUR

Wattle does not need to be fried or toasted as the nutty, roasted flavours have already been generated during processing. The flavour depends instead on the balance of water and fats within a dish.

Bitter

Wattle   *Fat*   *Lemon + Nuts*

Cooking in fats decreases the levels of bitter phenols, and releases lemony citral and the nutty, oil-soluble pyrazines.

Bitter

Wattle   *Water*   *Coffee + Cocoa*

Cooking in water-based liquids releases the water-soluble pyrazine and some of the bitter-tasting phenols, resulting in bitter, earthy, roasted-coffee flavours with hints of cocoa.

Stovetop espresso

Maximize water-based flavours while reducing bitterness by using ground wattle like coffee in an espresso machine and cooking with the liquid extract.

FOOD PARTNERS

⊕ **Potatoes** Sprinkle wattle over roasted sweet potato chips or potato wedges.

⊕ **Custard** Infuse custard with wattle, and then turn it into ice cream or serve it warm over sweet sponge pudding.

⊕ **Meat** Add wattle to a dry spice rub or marinade for chicken, lamb, or beef.

⊕ **Breads** Add a sprinkle of wattle to give a nutty sweetness to bread doughs and sweet yeast breads.

⊕ **Tuna** Include wattle in a spice crust for tuna before pan searing.

⊕ **Chocolate** Wattle works well in anything chocolatey – try adding it to chocolate mousse or a chocolate ganache.

SESAME

Nutty | Bittersweet | Rich

BOTANICAL NAME
Sesamum indicum

ALSO KNOWN AS
Benne.

MAJOR FLAVOUR COMPOUNDS
Pyrazine compounds.

PARTS USED
Seeds.

METHOD OF CULTIVATION
Whole plants are cut just before the seed capsules (technically fruits) are fully ripe.

COMMERCIAL PREPARATION
Stalks are dried, threshed, capsules split open, and the seeds shaken out.

NON-CULINARY USES
Sesame oil is used as a base in cosmetics and perfumery. The mildly laxative seeds are used in Ayurvedic medicine to treat indigestion and arthritis.

The plant
Sesame is a tropical, annual plant in the pedalium family. It grows to a height of 1–2m (3–6ft).

Flowers *are trumpet-shaped and can be white, pale pink, or purplish*

Seed capsules *are oblong and contain 50–100 flat seeds*

White
These are sold hulled or unhulled, and toasted or untoasted. Raw seeds have almost no aroma; roasting brings out their nutty taste.

Black
This type of unhulled seed is popular in Chinese and Japanese cookery, and sold toasted or untoasted.

Spice story

Sesame was first cultivated more than 4,000 years ago and was prized by many ancient civilizations. The Babylonians and Assyrians used sesame both in cooking and in religious rituals – in Assyrian mythology, the gods drank sesame wine the night before they created the world. Ancient Egyptians used the oil as a medicine, and ground the seeds for flour. Seed remains were found in Tutankhamun's tomb. In Rome, soldiers carried the energy-giving seeds as emergency rations, and cooks ground them into a paste-like condiment flavoured with cumin. In the famous Arabian folk tale, when Ali Baba cries "Open, sesame!" a cave is unsealed to reveal a stash of jewels. This probably alludes to the way ripe seed pods burst open at the slightest touch, scattering their seeds. Sesame travelled to North America and Mexico with the slave trade, and was being grown in colonial America by 1730.

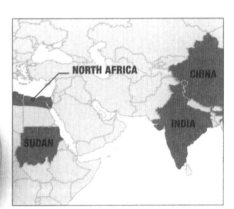

Region of cultivation
Sesame plants originated in sub-Saharan Africa. Sesame is cultivated in China, India, North Africa, North America, Central and South America, and Sudan.

Kitchen creativity }

Sesame is used in everything from sweets such as Indian *til laddoos* and Middle Eastern *halva* to savoury dips and dressings such as tahini and hummus. The Japanese sprinkle *gomashio*, a sesame-and-salt condiment, over rice and noodles.

BLENDING SCIENCE

Untoasted sesame seeds carry very subtle flavours from compounds such as furfural and hexanal. When roasted or toasted, proteins and sugars on the outer layers of the seed react with one another to form hundreds of new compounds, including nutty, flavourful pyrazines.

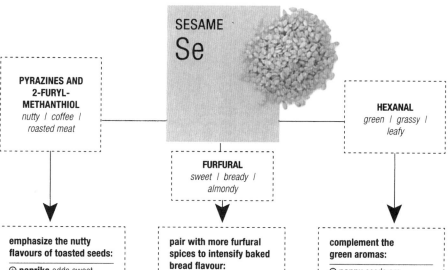

SESAME
Se

PYRAZINES AND 2-FURYL-METHANTHIOL
nutty | coffee | roasted meat

FURFURAL
sweet | bready | almondy

HEXANAL
green | grassy | leafy

emphasize the nutty flavours of toasted seeds:
- ⊕ **paprika** adds sweet earthiness
- ⊕ **wattle**'s pyrazines overlap with toasted sesame seed, bringing in notes of wood smoke and chocolate

pair with more furfural spices to intensify baked bread flavour:
- ⊕ **tamarind** brings caramel-like furfural flavour
- ⊕ **vanilla**'s complex mix of compounds adds depth to sweet flavours

complement the green aromas:
- ⊕ **poppy** seeds are packed with similar grassy aldehyde compounds
- ⊕ **bay**'s green, fresh flavour is heightened by shared hexanal

FOOD PARTNERS

⊕ **Bananas and apples** Sprinkle toasted seeds over apple or banana fritters.

⊕ **Vegetables** Sprinkle black seeds over a noodle and vegetable salad with a spicy Szechuan dressing, or scatter over roasted kale or asparagus.

⊕ **Oily fish** Coat tuna or salmon in seeds before pan frying.

⊕ **Chicken** Coat chicken legs in a ground black sesame, soy, and honey glaze before baking or grilling.

⊕ **Pulses** Roll falafel in raw seeds before cooking.

⊕ **Baking and sweets** Sprinkle raw seeds over bread dough before baking, or make sesame brittle with honey, butter, and white seeds.

RELEASE THE FLAVOUR

When sesame seeds are toasted, proteins and sugars on the outer layers react to form new compounds, including roasted-nut pyrazines and the sulphurous, coffee- and roasted meat-like 2-furylmethanethiol.

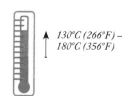

130°C (266°F) – 180°C (356°F)

Proteins and sugars react together at temperatures above 130°C (266°F). Fats inside the seeds burn and produce acrid flavours at around 180°C (356°F), so toast with care.

Black or white?

Darker seeds carry heavier, spicier aromas, and are better suited for savoury recipes. Pale varieties are ideal for mixing with milder spices and for cooking with butter. Unhulled seeds have a faint bitterness, due to oxalates in the external layers, designed to deter pests.

work best for strongly flavoured recipes

Higher concentrations of phenolic defence compounds alongside the pigments convey a stronger, slightly bitter flavour.

used to make pastes and added to sweets

Pale sesame seeds varieties have slightly less oil and more moisture, giving them gentler flavours of honey, caramelized milk, and vanilla.

BLACK SESAME, LIQUORICE, AND CARDAMOM ICE CREAM

This recipe blends three spices to create a creamy, subtly aromatic ice cream that is flavoursome and not too sweet. Its nutty, toasted-sesame taste is enhanced by a hint of liquorice and floral cardamom. Adding alcohol makes the ice cream softer straight from the freezer, but you can omit it if you prefer.

SPICE IDEAS

Use white sesame seeds instead of black for less bitterness, and **leave untoasted** to allow honeyed, more floral flavours to gain greater prominence.

Replace a proportion of sesame seeds with **wattle** to bring in notes of chocolate and wood smoke.

Pick up on leafy green hexanal in sesame and eucalyptus-like cineole in cardamom by using **ground bay leaves** in place of liquorice.

Serves 4

Prep time 20 mins

Freezing time 20–30 mins in ice-cream maker (remember to pre-freeze the bowl, if applicable); 3–4 hours minimum in freezer

3 heaped tbsp black sesame seeds

300ml (10fl oz) double cream

300ml (10fl oz) Greek yogurt

300ml (10fl oz) condensed milk

seeds of 30 cardamom pods, ground

1½ tsp liquorice root powder

1½ tbsp white rum or other lightly flavoured spirit (optional)

1 Toast the sesame seeds in a dry frying pan over a medium heat for about 5 minutes, then leave to cool.

2 Using a spice grinder or small food processor, grind the seeds until they form a powdery paste – this will take about 1 minute.

3 In a large bowl, whip the double cream until it forms soft peaks. Set aside.

4 In another bowl, beat together the yogurt, condensed milk, ground cardamom, liquorice powder, and sesame paste. Gently fold this mixture into the cream. Stir in the alcohol, if using.

5 Pour the mixture into an ice-cream maker and churn according to the instructions. Transfer the ice cream to a freezerproof container and freeze until ready to serve. Alternatively, pour the mixture into a freezerproof container and freeze for 3–4 hours, stirring at regular intervals to break up the ice crystals and ensure a smooth ice cream.

GARLIC

Pungent | Sulphurous | Sweet

BOTANICAL NAME
Allium sativum

ALSO KNOWN AS
Camphor of the poor, stinking rose.

MAJOR FLAVOUR COMPOUND
Allicin.

PARTS USED
Bulb.

METHOD OF CULTIVATION
The bulbs are harvested when around half
the leaves have turned yellow.

METHOD OF PREPARATION
Bulbs are stored in a cool, shady place
for 10–20 days so that they lose about
one-fifth of their water content.

NON-CULINARY USES
Modern research shows garlic improves
cholesterol levels and slightly reduces
high blood pressure.

The plant
Garlic is a bulbous
perennial herb in the
onion family that
grows to a height of
0.6m (2ft). Bulbs are
ready to harvest 5–9
months after planting.

◄ *Powdered*

Flaked ►

Dried
Dried garlic can be flaked, powdered, or
in granule form but all lack the pine and
citrusy subtleties of the fresh spice, leaving
only the main garlicky sulphur flavours. .

Skin *of the bulb
can be white,
yellow, pink,
or mauve*

Bulbs *consist
of up to 24
segments known
as cloves*

Store *in a cool,
dark place, but
no need for
refrigeration*

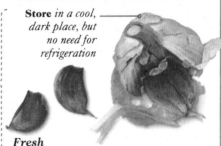

Fresh
Mature bulbs tend to have more potent
flavour, but avoid any that are showing
green shoots (see right).

Spice story

This most potent spice has been
prized for over five millennia, by
virtually every civilization – the Greek
physician Galen praised it as "the
great panacea". An Egyptian medical
papyrus from about 1550 BCE features
22 different garlic formulas for various
ailments. The slaves who built the
Egyptian pyramids were given garlic
to sustain them and prevent disease.
The Chinese cultivated garlic for its
stimulating and healing properties,
while Roman soldiers ate it before
battle for courage and strength. In
folklore, garlic has been seen both as a
protector from evil spirits or vampires,
and as a symbol of the Devil. As a food,
its popularity has waxed and waned; it
was shunned at Roman and Greek
feasts because of its powerful odour,
but over time, garlic became integral
to many regional cuisines, including
Indian and Mediterranean.

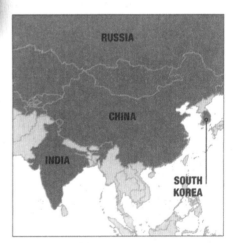

Region of cultivation
Probably native to Central Asia, China
is now the largest producer and exporter
of garlic, followed by India, South Korea,
Russia, and the USA.

Kitchen creativity }

Garlic amplifies and unites other flavours while having its own distinctive taste that gives depth to many savoury dishes. Essential to many cuisines, with onions and ginger it forms the "trinity" at the heart of much Asian cooking.

BLENDING SCIENCE

Garlic's pungency derives mainly from its sulphur-containing flavour compounds; these have significant cross-over with cooked meats, which also contain sulphur compounds. Smaller amounts of gently aromatic terpenes are also present, including limonene and sabinene. Toasting creates nutty-flavoured pyrazines.

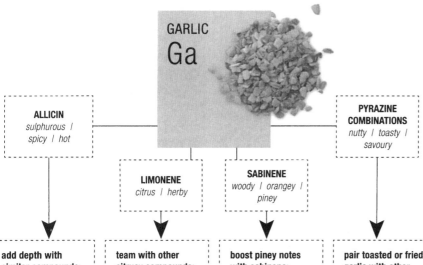

GARLIC
Ga

ALLICIN
sulphurous | spicy | hot

LIMONENE
citrus | herby

SABINENE
woody | orangey | piney

PYRAZINE COMBINATIONS
nutty | toasty | savoury

add depth with similar compounds:

⊕ **asafoetida** has a potent range of similar sulphur compounds

⊕ **chilli's** capsaicins give depth to garlic heat by stimulating the tongue's temperature receptors

team with other citrusy compounds:

⊕ **ginger** has citral, which shares garlic's lemony sweetness, and also carries heat

⊕ **lemongrass** adds citrus, a sweet, floral aroma and gentle pepperiness

boost piney notes with sabinene:

⊕ **black cardamom** shares sabinene and adds a nose-filling camphor quality and smokiness

⊕ **nutmeg, mace** bring notes of earthy sweetness

pair toasted or fried garlic with other pyrazine-laden spices:

⊕ **toasted sesame** intensifies garlic's nutty accents

⊕ **wattle** brings charred wood aromas and hints of popcorn

FOOD PARTNERS

⊕ **Roast lamb** Before roasting, make slits all over the joint and insert slices of fresh garlic.

⊕ **Soup** Roast a foil-wrapped garlic head in the oven, then squeeze out the sweet pulp and add to pumpkin or other vegetable soups.

⊕ **Prawns** Add to an oily marinade for grilled or barbecued prawns.

⊕ **Raw vegetables** Pound garlic with anchovies and olive oil to make the Provençal paste *anchoïade*, and serve with crudités.

⊕ **Chickpeas** Add roasted or raw cloves to the mortar or blender when making hummus.

BLENDS TO TRY

Use or adapt these recipes for classic blends featuring garlic:

Niter kibbeh p32

Mbongo mix p35

Nuoc cham p50

Shichimi-togarashi p57

BBQ rub p68

Bitter sprouts

When garlic cloves sprout, they become more bitter. The plant has begun stockpiling defensive bitter-tasting substances, such as phenols and sulphur compounds. Reduce bitterness by cutting out the green shoot before cooking.

Green shoot has bitter compounds

RELEASE THE FLAVOUR

A damaged garlic clove releases chemicals that react together to create allicin, the pungent compound we most associate with a "garlicky" flavour. Chopping, crushing, and puréeing produce progressively higher amounts of allicin.

Leave for 60 seconds after crushing or chopping, so allicin levels rise to a peak.

Uninjured cloves do not contain allicin. Cook whole for mild, sweet flavours.

Vegetable oils spread the strongest compounds while butter aids its gentler flavours.

Below 180°C (350°F)

Avoid cooking garlic above 180°C (350°F) to prevent bitterness.

ASAFOETIDA

Sulphurous | *Oniony* | *Garlic-like*

BOTANICAL NAME
Ferula assa-foetida

ALSO KNOWN AS
Devil's dung, stinking gum, *hing*.

MAIN FLAVOUR COMPOUNDS
Sulphides.

PARTS USED
Taproot: a resin is produced from the coagulated sap.

METHOD OF CULTIVATION
In spring, the stalk base is cut to expose the top of the taproot, which is "milked" every few days for its sap.

COMMERCIAL PREPARATION
The sap is dried to form a dark resin, most of which is ground to a powder and mixed with rice flour and gum arabic.

NON-CULINARY USES
In traditional medicine to relieve flatulence and to treat lung conditions.

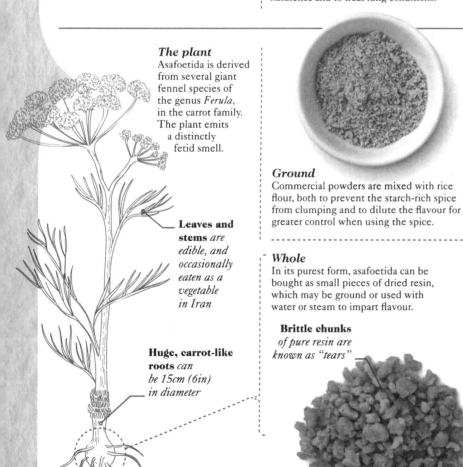

The plant
Asafoetida is derived from several giant fennel species of the genus *Ferula*, in the carrot family. The plant emits a distinctly fetid smell.

Leaves and stems *are edible, and occasionally eaten as a vegetable in Iran*

Huge, carrot-like roots *can be 15cm (6in) in diameter*

Ground
Commercial powders are mixed with rice flour, both to prevent the starch-rich spice from clumping and to dilute the flavour for greater control when using the spice.

Whole
In its purest form, asafoetida can be bought as small pieces of dried resin, which may be ground or used with water or steam to impart flavour.

Brittle chunks *of pure resin are known as "tears"*

Spice story

Asafoetida was discovered in Persia in the 4th century BCE by Alexander the Great's soldiers, who mistook it for silphium, a widely used ancient spice from a similar, and now extinct, plant. They took it to Asia and the Mediterranean region, where it became very popular with the Greeks and Romans as a substitute for silphium. Asafoetida was prized both as a seasoning and for its health-giving properties, and is cited in many of the recipes in *Apicius*, a Roman cookbook from the 1st century CE. After the fall of the Roman Empire it never regained popularity in Europe, but its use was recorded again, centuries later, in the *Baghdad Cookery Book* (1226). In the 16th century, the Mughals are reported to have taken the spice to India, where it became an indispensable element of vegetarian and Ayurvedic cuisine throughout the subcontinent.

Region of cultivation
Asafoetida is native to the mountains of Central Asia, from Turkey, Iran, and Afghanistan to Kashmir. It is cultivated mainly in Afghanistan, but also in Iran, Pakistan, and Kashmir. Most of the world's crop is imported by India.

Kitchen creativity }

When asafoetida is heated in fat, it develops a similar flavour to fried onions and garlic. Because traces of the same sulphurous flavour compounds (sulphides) are found in meat, asafoetida can also bring a meaty depth to vegetarian cooking.

BLENDING SCIENCE

Asafoetida's flavour-carrying oils are dominated by sulphides, which provide its fried onion smell, making it a suitable partner for similarly flavoured spices, such as garlic. Minor flavour compounds contribute more subtle hints of flavour but serve as a helpful guide for further pairings.

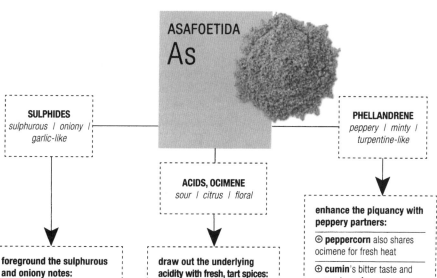

ASAFOETIDA
As

SULPHIDES
sulphurous | oniony | garlic-like

PHELLANDRENE
peppery | minty | turpentine-like

ACIDS, OCIMENE
sour | citrus | floral

foreground the sulphurous and oniony notes:
⊕ **garlic** shares several sulphur-containing flavour compounds
⊕ **mustard** has a flavour profile dominated by sulphur-containing flavour compounds
⊕ **nigella** has a similar onion-like taste profile

draw out the underlying acidity with fresh, tart spices:
⊕ **barberry** contributes a fruity sharpness
⊕ **coriander** adds citrus and floral notes

enhance the piquancy with peppery partners:
⊕ **peppercorn** also shares ocimene for fresh heat
⊕ **cumin**'s bitter taste and pepperiness from myrcene match those of asafoetida
⊕ **grains of Selim** add a complementary penetrating character due to cineole
⊕ **bay** highlights fresh woody notes from shared pinene

FOOD PARTNERS

⊕ **Beans and pulses** Fry asafoetida in ghee with other warm spices for a moong lentil dhal.

⊕ **Chicken and lamb** Add asafoetida to a yogurt marinade for baked or barbecued chicken or lamb.

⊕ **Fish** Sprinkle asafoetida over fish kebabs before grilling.

⊕ **Vegetables** Add a small pinch of ground asafoetida to give depth to a slow-cooked onion soup; sprinkle a little ground asafoetida into cooling oil when making a cauliflower, mushroom, or potato curry.

⊕ **Preserves** Add a pinch of asafoetida and turmeric to a pineapple, tomato, or mango pickle or chutney.

BLENDS TO TRY

Try these recipes for classic blends featuring asafoetida, and why not adapt them with some blending science?

Chaat masala p42
Gunpowder p45

CONTROL THE FLAVOUR

Asafoetida's potent oil-based sulphur compounds dissolve very slowly in water, a fact that can be exploited to control the strength of flavour when using whole chunks of resin.

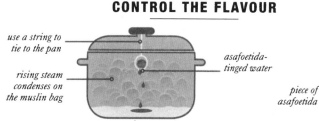

use a string to tie to the pan

rising steam condenses on the muslin bag

asafoetida-tinged water

Place a "tear" in a muslin bag and tie it to the underside of the pan lid. Drops of asafoetida-tinged water will drip down into the cooking liquid.

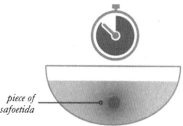

piece of asafoetida

Steep a "tear" of the spice in water for several hours to give a flavoured water that will be much milder than the raw spice.

CURRY LEAF

Meaty | Warm | Floral

BOTANICAL NAME
Murraya koenigii

ALSO KNOWN AS
Karapincha, meetha neem, kari patta. Not to
be confused with the inedible "curry plant".

MAJOR FLAVOUR COMPOUND
1-phenylethanethiol.

PARTS USED
Leaves (more accurately leaflets).

METHOD OF CULTIVATION
The leaves are harvested in early summer,
before flowering, from trees that are at
least three years old.

COMMERCIAL PREPARATION
Fresh leaves are vacuum-packed on their
stems and chilled or frozen, or washed and
air-dried for 4–5 days.

NON-CULINARY USES
In cosmetics and in traditional medicine
as a digestive aid.

The plant
Curry leaves come from a
small, deciduous tropical
tree in the citrus family.

Black berries
*are borne at the
ends of branches*

Dried
Although some recipes say dried leaves
can substitute for fresh if double the
quantity is added, they really have very
little flavour and are best avoided.

Leaves *are
divided into
pairs of leaflets*

Fresh
Leaves are best
bought fresh, on
the stem. Store
in a sealed bag
for a week in
the fridge, or
near indefinitely
in the freezer.

Leaves
*should be
bright green
without dark
blotches*

Leaflets *are
dark green, shiny,
and strongly
aromatic*

Spice story

Curry leaf has a special place in the
cuisines of southern India, Sri Lanka,
and Malaysia. When the Dravidians
of northwest India moved south in
around 1000 BCE, they brought with
them rice, mustard seeds, and pulses
to plant in their new home, and then
started combining them with the
indigenous curry leaves. The use of
curry leaf as flavouring for vegetables
is documented in early Tamil
literature from the 1st century CE.
The botanical name, *Murraya koenigii*,
refers to two 18th-century botanists,
Johann Andreas Murray and Johann
Gerhard König, rather than in tribute
to the "kingly" aromatic qualities of
the plant. It is grown prolifically in
southern India as an ornamental and
kitchen garden plant.

Region of cultivation
Native to the foothills of the Himalayas,
but spread over millennia to naturalize across
India, Sri Lanka, Bangladesh, and Myanmar.
It is cultivated mainly in southern India, but
also across southeast Asia, in northern Australia,
and the Middle East.

Kitchen creativity }

Picked when fresh, curry leaves have a mild, citrusy fragrance that erupts into a musky, floral aroma when bruised or sliced – not at all like curry powder! The flavour is subtle, so the leaves can be used liberally.

BLENDING SCIENCE

Sulphurous compound 1-phenylethanethiol dominates the flavour, which conveys a meaty taste, hyacinth aroma, and sulphurous bite. Smaller amounts of terpenes include floral linalool, pine-scented pinene, penetrating cineole, and peppery myrcene. "Green" hexanal and limonene provide citrusy flavours, present especially in fresh leaves.

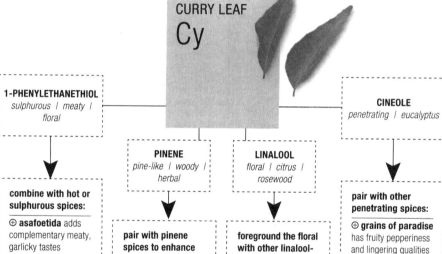

CURRY LEAF Cy

1-PHENYLETHANETHIOL
sulphurous | meaty | floral

PINENE
pine-like | woody | herbal

LINALOOL
floral | citrus | rosewood

CINEOLE
penetrating | eucalyptus

combine with hot or sulphurous spices:

⊕ **asafoetida** adds complementary meaty, garlicky tastes

⊕ **garlic** contributes heat, a sulphuric tang, and some sweetness

⊕ **mustard** brings heat from sulphur compounds and shares subtle pine

⊕ **chilli** brings heat and fresh fruitiness

pair with pinene spices to enhance woody aromas:

⊕ **nutmeg** has an undercurrent of pinene, bringing a bittersweet warmth

⊕ **black pepper** has both punchy heat and an aroma underpinned by pinene

foreground the floral with other linalool-carrying spices:

⊕ **coriander** is highly floral with a pine-like aroma and citrus edge

⊕ **lemongrass** has floral aromas from linalool and nerol; its woody myrcene also complementing pinene

pair with other penetrating spices:

⊕ **grains of paradise** has fruity pepperiness and lingering qualities compatible with cineole

⊕ **cardamom** shares eucalyptus qualities

⊕ **black cardamom** adds smoky layers

⊕ **bay** has a herby aroma, bitter notes, and penetrating tastes

FOOD PARTNERS

⊕ **Aubergine, okra** Fry fresh curry leaves with mustard seeds, cumin, and ginger before adding aubergine or okra and coconut milk, cooking until tender for a simple vegetable side dish.

⊕ **Lamb** Add fresh curry leaves to a garlicky yoghurt marinade for lamb, before slow-cooking.

⊕ **Seafood** Stir curry leaves into a tomato-based prawn or crab curry; swap European aromatics for curry leaves in *moules marinières*.

⊕ **Eggs** Fry fresh leaves in oil or ghee and drizzle over scrambled eggs.

⊕ **Pulses** Fry fresh leaves in ghee or butter with mustard seeds before stirring into a red lentil dhal.

⊕ **Baking** Add chopped leaves to flatbread dough before baking.

BLEND TO TRY

Use and adapt this classic south Indian spice blend featuring curry leaves:

Gunpowder p45

RELEASE THE FLAVOUR

Fresh curry leaves are best plucked from the stem and lightly bruised just before adding to hot oil. If using dried leaves, they can be ground to increase flavours from this less aromatic form.

Cook immediately in oil or ghee to ensure all the flavoursome oils can escape.

For slow-cook dishes, pluck out the leaves after frying and add later to ensure lighter floral notes don't entirely evaporate.

For quick-cook dishes, finely slice or pulverize leaves to ensure the flavour is imparted faster.

MUSTARD

Pungent | Earthy | Sharp

BOTANICAL NAMES
Brassica alba (white), *B. juncea* (brown),
B. nigra (black)

ALSO KNOWN AS
Indian mustard (brown).

MAJOR FLAVOUR COMPOUNDS
Isothiocyanates.

PARTS USED
Seeds. Leaves are also edible,
raw or cooked.

METHOD OF CULTIVATION
The green seed fruits ("pods") are harvested
about 4 months after sowing, when full-size
but not quite ripe, so they don't split open.

COMMERCIAL PREPARATION
Fruits are stacked in sheaves to dry for
about 10 days, then threshed and graded.
Seeds for grinding will have their bitter,
papery seed coats stripped off.

NON-CULINARY USES
Mustard oil is applied topically to treat
muscular aches and arthritis.

Spice story

Mustard seeds have been found in
prehistoric sites from China to Europe.
First records of the use of mustard as
a condiment date back to the ancient
Greeks and Romans, who chewed the
seeds whole, pulverized and sprinkled
them over food, or steeped them in
wine. By the Middle Ages, white
mustard had made its way to India and
China via the Arab trade routes, and
brown mustard had travelled overland
from its native India to Europe. One
method of transporting the powder was
to mix it with flour and other spices and
form it into balls using honey, wine, or
vinegar. The term mustard is thought
to come from the Latin *mustum*, the
name for the young wine used to mix
the ground seeds to a paste.

The plant
Mustard is a fast-growing
annual plant in the
cabbage family. It grows
up to 60cm (2ft) tall.

Whole
White mustard seeds are light brown
rather than white. Brown and black
mustard seeds are smaller.

**Yellow
flowers** *turn
into green
seed fruits*

**Each
fruit**
*contains
around
6 seeds*

Powder
Yellow mustard powder is often
made from a mixture of white and
brown seeds. Once moistened,
flavour develops within 10
minutes, but loses its
potency after an hour
or so unless vinegar
is added.

Region of cultivation
White mustard is probably native to
the Mediterranean region. It is cultivated
in most temperate regions of Europe,
and in North America, mainly in Canada.
Brown mustard is probably native to the
foothills of the Himalayas. It is cultivated
throughout India.

Kitchen creativity }

White mustard seeds have a mild taste and are used in pickling and to make American yellow mustard. Brown mustard seeds are much hotter, often featuring in Indian cuisine. Black seeds have a fine aroma but are less common.

BLENDING SCIENCE

Mustard's heat is produced by sulphur-containing isothiocyanates, which, unlike other pungent compounds, vaporize at body temperature to have a nose-filling pungency. The complex flavour profile also includes pine-like pinene, ground-coffee-like furanmethanethiol, malty, peachy 3-methylbutanal, and popcorn-like 2-acetyl-1-pyrroline. Nutty, roasted pyrazine flavours are produced by toasting the seeds.

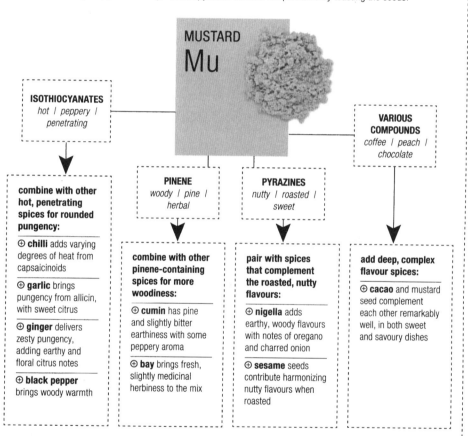

MUSTARD
Mu

ISOTHIOCYANATES
hot | peppery | penetrating

VARIOUS COMPOUNDS
coffee | peach | chocolate

PINENE
woody | pine | herbal

PYRAZINES
nutty | roasted | sweet

combine with other hot, penetrating spices for rounded pungency:

⊕ **chilli** adds varying degrees of heat from capsaicinoids

⊕ **garlic** brings pungency from allicin, with sweet citrus

⊕ **ginger** delivers zesty pungency, adding earthy and floral citrus notes

⊕ **black pepper** brings woody warmth

combine with other pinene-containing spices for more woodiness:

⊕ **cumin** has pine and slightly bitter earthiness with some peppery aroma

⊕ **bay** brings fresh, slightly medicinal herbiness to the mix

pair with spices that complement the roasted, nutty flavours:

⊕ **nigella** adds earthy, woody flavours with notes of oregano and charred onion

⊕ **sesame** seeds contribute harmonizing nutty flavours when roasted

add deep, complex flavour spices:

⊕ **cacao** and mustard seed complement each other remarkably well, in both sweet and savoury dishes

RELEASE THE FLAVOUR

Whole seeds are bland: the hot spicy isothiocyanates are only formed when a defensive enzyme called myrosinase breaks out of damaged cells to act on specific molecules – sinalbin in white mustard, stronger singrin in black and brown. However, myrosinase only functions when water is present.

Create a rich variety of nutty and roasted pyrazine flavour compounds by toasting the seeds before use.

Damage mustard seeds to release the myrosinase enzyme by crushing or cooking them.

Soak cracked mustard seeds in water for several minutes before cooking to allow the myrosinase enzyme to work and so obtain maximum flavour and heat.

FOOD PARTNERS

⊕ **Parsnips** Add a spoonful of wholegrain mustard to a creamy parsnip bake.

⊕ **Haricot beans** Combine English mustard powder with molasses and add to a haricot bean casserole.

⊕ **Rabbit** Add a spoonful of mustard to braised rabbit with tarragon.

⊕ **Fish** Fry brown mustard seeds in ghee with other warming spices, adding tomatoes and onion to make a sauce for fried or steamed fish.

⊕ **Cheese** Sprinkle mustard seeds over strips of puff pastry with grated strong cheese to make cheese straws.

BLENDS TO TRY

Try these recipes for classic blends featuring mustard, or why not adapt them with some blending science?

Panch phoran p43

Vindaloo paste p44

GRAINS OF PARADISE

Peppery | Pungent | Fruity-floral

BOTANICAL NAME
Aframomum melegueta

ALSO KNOWN AS
Guinea pepper, Melegueta pepper, ossame.

MAJOR FLAVOUR COMPOUND
Paradol.

PARTS USED
Seeds.

METHOD OF CULTIVATION
Seed pods (fruits) are harvested when the fruit has turned from green to red.

COMMERCIAL PREPARATION
Seed pods are typically dried in the sun. Pods are then opened and the seeds are removed for further drying.

NON-CULINARY USES
To relieve flatulence, freshen breath, and as a stimulant. *Gerard's Herbal* states that the seeds "rid the body of infection".

The plant
This herbaceous, perennial, reed-like plant is a member of the ginger family. It grows to a height of 1.5m (5ft).

Fruits *are fig-shaped and contain 60–100 seeds*

Seeds *inside the fruits are similar in size to cardamom seeds*

Whole
Seeds are a reddish-brown colour and pyramid-shaped.

The tiny seeds are milky-white inside

Powder
Ground seeds are greyish in colour.

Spice story

Grains of paradise originated in West Africa. The spice was first brought to Europe by Arab, Berber, or Jewish merchants, via trade caravan routes across the Sahara Desert. In Europe, it reached its peak of fashionability during the 14th and 15th centuries, when merchants gave it the heavenly epithet as a marketing ploy to increase sales. It was used as a less expensive substitute for black pepper, to spice wine, beer, and as a seasoning for food. Production of the spice was so important that the area of West Africa where it was grown became known as the Grain (or Pepper) Coast. The spice's popularity in Western cuisine had dwindled by the 19th century, but in its native West Africa it remains an important spice in ritual and food; in the Nigerian Yoruba culture it is used as an offering to the spirits.

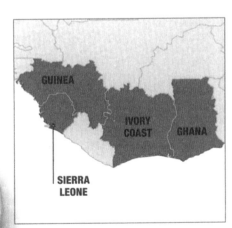

Region of cultivation
Grains of paradise are native to the coastal regions of West Africa, where they grow in forest margins. Ghana is the main producer of the spice.

Kitchen creativity }

This spice, with its heat and fragrant, herbaceous notes, is often used in seasoning blends for meat stews and soups in North and West Africa. It can be used instead of or combined with black peppercorns – try adding a few seeds to your pepper grinder.

BLENDING SCIENCE

The slowly developing heat of grains of paradise comes mainly from the pungent compound paradol, and to a lesser extent from gingerol, which gives heat in ginger. Bitterness derives from an acid called humulone, and fragrance from the terpene molecule caryophyllene.

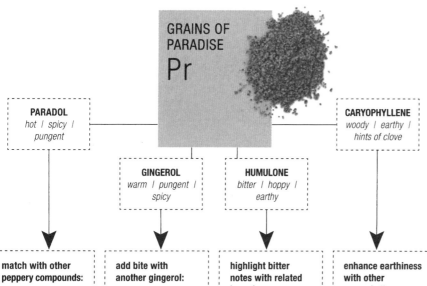

GRAINS OF PARADISE
Pr

PARADOL
hot | spicy | pungent

CARYOPHYLLENE
woody | earthy | hints of clove

GINGEROL
warm | pungent | spicy

HUMULONE
bitter | hoppy | earthy

match with other peppery compounds:

⊕ **black pepper** has a similar heat to paradol from the piperine compound, and also brings floral notes

⊕ **curry leaf** makes an excellent pairing as it also shares caryophyllene

add bite with another gingerol:

⊕ **ginger** brings a raft of flavour compounds from sweet to citrusy, and its own pungency adds depth to the heat

highlight bitter notes with related humulene:

⊕ **celery seed** also adds warmth and earthy aromas, and a savoury quality

enhance earthiness with other caryophyllenes:

⊕ **cinnamon** intensifies woodiness and adds warmth with cinnamaldehyde

⊕ **allspice** brings sweetness and clove-like penetrating eugenol

RELEASE THE FLAVOUR

The flavour compounds in these small seeds evaporate very quickly and most dissolve poorly in water.

Fat   *Alcohol*

Cooking with oil is essential – most of the flavour and pungency compounds dissolve well in oil and/or alcohol.

Grind seeds immediately before use and add them towards the end of cooking to minimize loss of flavour from evaporation.

BLEND TO TRY

Use and adapt this classic blend featuring grains of paradise.
Mbongo mix p35

Pepper substitute

If using grains of paradise as an alternative to black pepper, add two to three times more than you would of pepper.

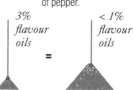

3% flavour oils   **=**   *< 1% flavour oils*

Black pepper   *Grains of paradise*

Black pepper contains three times more flavour-containing oil than grains of paradise.

FOOD PARTNERS

⊕ **Vegetables** Sprinkle ground seeds over an aubergine and tomato stew; grind liberally over root vegetables after roasting.

⊕ **Apples** Grind a couple of seeds and add to apple compote for a citrusy, herbaceous flavour.

⊕ **Rice** Add plenty of ground seeds to the cooking liquid for jollof rice, a West African dish.

⊕ **Lamb** Toast and grind the seeds and sprinkle them over Moroccan-style stewed lamb just before serving.

⊕ **Oily fish** Sprinkle crushed seeds over salmon or tuna steaks before grilling.

⊕ **Drinks** Steep a few seeds in a warm sugar syrup with other aromatics such as pared lemon peel. Allow to cool, then use in gin or vodka cocktails.

SWEET <u>AND</u> SPICY APPLE PASTRY ROSETTES

This beguiling take on a popular pastry treat is inspired by the sweet and peppery flavours of East and West African spiced teas. The sweetness of the apples balances the lingering heat supplied by Scotch bonnet chillies; if you can't find them, use African or Thai bird's eye chillies instead.

Makes 6 pastries

Prep time 30 mins

Cooking time 35–40 mins

2 red apples, such as Empire, Jazz, or Pink Lady

juice of ½ lemon

3 tbsp apricot jam

½ Scotch bonnet chilli, deseeded and thinly sliced

1 tsp grated fresh ginger

½ tsp ground cinnamon

¼ tsp ground cloves

¼ tsp ground grains of paradise

¼ tsp ground cardamom seeds

375g (13oz) sheet ready-rolled puff pastry

butter, for greasing

1. Remove the puff pastry from the freezer or fridge and allow it to thaw or come to room temperature, so that it is pliable. Preheat the oven to 210°C (410°F/Gas 6½).

2. Cut the apples in half and remove the cores. Cut each half into 3mm (⅛in) thick, half-moon-shaped slices.

3. Put the apple slices in a saucepan with the lemon juice, cover with water, bring to the boil, and simmer gently for 2–3 minutes until the slices are just soft enough to roll up. Drain and dry the slices, then set them aside to cool. Alternatively, place the apple slices in a microwave-safe bowl with the lemon juice and 2 tablespoons of water. Cover with cling film and pierce a hole to let the steam escape. Heat for 2–3 minutes on high (900W), until the slices are softened.

4. Place the apricot jam with the chilli and spices in a small saucepan, and heat gently until melted.

5. On a lightly floured surface, roll out the pastry into a rectangle measuring about 30 x 36cm (12 x 15in). Slice the dough lengthways into six equal strips.

6. Spread the spiced jam over each strip. Arrange the apple slices lengthways along each strip, overlapping a little, with the skin side of the slices slightly extending beyond the top edge of the strip.

7. Fold the bottom edge of each strip up to meet the top edge. Now roll up the strips to make rose shapes, taking care to keep the apple slices in place.

8. Grease a cupcake tin with butter and place the roses in the holes. Bake for 35–40 minutes until crisp and golden. Serve immediately.

BLACK PEPPER
Hot | Spicy | Citrusy

BOTANICAL NAME
Piper nigrum

ALSO KNOWN AS
Peppercorn.

MAJOR FLAVOUR COMPOUND
Piperine.

PARTS USED
Dried berries, known as "peppercorns".

METHOD OF CULTIVATION
The berries are harvested from vines at different stages of maturity.

COMMERCIAL PREPARATION
Underripe berries are either blanched and left to darken and dry for black pepper, or picked earlier and preserved without darkening for green pepper. Pink pepper is picked after fully ripening.

NON-CULINARY USES
In traditional medicine as a digestive aid.

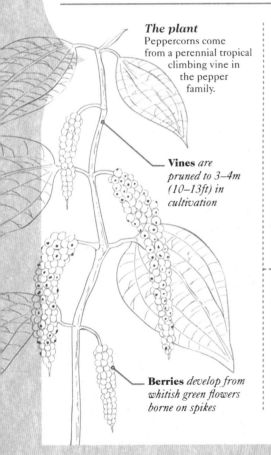

The plant
Peppercorns come from a perennial tropical climbing vine in the pepper family.

Vines *are pruned to 3–4m (10–13ft) in cultivation*

Berries *develop from whitish green flowers borne on spikes*

Whole black
Black peppercorns are dried with their browned, aromatic outer layer intact. Green pepper is less fiery and has more abundant herbaceous flavours.

Whole white
The outer layer of white pepper is stripped by bacterial fermentation, leaving it harsher, less aromatic, and with dung-like nuances.

Spice story

Black pepper is native to southern India and has been cultivated and traded for over 3,500 years. In the 4th century BCE, after Alexander the Great had reached India, black pepper was brought to Europe along newly established trade routes. The highly valued spice quickly became commercially important, and Arab traders established a monopoly on its transport to Europe. By the Middle Ages, black peppercorns had not only become a culinary status symbol, but were also accepted as currency. The Portuguese explorer Vasco de Gama set off to find and take control of the source of this costly spice, and discovered a sea route to southwest India in 1498. For the next century the Portuguese controlled the black pepper trade. In the 17th century they lost their monopoly to the Dutch, who lost it to Britain in the 18th century, when the British Empire took control of the spice trade in the tropics.

Region of cultivation
Black pepper is native to the Malabar coast of southwest India. It is now cultivated mainly in Vietnam, but also in India, Indonesia, Malaysia, and Brazil.

Kitchen creativity }

Black pepper produces a pungent heat that is neither flavour nor fragrance, but a pain-like sensation very similar to chilli heat. The spice also has a woody aroma with floral, fruity, and citrus elements, and some bitterness.

BLENDING SCIENCE

The warming quality of pepper is produced by a pungent alkaloid called piperine. The spice's more subtle flavours are created by terpene compounds, including woody rotundone, pine-scented pinene, lemony limonene, spicy myrcene, floral linalool, and phellandrene, which has fresh lime and green notes.

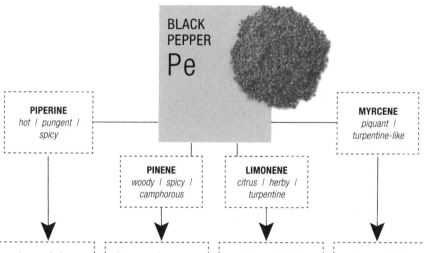

BLACK PEPPER

Pe

PIPERINE
hot | pungent | spicy

PINENE
woody | spicy | camphorous

LIMONENE
citrus | herby | turpentine

MYRCENE
piquant | turpentine-like

create rounded, complex heat with other spices in the pungent group:

⊕ **chilli** offers fruity, grassy, or toasted flavours, depending on variety and if fresh or dried

⊕ **mustard** adds bitter warmth and, if toasted, nutty flavours

⊕ **Sichuan pepper** has a mouth-tingling quality as well as heat, and also shares citrus-floral elements

⊕ **ginger** brings a characteristic heat and additional sweet, citrus notes

foreground coniferous notes other pinene scented spices:

⊕ **bay** brings a floral-herbal aroma, penetrating eucalyptus flavour, and slight bitterness

⊕ **black cardamom** contributes meaty and smoky aromas, clove-like taste and eucalyptus

⊕ **nutmeg** adds sweetness, musky aroma and a strong, woody earthiness

combine with other sources of limonene or spices that enhance the citrus component:

⊕ **cardamom** is sweet, minty, and penetrating

⊕ **lemon myrtle** brings intensity to the lemon flavour and lingering eucalyptus

⊕ **turmeric** gives earthy warmth with hints of ginger and citrus from citral

⊕ **coriander** adds floral and spicy citrus notes

spices containing myrcene make excellent matches, particularly sweet spices with pink peppercorns:

⊕ **cinnamon, anise** both have sweet, warming fragrance and, surprisingly, are among the best pairings for pepper

⊕ **allspice** brings sweetness and clove-like tastes

⊕ **anardana** adds tart fruitiness, sharing both myrcene and limonene

⊕ **juniper** offers strong pine-like flavour with fruitiness and overtones of citrus

FOOD PARTNERS

⊕ **Preserved vegetables** Add whole black or green peppercorns to a brine for preserving roasted bell peppers or fresh cucumber.

⊕ **Fruit** Sprinkle ground pepper over peaches or melon, or macerate strawberries with sugar and a few grinds of black pepper.

⊕ **Steak** Swap black pepper for dried or pickled green peppercorns for a fruitier bite to *steak au poivre*.

⊕ **Shellfish** Add white pepper to a clam chowder or *moules marinières*.

⊕ **Ice cream** Grind black pepper into vanilla custard before churning to make ice cream.

RELEASE THE FLAVOUR

To enjoy pepper's full complexity it is vital to preserve subtle terpene compounds, which quickly break down and evaporate when exposed to air.

Grind whole peppercorns immediately before use to minimize flavour loss.

Pre-ground spice is only good for adding heat.

BLENDS TO TRY

Use and adapt these classic blends featuring black pepper:

Turkish baharat p23
Chaat masala p42
Nanjing spice bag p59
Quatre épices p74

SICHUAN PEPPER

Pungent | Citrusy | Floral

BOTANICAL NAME
Zanthoxylum simulans

ALSO KNOWN AS
Chinese coriander, Chinese pepper, mountain pepper, *hua jiao, fagara*.

MAJOR FLAVOUR COMPOUNDS
Sanshools.

PARTS USED
Fruit rinds (termed "peppercorns"), leaves.

METHOD OF CULTIVATION
Berry-sized fruits are picked in autumn when red and mature.

COMMERCIAL PREPARATION
Fruits are sun-dried until they split open and pounded to free the bitter seeds, which are are discarded. The fruits are dried further.

NON-CULINARY USES
Used in Chinese herbal medicine as a stimulant to promote digestion. Also used as a diuretic and to treat rheumatism.

Spice story

Sichuan pepper has long featured in the culture and cuisine of China. More than 2,000 years ago, during the Han Dynasty, it was reportedly mixed into plaster to perfume the walls of "pepper houses" – buildings that housed the Emperor's concubines – to warm the rooms and perfume the air. It has also been found in tombs in northern China dating back to a similar period. The pepper was used to spice luxury foods and wines; Hanshan, an 8th century Chinese poet, described lavish dishes of "roast duck tinctured with Sichuan pepper and salt". It was also key in foods prepared as offerings to the gods. Perhaps because the plant bears many fruits and seeds, it was adopted as a fertility symbol, and in some rural areas of China today the spice is still thrown over newlyweds, like rice or confetti.

The plant
Sichuan pepper comes from a shrub or small tree in the citrus family.

Fruits *are small and rust-red*

Leaves *are used as a lemony spice in Japan*

Seeds *in the fruits are black and shiny*

Seeds *are slightly bitter but harmless, and need not be picked out*

Surface *is prickly, with bits of stalk attached*

Whole
The spice flavour comes from the fruit's dried husk, rather than from the black seeds inside it.

Powder
Pre-ground Sichuan pepper is available to buy, but is best avoided as the flavours quickly degrade.

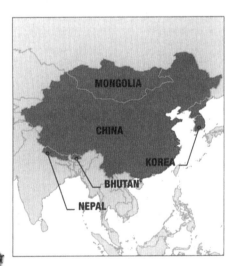

Region of cultivation
Sichuan pepper is native to the Sichuan region of China. It is now cultivated throughout China, Korea, Mongolia, Nepal, and Bhutan.

Kitchen creativity }

Sichuan pepper is an essential ingredient in Chinese cooking. It comprises two of the five key flavours of Chinese food, namely hot (or pungent) and bitter (or numbing), the others being salt, sweet, and sour.

BLENDING SCIENCE

Sichuan pepper contains a group of compounds called sanshools, which act on nerves in the mouth and lips to cause numbing, tingling sensations. Fragrance is added by a combination of flavour compounds: linalool, geraniol, limonene, and terpineol. Its sharp qualities come from myrcene and cineole.

SICHUAN PEPPER
Si

SANSHOOLS
hot | numbing | tingling

LINALOOL
floral | woody

LIMONENE
citrus | herby

CINEOLE
eucalyptus | mildly medicinal | penetrating

round out the heat with warming or sweet compounds:

⊕ **star anise**'s mix of penetrating, woody, and sweet compounds adds complexity

⊕ **nutmeg**'s penetrating eugenol and camphene pack enough power to make a match with sanshool

play up floral notes:

⊕ **coriander** shares limonene, plus linalool and peppery myrcene

⊕ **cinnamon** shares linalool and adds spicy woody caryophyllene

add complexity to the citrus profile

⊕ **lemongrass**'s powerful citrus and myrcene components make it an ideal pairing

enhance eucalyptus notes with spices containing cineole:

⊕ **bay** also adds clove-like eugenol

⊕ **galangal** also adds powerful camphor notes

⊕ **cardamom** pairs excellently, sharing linalool and limonene, as well as cineole

FOOD PARTNERS

⊕ **Vegetables** Fry crushed pepper in oil before using it to stir-fry green beans, asparagus, or cabbage. Sprinkle with ground, toasted pepper.

⊕ **Citrus** Sprinkle toasted, crushed pepper over a tart blood-orange sherbet or lemon sorbet.

⊕ **Pork, beef** Add whole to slow-cooked pork belly or oxtail with ginger, spring onions, star anise, sugar, and soy.

⊕ **Squid** Add crushed pepper to the batter for deep-fried squid.

⊕ **Noodles** Combine cold cooked noodles, roasted peanuts, spring onions, stir-fried greens, and chilli, then drizzle with a pepper- and sesame-infused oil.

RELEASE THE FLAVOUR

The thick husks of the peppercorns can impede the release of flavours. Toasting helps the compounds to escape. They can also be ground in a pepper mill and used as a condiment.

Toasting also develops nutty pyrazines

Avoid over-roasting, which can cause the loss of the limonene molecules and mask subtler scents with strong pyrazines.

BLENDS TO TRY

Use and adapt these classic blends featuring Sichuan pepper.

Timur ko chhop p41
Shichimi-togarashi p57

Zanthoxylum variations

There are regional variants of Sichuan pepper, which come from slightly different tree species. They have the same core features but can have significantly different flavour profiles.

Sanshō	**Timur**	**Andaliman**	**Tirphal**
(Zanthoxylum piperatum) is the milder version from Japan, with pronounced citrus flavours.	*(Zanthoxylum alatum)* comes from Nepal and has distinctly grapefruit notes.	*(Zanthoxylum acanthopodium)* is from Indonesia and has notes of lime and mandarin.	*(Zanthoxylum rhetsa)* is grown in the coastal rainforests of India and has a lingering bitterness.

GINGER

Hot | Citrusy | Woody

BOTANICAL NAME
Zingiber officinale

ALSO KNOWN AS
Ginger root, Canton ginger.

MAJOR FLAVOUR COMPOUNDS
Gingerol, shogaol, and zingiberene.

PARTS USED
Rhizomes (fleshy underground stems).

METHOD OF CULTIVATION
Rhizomes are harvested 2–5 or 8–10 months after planting if they are to be sold fresh, or are to be dried, respectively.

COMMERCIAL PREPARATION
Fresh: Young rhizomes are cleaned, sometimes bleached, and dried for a day or two. *Dried*: Mature rhizomes are peeled, dried, and ground.

NON-CULINARY USES
Perfumery and cosmetics; in traditional medicine for indigestion and nausea.

Spice story

Ginger was one of the first Asian spices to reach Europe, from around the 4th century BCE, when Arab traders transported dried and preserved ginger to ancient Greece and Rome. The Greeks prescribed it for stomach complaints, and the Romans used it in sauces and to make aromatic salt. By the 9th century CE, dried ginger was regarded as an everyday condiment in Europe. By the Middle Ages it was being widely used in savoury and sweet cooking (notably gingerbread), and for flavouring beer and ale. By the 13th century, ginger was being grown in East and West Africa, and by the 16th century it was being cultivated in Jamaica, which still has a reputation for producing quality ginger.

The plant
Ginger is a tropical, rhizomatous flowering plant in the same family as turmeric and cardamom. It grows up to 1m (3ft) tall.

Flowers *consist of cone-shaped clusters of yellowish bracts.*

Shoots *are a series of tightly overlapping leaf bases*

Powder
Do not use ground dried ginger in place of the fresh spice, as it has a different flavour profile (see Dry heat, opposite).

Fresh
Avoid older rhizomes with signs of shriveling, which can mean the flesh is fibrous.

Region of cultivation
Ginger is native to tropical Asia, possibly India. Today it is mainly cultivated on India's Malabar Coast (which produces 50 per cent of the world's fresh crop) and throughout tropical and subtropical Asia, but also in parts of Africa, Jamaica, Mexico, North America, and Peru.

Kitchen creativity }

Ginger has a hot-spice, citrusy, woody taste. The dried form has a stronger, more aromatic flavour than fresh ginger, and is commonly used in baking and in spice blends. Fresh ginger is widely used in Asian cuisine.

BLENDING SCIENCE

The terpene compound zingiberene carries the characteristic aroma of ginger, but the taste is made more complex thanks to a cornucopia of other compounds, including spicy-hot gingerols, as well as floral linalool and geraniol, herbal curcumene, lemony citral, and eucalyptus-like cineole.

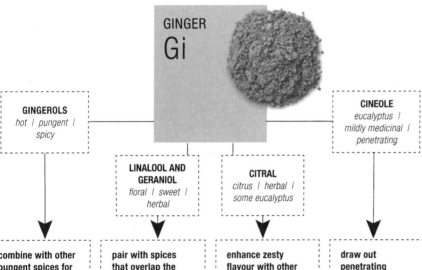

GINGER
Gi

GINGEROLS
hot | pungent | spicy

LINALOOL AND GERANIOL
floral | sweet | herbal

CITRAL
citrus | herbal | some eucalyptus

CINEOLE
eucalyptus | mildly medicinal | penetrating

combine with other pungent spices for added depth:

⊕ **chilli** adds varying degrees of heat from capsaicinoids

⊕ **black pepper** brings a woody warmth from piperine, and some citrus

pair with spices that overlap the floral qualities:

⊕ **cinnamon** shares linalool and brings sweet, warming qualities

⊕ **nutmeg** shares geraniol and cineole for warm spicy notes

⊕ **cacao** adds strong bittersweet and roasted flavours

enhance zesty flavour with other citrusy spices:

⊕ **lemongrass** shares citral and adds mild pepperiness

⊕ **lemon myrtle** brings intense lemon, sharing citral and lingering eucalyptus

⊕ **coriander** harmonizes with lemony notes

draw out penetrating freshness with cineole-rich spices:

⊕ **bay** adds a lingering, clove-like background

⊕ **cardamom** provides sweet and herby hints of mint

FOOD PARTNERS

⊕ **Squash and coleslaw** Mix grated fresh ginger into Asian-style coleslaws, or fry with the onion base of a squash soup.

⊕ **Mango, pears, rhubarb** Pair with mango in creamy puddings, and poach fresh slices with pears and rhubarb.

⊕ **Pork** Add slices of fresh ginger to slow-cooked pork dishes to offset the fattiness.

⊕ **Fish** Use julienned ginger with shredded leek or spring onions when steaming fish.

⊕ **Baking** Try adding ground ginger to carrot cake, lemon cake, and coconut or dark chocolate cookies.

BLENDS TO TRY

Use and adapt these classic blends featuring ginger.

Advieh p27

Yaji p36

Leche de tigre p69

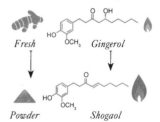

Dry heat

When fresh ginger is dried, its heat pungency increases and a fifth of the flavour molecules evaporate.

Fresh — *Gingerol*

Powder — *Shogaol*

The drying process converts gingerol to shogaol, which has twice the heat. The dry spice also has fewer citrus notes.

RELEASE THE FLAVOUR

Peel fresh ginger shortly before use in order to retain the complex flavour profile. Heat breaks both gingerols and shogaols into mild zingerone, so the longer that ginger is cooked, the gentler its spicy-heat.

Stripping the skin bursts open the outer layer of cells, allowing fragrant oils to evaporate.

Cooking converts ginger's mouthwarming flavor compounds into the much milder zingerone.

CHILLI

Hot | Pungent | Fruity

BOTANICAL NAME
Capsicum annuum, *C. frutescens*, and several
other species.

ALSO KNOWN AS
Chilli pepper, red pepper, hot pepper, chile
or chili.

MAJOR FLAVOUR COMPOUND
Capsaicin.

PARTS USED
Fruits (which are in fact berries).

METHOD OF CULTIVATION
Green chillies are harvested unripe, about 3
months after planting. Chillies for dry spice
are usually harvested when red and fully ripe.

COMMERCIAL PREPARATION
Chillies are washed and either sun- or
oven-dried, pickled, or sold fresh.

NON-CULINARY USES
In creams and ointments to reduce
muscle pain; in Ayurvedic medicine to
stimulate digestion.

The plant
Chillies are borne
by annual or
perennial plants
in the nightshade
family. Around
32 species are
cultivated for
their fruits.

Powder
Grinding causes
many flavour
compounds to
evaporate and
powders are
best used for
adding heat.

Whole dried
Some fragrant substances
are lost through the
drying process, but new
compounds are created,
ranging from sweet
anise-like flavours
to nutty, woody, and
roasted nuances.

Fresh
Fruity, citrus,
green flavours and
sweetness are
often prominent
in fresh chillies,
depending on
type and ripeness.

Unripe fruits
*are green; ripe
fruits range
from yellow to
almost black*

Spice story

Evidence suggests chillies were being
cultivated as early as 5000 BCE in South
America. According to the Spanish
conquistador Hernan Cortez, the
ancient Aztecs cultivated a vast range
of chillies for use in rituals and adding
to chocolate beverages. Columbus
brought the newly discovered spice
back to Spain at the end of the 15th
century CE; he wrongly assumed
chillies were related to peppercorns
because of their heat and the name has
stuck. Portuguese traders transported
the spice to their colony in Goa, India,
and to Asian and African trading posts,
where chillies rapidly replaced black
pepper as the hot spice of choice.
In 1912, the pharmacologist William
Scoville devised a way of measuring
chilli pungency, which became known
as the Scoville Heat Index, but this is
now being replaced by more accurate
lab-based measures.

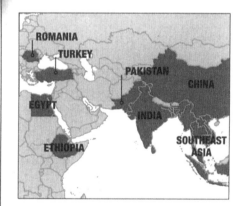

Region of cultivation
Chillies are native to Mexico and Central
and South America. Production of the dried
spice is concentrated in China, South Asia,
mainland Southeast Asia, Egypt, Ethiopia,
Turkey, and Romania. Indonesia, North Africa,
Spain, Mexico, and the USA are more noted
for growing fresh chillies.

Kitchen creativity }

Chillies appear in countless cuisines around the world, and are used as much for their flavour as for their heat, particularly in Mexican cooking. Some powders are actually spice blends; "chile" powder and cayenne pepper are generally pure.

BLENDING SCIENCE

Capsaicin is responsible for the heat pungency that can numb the mouth to more subtle flavours. The latter are best appreciated in milder and/or fresh chillies and are produced by plentiful fruity esters, and less common floral undecanol, grassy aldehydes, and citrusy limonene. Drying and smoking chillies creates new flavour compounds, notably earthy, toasty pyrazines and nutty, bread-like furfural.

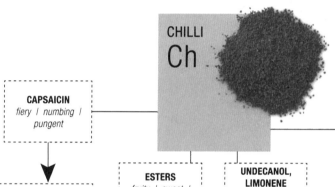

CHILLI
Ch

CAPSAICIN
fiery | numbing | pungent

PYRAZINES, FURFURAL
nutty | roasted | earthy

ESTERS
fruity | sweet | waxy

UNDECANOL, LIMONENE
citrus | floral | herby

create rounded, complex heat with other pungent compounds:

⊕ **mustard** adds sharp, penetrating pungency and bitterness

⊕ **black pepper** adds a woody, lingering heat and citrus notes

⊕ **grains of paradise** bring hints of tropical fruit beneath a peppery warmth

⊕ **Sichuan pepper** offers woody, citrusy, and floral notes, and causes a tingling sensation

enhance the fruity side of mild and fresh chillies:

⊕ **cinnamon** adds sweet, penetrating fragrance and warmth

⊕ **allspice** brings sweet pepperiness

⊕ **cardamom** has penetrating mintiness

⊕ **caraway** adds bittersweet, anise-like, citrus flavours

draw out citrus and floral sides of mild and fresh chillies:

⊕ **coriander** offers strong, floral citrus

⊕ **ginger** brings sweet citrus notes and refreshing pungency

⊕ **lemongrass** has similar citral and slight pepperiness

⊕ **ajwain** offers strong, herbal, thyme-like flavour

complement the earthy, roasted flavours of dried and smoked chillies:

⊕ **cacao** nibs add toasted, nutty flavours, with floral and citrus notes

⊕ **cumin** adds slightly bitter earthiness

⊕ **sesame** seeds share furfural and bring harmonizing nuttiness when toasted

⊕ **turmeric** adds a musky, earthy flavour with hints of ginger

FOOD PARTNERS

⊕ **Tropical fruit** Dust chilli powder over sliced tropical fruit.

⊕ **Tomatoes** Sprinkle smoked chilli flakes over chilled gazpacho.

⊕ **White fish** Blitz soaked, dried chillies and add them to a cherry tomato sauce for grilled or fried white fish.

⊕ **Chicken, tofu** Combine dried red chilli and Sichuan pepper in a fragrant chicken stir-fry, or substitute tofu.

⊕ **Chocolate** Mix small amounts of ground chilli into dark chocolate desserts, tarts, cookies, or ganache.

BLENDS TO TRY

Try these blends featuring chilli and adapt them with blending science:

Harissa p33

Yaji p36

Timur ko chhop p41

Vindaloo paste p44

Gunpowder p45

Shichimi-togarashi p57

Chilli black bean sauce p61

Mole mix p65

BBQ rub p68

Arrabiata sauce p76

CONTROL THE HEAT

Don't underestimate chilli heat: add with caution! Less fat in a dish will curb heat as capsaicin dissolves in oil, though some related capsaicinoids do dissolve in water.

Dried chillies have more heat than their fresh equivalent: capsaicin concentration roughly doubles after drying.

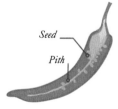

Seed

Pith

Remove the inner white pith (or placenta) to reduce heat. "Deseeding" is effective only if the pith is removed in the process.

CHILLI
varieties

Chillies come in many shapes, sizes, and colours. As a rule of thumb, the smaller and riper a chilli is, the hotter it will be. Mexico is unique in having distinct uses for their many varieties. Mexican dried chillies should be pliable, not brittle. Wipe them clean, remove the stems and bland seeds, dry-toast, then soak before use.

FRESH CHILLIES

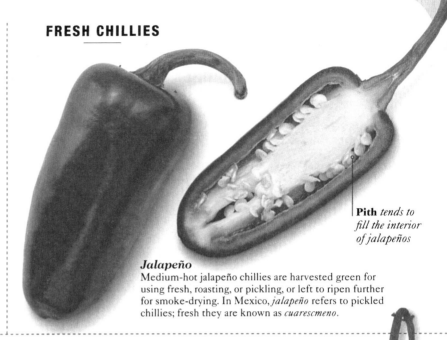

Pith *tends to fill the interior of jalapeños*

Jalapeño
Medium-hot jalapeño chillies are harvested green for using fresh, roasting, or pickling, or left to ripen further for smoke-drying. In Mexico, *jalapeño* refers to pickled chillies; fresh they are known as *cuarescmeno*.

DRIED CHILLIES

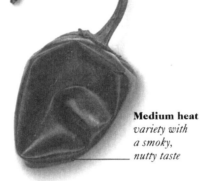

Medium heat *variety with a smoky, nutty taste*

Dried version *of the Mexican poblano pepper*

Cascabel
This cherry-tomato-shaped Mexican chilli – nicknamed the "rattle chilli" because its seeds rattle when shaken – is prized for its tropical sweetness without excessive heat.

Ancho
A sweet, fruity, and mild dried chilli, with a hint of tobacco, it can be soaked and stuffed, or blitzed and added to *mole* sauce. Goes well with pulled pork in a burrito.

Use crumbled *or ground in cornbread or pork stews*

Guajillo
This is the dark, sun-dried form of the *mirasol* chilli. Its smoky sweetness – with just a little heat – peps up classic Mexican tamales, enchiladas, and salsas.

Arbol
This slender, sun-dried chilli is widely used in Mexican cuisine to add a bright, fiery flavour with smoky notes. Fry in oil and finely chop, or crushed and use as chilli flakes.

Kashmiri
The dried Kashmiri chilli has an attractive deep crimson colour, and unlike many Indian chillies it is only mildly spicy. An essential part of rogan josh and Kashmiri biryani.

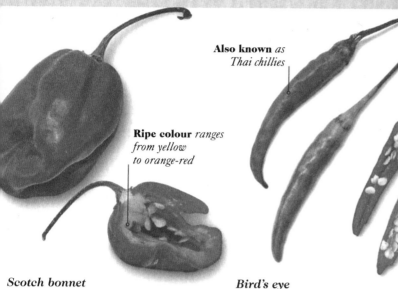

Also known *as Thai chillies*

Ripe colour *ranges from yellow to orange-red*

Scotch bonnet
Related to the habanero, Scotch bonnet is also extremely hot – it is known in Guiana as "ball of fire" – and has a deep, fruity flavour. It is the preferred chilli of the Caribbean.

Bird's eye
Available fresh or dried, this fiery chilli is ubiquitous in Asian cooking, especially in the soups, salads, and sambals of southeast Asia and in Chinese stir-fries.

GROUND CHILLIES

Smoked chipotle
Chipotle is the name given to smoke-dried ripe jalapeños. In addition to smokiness, they have a chocolate-like sweetness. Use ground for fast intensity or whole in slow-cook stews.

Resembles *a mini bell pepper but is one of the hottest chillies*

Meaty texture *and pliable flesh*

Mulato
Closely related to *ancho*, the *mulato* chilli has a smokier taste. Deseeded, toasted, soaked, and ground into a paste, it adds intense ripe fruit flavours and a rich, dark colour.

Habanero
Bright orange with an intensely fruity aroma, habaneros are an essential part of *cochinita pibil*, a slow-cooked pork dish from Mexico's Yucatán peninsula.

Cayenne
The clean, sharp heat of cayenne pepper is typically enjoyed dried and ground. It is an inportant ingredient in Indian and South American cuisine.

Used in African *cuisine to spice meat dishes*

Also known *as "little raisin"*

Pasilla
This Mexican staple spice is medium-hot, with a complex, sweet flavour resembling liquorice. Works well in sweet recipes, such as chocolate cake.

Piri piri
The tiny piri piri chilli (also known as African bird's eye) is milder than the true bird's eye but still intensely spicy. Essential to *molho de piri-piri*, a Portuguese sauce.

Espelette
A legally- protected variety only cultivated in the commune of Espelette in France, it has a citrusy flavour and medium heat. Used in Basque cuisine in meat cures, piperade, and fish stew.

SAFFRON

Grassy | Bitter | Honeyed

BOTANICAL NAME
Crocus sativus

ALSO KNOWN AS
Red gold.

MAJOR FLAVOUR COMPOUND
Picrocrocin.

PARTS USED
Flower stigmas (female pollen-catching reproductive parts).

METHOD OF CULTIVATION
Harvesting takes place over two weeks in late autumn. Flowers are hand-picked pre-dawn, before they open for the day.

COMMERCIAL PREPARATION
The stigmas are laid out on a sieve, dried, and then transferred to airtight tins.

NON-CULINARY USES
Cosmetic colouring agent and fabric dye; in Ayurvedic medicine as a sedative and to treat coughs and asthma.

Spice story

Grown since the Early Bronze Age, saffron has been prized for millennia. Cleopatra is said to have bathed in saffron-scented mare's milk, China's Buddhist monks used it to colour their robes, and it was adored by Greeks, Romans, and Indian emperors as food and medicine. As trade routes opened up in medieval times, Arabs took it to Spain and Crusaders to France and England. Britain cultivated it in the Middle Ages, and the Essex town of Saffron Walden is named after the spice that grew there. Owing to its value, saffron has been adulterated for as long as it has been traded and imitations (turmeric, marigold petals, and safflower) are rife even today. Kashmiri saffron is particularly prized, as is saffron from La Mancha in Spain, which has been granted EU Protected Designation of Origin (PDO) status. Saffron's modern name derives from the Arabic for yellow: *asfar*.

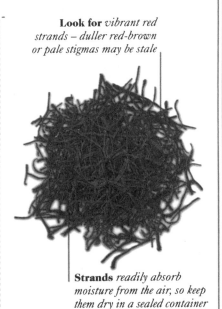

Each flower *contains three red stigmas and three yellow stamens (the flower's male sexual organs)*

Look for *vibrant red strands – duller red-brown or pale stigmas may be stale*

Up to five pale mauve flowers *are produced by each corm*

Strands *readily absorb moisture from the air, so keep them dry in a sealed container*

The plant
Saffron is a bulbous perennial crocus plant in the iris family, which grows to around 15cm (6in) high and blooms in autumn. The six-petalled flowers sprout from a corm (swollen stem base).

Whole strands
More than 6,000 flowers and over 12 hours labour makes just 30g (1oz) of saffron, so if it's cheap, be suspicious. Imitation saffron is often odourless and may taste sweet, rather than bitter. Pre-ground saffron is easily adulterated and best avoided.

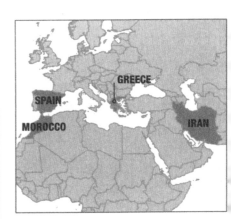

Region of cultivation
Native to parts of the Mediterranean and originally cultivated in Greece, saffron is now mainly grown in Iran, which accounts for 90 per cent of world production, as well as Kashmir, Spain, Greece, Afghanistan, and Morocco.

Kitchen creativity }

Warm, musky, with the distinctive aroma of cut hay and a slightly metallic tang, saffron's flavour comes in part from compounds unique among the spices. With correct handling, just a pinch will transform a meal.

BLENDING SCIENCE

Picrocrocin gives saffron its lingering, slightly bitter taste, and safranal produces much of its distinctive aroma. Both picrococin and safranal are unique to saffron, but their qualities help to determine pairings, as does the small amounts of pinene and the tenacious eucalyptus-like compound cineole.

SAFFRON
Sa

PICROCROCIN
musky | earthy | warm | bitter

PINENE
pine-like | woody

SAFRANAL
honeyed | hay-like | floral

CINEOLE
penetrating | eucalyptus-like

the bitterness withstands other potent compounds:

⊕ **caraway** harmonizes through shared pinene and its S-carvone has parallels to picrococin

⊕ **paprika** brings earthy, smoky aromas that combine with saffron's muskiness

⊕ **black pepper** has gentle pungency, slight bitterness, and shares pinene

harmonize with the aroma of safranal:

⊕ **coriander**'s flowery aroma from lilac-scented linalool complements the hay notes of safranal

⊕ **cinnamon, vanilla, allspice, nutmeg** are all sweet spices that work beautifully with the hints of honey in safranal

cineole provides a crucial flavour link:

⊕ **ginger** is a potent, warming match, sharing cineole along with pinene, floral linalool, and sweetly scented geraniol

⊕ **bay** has great synergy thanks to shared cineole and other complementary minor compounds

draw parallels with other pine and/or fir aromas:

⊕ **garlic** cooked gently has sweetness that, combined with piney, orange-hinted sabinene, make this an important spice for savoury saffron dishes

⊕ **sumac** carries a notable pine-like and woody flavour, and its high tannin content mirrors musky, earthy aromas

FOOD PARTNERS

⊕ **Vegetables** Saffron has a particular affinity to earthy vegetables, such as carrots, leeks, mushrooms, squash, and spinach. For rich colour and depth of flavour to roast potatoes, parboil in saffron-infused water then roast with oil mixed with ground saffron.

⊕ **Lemon** Pair saffron and preserved lemon in a Moroccan-style tagine.

⊕ **Rice** Essential to Spanish paellas, saffron also enriches Iranian pilaus, Indian biryanis, and Italian risotto.

⊕ **Lamb** Use to flavour a yoghurt marinade for slow-roast leg of lamb.

⊕ **Fish, shellfish** Poach fish in saffron-infused milk, or add steeped strands to a crab or lobster bisque, *moules marinières*, or Marseille bouillabaisse.

⊕ **Milk** Infuse into milk to make Indian custard-like puddings, ice cream, or reduced-milk sweets.

BLEND TO TRY

Use and adapt this classic blend featuring saffron:
Paella mix p75

RELEASE THE FLAVOUR

The key flavour compounds (safranal and picrocrocin) and pigments (crocin) dissolve in water better than in oil, but need time to escape and benefit from steeping; adding directly may leave much still trapped in the threads.

Grind in a pestle and mortar before steeping to speed the release of compounds.

Steep in warm or hot water for at least 20 minutes or up to 24 hours.

Add alcohol to the soaking water to draw out the lesser compounds.

Use milk to help dissolve the lesser flavour molecules through the presence of fat.

SPICED SCALLOPS WITH SAFFRON BEURRE BLANC

Kashmiri cooking is often characterized by the contrast of warm roasted fennel seeds, astringent ginger, and sweet saffron. This trio travels well across global cooking styles, and is a great match for mushrooms and seafood – both feature in this indulgent dish of scallops in a vibrant take on French butter sauce.

SPICE IDEAS

Make a more **earthy, South Indian-style** spice seasoning by replacing the fennel and ginger with curry leaves and mustard and cumin seeds.

Use a **Mediterranean spice palette** and pair fennel seeds with cumin and hot paprika – smoked if you prefer – instead of ginger.

For **stronger pepper notes**, lightly crack the whole peppercorns, to release more flavour oils, before adding to the *beurre blanc*.

Serves 6 as a starter

Prep time 30 mins, plus 1 hour soaking

Cooking time 2 hours 25 mins, plus cooling

For the mushroom and spice seasoning
200g (7oz) chestnut mushrooms
2 tsp fennel seeds
1 tsp ground ginger
1 tsp salt

For the *beurre blanc*
small pinch of saffron strands
3 tbsp white wine vinegar
4 tbsp white wine
1 shallot, finely diced
175g (6oz) unsalted butter, cubed
6 black peppercorns
½ lemon

For the scallops
12 large scallops, roe removed
2 tbsp extra virgin olive oil
4 tbsp mushroom and spice mix
2 tbsp chives, snipped

1 Grind the saffron strands to a powder using a pestle and mortar, and leave to soak in 2 tablespoons of warm water for 1 hour.

2 For the spiced mushroom seasoning, heat the oven to 120°C (250°F/Gas ½). Thinly slice the mushrooms and spread out in a single layer on a baking tray lined with baking parchment. Bake for 2 hours, or until the mushrooms are crisp. Remove from the oven and leave to cool.

3 Heat a small frying pan over a medium heat and toast the fennel seeds for 1 minute, until fragrant. Grind the toasted seeds to a powder.

4 Put the dried mushrooms in a small food processor and add the fennel, ginger, and salt. Process until coarsely ground, and set aside. The mix will keep for 2–3 weeks in a tightly lidded jar.

5 For the *beurre blanc*, pour the vinegar and wine into a small pan and add the diced shallot and peppercorns. Bring to the boil, and then simmer for 4–6 minutes, until it has reduced to 1–2 tablespoons and looks syrupy.

6 Strain the liquid and discard the shallots. Whisk in the saffron and its soaking water. Return the liquid to the rinsed-out pan and cook for about 15 minutes over a low heat, whisking in the butter gradually, one cube at a time. The sauce will emulsify and thicken so that it just coats the back of a spoon. Season and sharpen the sauce with a squeeze of lemon, and keep it warm.

7 Heat a dry frying pan over a medium heat. Brush both sides of each scallop with olive oil and lightly coat with the spiced mushroom mix. Cook the scallops for 1–2 minutes on each side, depending on their size. Take care not to overcook – they are ready when they are opaque but still tender.

8 Divide the *beurre blanc* between six shallow bowls and top each with two scallops. Scatter with the chives and serve immediately.

POPPY

Nutty | Mild | Green

BOTANICAL NAME
Papaver somniferum

ALSO KNOWN AS
Opium poppy, maw seed.

MAJOR FLAVOUR COMPOUND
2-Pentylfuran.

PARTS USED
Seeds.

METHOD OF CULTIVATION
Seed pods are harvested mechanically in the autumn when the petals fade and the seed heads turn from green to yellow-brown.

COMMERCIAL PREPARATION
The pods are dried, then cracked open to collect the seeds.

NON-CULINARY USES
Poppy seed oil is used in the cosmetics industry. Several painkillers and sedatives are manufactured from the plant's unripe seed pods.

Spice story

Poppy seeds were cultivated as early as 3,500 BCE by the Sumerians of modern-day southern Iraq, and later, in around 2,000 BCE, the Hittites of Anatolia used them in breadmaking. In a first-century novel by Petronius, a wealthy Roman serves dormice at his banquet, glazed in honey and rolled in poppy seeds. Through Arab traders, poppy cultivation spread along the Silk Road from Arabia and Persia to India and China. Although its use declined after the fall of the Roman Empire, the spice regained popularity in Europe in the Middle Ages. The botanical name "somniferum" translates as "sleep bearing", and refers to the use of the plant to produce the drug opium. However, opium is made from the "sap" of unripe seed pods rather than from the ripe seeds used for cooking, which do not have the same effect.

The plant
Opium poppy is a summer-flowering annual herbaceous plant that can grow to 1.2m (4ft) high.

Ripe pods *make a rattling sound when shaken*

Seed pods *have a ribbed outer shell containing several chambers holding hundreds of tiny seeds*

Leaves *can be cooked and eaten like spinach*

Seeds *appear round at first glance, but are in fact kidney-shaped*

Black
The blue-black variety of seeds is the most widely cultivated. The hard raw seeds have a mild taste and almost no aroma.

1 gram *contains about 3,300 tiny seeds*

White
The pale variety of seeds is popular in Indian cooking and is most often ground to add richness and as a thickener for sauces.

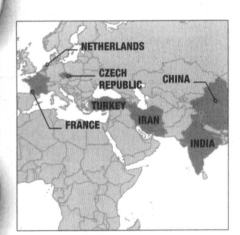

Region of cultivation
Native to the western Mediterranean and southwest Asia, poppy is cultivated in the Netherlands, France, the Czech Republic, Turkey, Iran, India, China, and Canada.

Kitchen creativity }

Poppy seeds lend themselves to a variety of dishes, from pickles and kormas to cakes, bagels, and buns. The blue-grey seeds are used in central and eastern European and Middle Eastern cuisines, and the creamy-yellow seeds are used in Asian cooking.

BLENDING SCIENCE

Poppy seeds are rich in linoleic acid, which makes the taste buds more sensitive to pleasant sweet, salty, and savoury tastes, while dampening down bitterness. The seeds are also packed with green and grassy aldehyde flavour compounds, in particular 2-pentylfuran and hexanal. Other important flavour compounds include balsamic vinyl amyl ketone, and citrusy limonene.

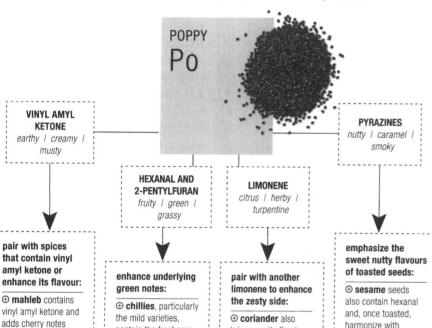

POPPY
Po

VINYL AMYL KETONE
earthy | creamy | musty

HEXANAL AND 2-PENTYLFURAN
fruity | green | grassy

LIMONENE
citrus | herby | turpentine

PYRAZINES
nutty | caramel | smoky

pair with spices that contain vinyl amyl ketone or enhance its flavour:

⊕ **mahleb** contains vinyl amyl ketone and adds cherry notes

⊕ **liquorice** is strongly sweet with penetrating aniseed

⊕ **cinnamon** contributes sweet, warming qualities

enhance underlying green notes:

⊕ **chillies**, particularly the mild varieties, contain the freshness of hexanal, and add warmth

⊕ **bay** is a good match thanks to it also carrying some leafy hexanal

pair with another limonene to enhance the zesty side:

⊕ **coriander** also brings gentle floral qualities

emphasize the sweet nutty flavours of toasted seeds:

⊕ **sesame** seeds also contain hexanal and, once toasted, harmonize with the pyrazine flavours

⊕ **paprika** brings earthy sweetness; smoked varieties work particularly well with toasted poppy seeds

RELEASE THE FLAVOUR

Poppy seeds contain a particularly diverse range of amino acids, which means that, when toasted, they produce a remarkable mix of sweet, earthy, nutty, onion-like, and smoky flavours.

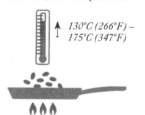

↑ *130°C (266°F) – 175°C (347°F)*

Temperatures over 130°C (2 66°F) are needed to create new compounds, but burnt, bitter flavours will predominate over 175°C (347°F), due to the small seed size and fragile oils.

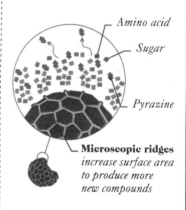

Amino acid

Sugar

Pyrazine

Microscopic ridges *increase surface area to produce more new compounds*

When heated, amino acids and sugars in the seeds react with each other to produce new flavour compounds, most importantly pyrazines.

FOOD PARTNERS

⊕ **Vegetables** Sprinkle the black seeds over potato purée or celeriac remoulade to add visual and textural contrast. Scatter over carrots before roasting.

⊕ **Sweet bakes** Give the moist crumb of an almond and lemon or orange cake a nutty crunch by adding a spoonful of seeds to the batter. Combine with honey and drizzle over baklava.

⊕ **Pastry** Add a spoonful of seeds to savoury shortcrust pastry dough for a quiche or a cheese and leek tart.

⊕ **Fruit** Add to a honey and citrus dressing for fruit salad.

⊕ **Oily fish** Ground white seeds work well with Indian spices to make a sauce for trout or salmon.

AJWAIN

Bitter | Herbaceous | Peppery

BOTANICAL NAME
Trachyspermum ammi

ALSO KNOWN AS
Ajowan, ajave, carom, Ethiopian cumin, omum, bishop's weed.

MAJOR FLAVOUR COMPOUND
Thymol.

PARTS USED
Seeds (technically fruits).

METHOD OF CULTIVATION
The stems are cut when the seeds are ripe, around two months after flowering.

COMMERCIAL PREPARATION
Stems are dried, threshed, and sieved; seeds are then graded and grouped by size.

NON-CULINARY USES
In perfumes; as an antiseptic agent in toothpastes; in Ayurvedic medicine to treat digestive disorders, rheumatism, arthritis, and fevers.

Spice story

Ajwain was valued as a medicinal spice from ancient times, and was probably first cultivated in Egypt. The Romans believed it to be a variety of cumin – hence the common name "Ethiopian cumin." It is believed to have reached India, where it became popular, via the spice caravans at around the same time as cumin seed, soon after 750 CE. It was given a number of misleading names – "celery seed" and "lovage seed" were the most common ones – which persist to this day, even though the taste is very different. For centuries, regions of India practising Ayurvedic medicine have been making a cure-all tonic "omam water" from ajwain seeds. Although the plant is now mainly cultivated for its potent essential oil, ajwain is one of the defining spices of the vegetarian cuisine of the west Indian state of Gujarat.

The plant
Ajwain is a small annual plant in the parsley family, and is closely related to caraway and cumin.

Flat heads *of small white flowers appear, which later develop into tiny "seeds"*

Powder
Ground ajwain is available to buy and is less bitter than whole or fresh ground seeds, but adds a much weaker flavour to a dish.

Oval seeds *are greyish-green and resemble those of caraway*

Whole
South Indian seeds have the highest levels of thymol (up to 98 per cent of the flavour compound molecules). Whole seeds retain a strong flavour for a very long time.

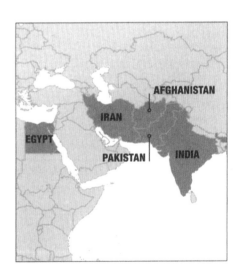

Region of cultivation
Ajwain is probably native to the Middle East, possibly Egypt. It is now cultivated mainly in India and Iran, but also in Pakistan, Afghanistan, and Egypt.

Kitchen creativity }

The flavour of ajwain has been described as a mixture of anise, oregano, and black pepper. Its bitterness can be reduced by toasting or frying it. Ajwain is highly aromatic and pungent, so use it cautiously.

BLENDING SCIENCE

Ajwain and thyme have similar taste profiles: they both share the same main flavour compound – thymol – which is also found in oregano. This powerful phenol works alongside equally penetrating or herbal spices, while the lesser terpene compounds provide opportunities for bringing out citrus and woody, spicy flavours.

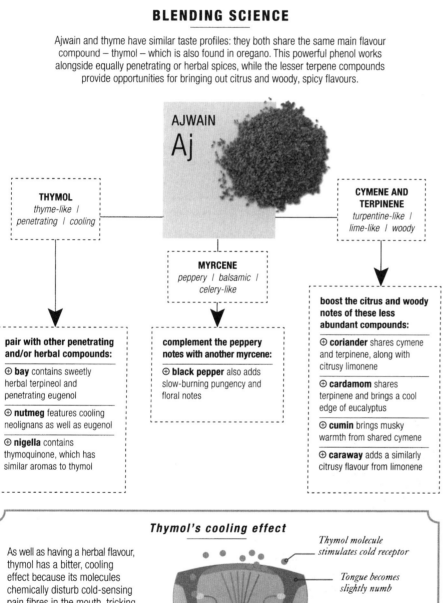

AJWAIN
Aj

THYMOL
thyme-like | penetrating | cooling

CYMENE AND TERPENE
turpentine-like | lime-like | woody

MYRCENE
peppery | balsamic | celery-like

pair with other penetrating and/or herbal compounds:

⊕ **bay** contains sweetly herbal terpineol and penetrating eugenol

⊕ **nutmeg** features cooling neolignans as well as eugenol

⊕ **nigella** contains thymoquinone, which has similar aromas to thymol

complement the peppery notes with another myrcene:

⊕ **black pepper** also adds slow-burning pungency and floral notes

boost the citrus and woody notes of these less abundant compounds:

⊕ **coriander** shares cymene and terpinene, along with citrusy limonene

⊕ **cardamom** shares terpinene and brings a cool edge of eucalyptus

⊕ **cumin** brings musky warmth from shared cymene

⊕ **caraway** adds a similarly citrusy flavour from limonene

FOOD PARTNERS

⊕ **Fish** Combine bruised ajwain seeds with chilli powder and turmeric to make a dry rub for whole or filleted fish. Then fry or oven bake.

⊕ **Vegetables** Add lightly crushed ajwain seeds to a chickpea flour batter for vegetable fritters or onion bhajis.

⊕ **Lentils** Add whole seeds to melted butter or ghee for an aromatic tempering for lentil soup or dhal.

⊕ **Breads** Fry ajwain seeds in oil, ghee, or butter and drizzle over flatbreads, chapatti, or naan.

⊕ **Eggs** Fry a pinch of seeds in butter or ghee, and add gently beaten eggs to make Parsi-style scrambled eggs.

RELEASE THE FLAVOUR

For a more rounded taste, dry roast the whole seeds to create compounds with nutty, roasted flavours, particularly pyrazines. This also dampens the penetrating icy quality because some of the thymol will evaporate and degrade.

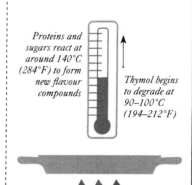

Proteins and sugars react at around 140°C (284°F) to form new flavour compounds

Thymol begins to degrade at 90–100°C (194–212°F)

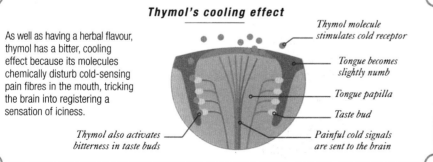

Thymol's cooling effect

As well as having a herbal flavour, thymol has a bitter, cooling effect because its molecules chemically disturb cold-sensing pain fibres in the mouth, tricking the brain into registering a sensation of iciness.

Thymol molecule stimulates cold receptor

Tongue becomes slightly numb

Tongue papilla

Taste bud

Thymol also activates bitterness in taste buds

Painful cold signals are sent to the brain

CELERY SEED

Bitter | Savoury | Lemony

BOTANICAL NAME
Apium graveolens

ALSO KNOWN AS
Smallage, wild celery.

MAJOR FLAVOUR COMPOUND
Sedanolide.

PARTS USED
Seeds (which are technically fruits).

METHOD OF CULTIVATION
The plant is cut at ground level when the seeds are mature and grey-brown in colour.

COMMERCIAL PREPARATION
The seeds are left to dry a few days, and then threshed, cleaned, and further dried.

NON-CULINARY USES
Perfumery; in herbal medicine for water retention, arthritis, and gout; in Ayurvedic medicine as a nerve stimulant and tonic.

The plant
Wild celery is a biennial herb. It has a thinner, less fleshy stem than cultivated celery. It grows up to 1m (3ft) tall.

Whole
Use whole seeds and grind them as required. They can be stored in a sealed container in a cool, dark place for up to 2 years.

Ridged *seeds are up to 5mm (¼in) long*

Tiny cream flowers *are produced in clusters called umbels*

Feathery, yellow-green leaves *are aromatic*

Powder
Ground celery seed is available to buy, but quickly loses its flavour.

Spice story

Wild celery has been cultivated for over 3,000 years, and was widely used by the ancient Egyptians, Greeks, and Romans as a panacea, and was grown in most of their herb gardens. The Romans also added the bitter seeds and leaves to bread, wine, soups, cheese, and other foods. By the 6th century CE, wild celery had been introduced to China. Meanwhile in Europe its use spread north to France and England. In medieval Europe it was believed to cure every kind of illness, and was reputed to be an aphrodisiac. By the 17th century, a new, sweeter form of the plant was being cultivated in Italy for use as a vegetable; this is the celery we know today. Its wild relative – smallage – was relegated to seed production, and is still the main source of celery seed.

Region of cultivation
Wild celery is thought to be native to temperate regions of Europe and western Asia. It is cultivated specifically for its seed mainly in India (which produces more than 50 per cent of the world's total crop), but also in China, Egypt, and France.

Kitchen creativity }

Celery seeds are more intensely flavoured than the stalks and leaves, with a warm, concentrated, earthy taste, lingering bitterness, and hints of grassiness, but without the freshness of the vegetable. Use them judiciously in soups, sauces, and vegetable dishes.

BLENDING SCIENCE

The most abundant flavour compound in celery seeds is citrus-scented limonene, with lesser amounts of herbal-tasting selinene and woody, spicy humulene. However, the unique herbal taste of this spice is produced by unusually potent lactone compounds called phthalides, which are present in only trace amounts but have a profound effect on the overall flavour.

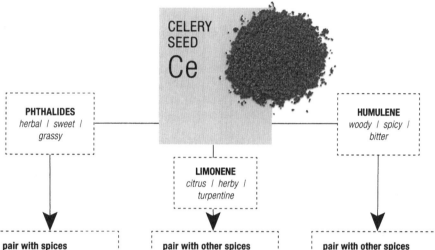

CELERY SEED
Ce

PHTHALIDES
herbal | sweet | grassy

LIMONENE
citrus | herby | turpentine

HUMULENE
woody | spicy | bitter

pair with spices that contain traces of these flavour compounds:

⊕ **caraway** brings complex, anise-like, peppery flavours

⊕ **cardamom** adds eucalyptus notes and a sweet mintiness

⊕ **cumin** lends an earthy warmth

⊕ **ajwain** contributes a strong thyme flavour

pair with other spices that carry some limonene to balance the bitterness:

⊕ **black pepper** gives lingering pungency and woody notes

⊕ **coriander** brings its distinctive floral qualities, with lemon and pine aromas

pair with other spices containing humulene, or with spices that also have woody nuances:

⊕ **grains of paradise** enhance the spicy bitterness

⊕ **allspice** provides sweet, clove-like warmth

⊕ **bay** has woody bitterness with complex eucalyptus, lemon, and floral scents

FOOD PARTNERS

⊕ **Tomatoes** Sprinkle seeds sparingly over grilled tomatoes or a tomato tarte tatin.

⊕ **Potatoes** Toss celery seeds in melted butter and drizzle over new potatoes.

⊕ **Fish** Add the seeds to a fish chowder, or to the batter for fish goujons.

⊕ **Beef** Add a few seeds to pepper as a spice rub for beef brisket.

⊕ **Savoury bakes** Add to savoury bread dough, cheese biscuits, or oat biscuits for serving with cheese.

⊕ **Eggs** Sprinkle lightly toasted seeds over scrambled or devilled eggs.

Homemade celery salt

Not just for a Bloody Mary, celery salt is a flavoursome alternative to ordinary salt that works well with soups, cold salads, and dips. Use a ratio of 1 part celery seed to 6 parts salt.

Toast the celery seeds lightly in a dry frying pan to remove moisture.

Crush the toasted seeds with sea salt using a pestle and mortar, adjusting the quantities to taste.

RELEASE THE FLAVOUR

Flavours dissolve best in oil, but several of the flavour compounds in celery seed are sensitive to temperatures at either end of the hot–cold spectrum.

Bitter substances are destroyed by heat. Toast seeds at the start of cooking to mellow the bitterness.

Phthalides turn to vapour when seeds are ground, but chilling beforehand helps to slow the rate of evaporation.

TURMERIC

Woody | Floral | Bitter

BOTANICAL NAME
Curcuma longa

ALSO KNOWN AS
Indian saffron, false saffron.

MAJOR FLAVOUR COMPOUNDS
Turmerone and ar-turmerone.

PARTS USED
Rhizomes (fresh, dried, or powdered); occasionally fresh leaves.

METHOD OF CULTIVATION
This annual crop is grown in heavily manured furrows; rhizomes are harvested when the leaves turn yellow.

COMMERCIAL PREPARATION
Rhizomes are boiled and dried; they are then sold whole or ground to a powder.

NON-CULINARY USES
Fabric dye; colouring agent in cosmetics; in traditional medicine as an anti-inflammatory and antimicrobial agent.

The plant
Turmeric is a leafy tropical plant in the ginger family, which grows as a perennial in the wild.

Fresh leaves *can be used to wrap foods or as a herb*

Rhizomes *look like smaller, thinner versions of ginger*

Ground turmeric *is less staining than the fresh spice*

Powder
There are two main types: Madras (above) is brighter yellow and sweeter in taste than the pungent, earthy, ochre-coloured Alleppey turmeric, which is more prized.

Fresh
Zesty flavours are more prominent in raw rhizomes. Peel and then chop or grate them, like ginger.

Spice story

The flavour and properties of turmeric were first appreciated by the ancient Vedic culture of India over 3,000 years ago. The spice still forms a major part of many Indian masala blends, and is used in Hindu rituals to symbolize the sun. Turmeric's influence on Persian and North African cooking dates back to the pre-Christian era, when it first reached these regions via the caravans and ships of the Spice Routes. Ottoman traders introduced turmeric to Europe in the early medieval period, although it was mainly used as a cheap alternative to saffron. The spice gained popularity in Britain during the era of Imperial India, when returning colonial officers recreated the flavours of the Raj with an all-purpose "curry powder", of which turmeric was (and still is) a major constituent.

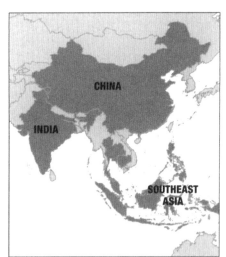

Region of cultivation
Turmeric is thought to be native to India. It is cultivated mainly in that country (which produces 90 per cent of all turmeric powder), but also in China, Thailand, Cambodia, Malaysia, Indonesia, and the Philippines.

Kitchen creativity }

Turmeric works well in complex blends, where its pungent earthiness acts as a base to help to bind other flavours together. Add sparingly if it is to be used on its own, so that the bitter notes do not overwhelm.

BLENDING SCIENCE

Turmeric's dominant earthy notes are produced by the flavour compounds turmerone and ar-turmerone ("ar-" for "aromatic"), which are found in few other spices. The minor compounds provide more opportunities for effective pairing. Focus on one compound for a particular taste effect, or mix and match several.

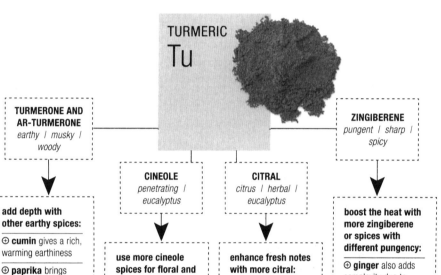

TURMERIC
Tu

TURMERONE AND AR-TURMERONE
earthy | musky | woody

CINEOLE
penetrating | eucalyptus

CITRAL
citrus | herbal | eucalyptus

ZINGIBERENE
pungent | sharp | spicy

add depth with other earthy spices:

⊕ **cumin** gives a rich, warming earthiness

⊕ **paprika** brings toasted, smoky, and sweet notes from pyrazines

⊕ **black cardamom** brings smokiness and penetrating menthol from shared cineole

use more cineole spices for floral and menthol notes:

⊕ **anise**, **star anise** easily overpower, so use sparingly

⊕ **nutmeg** will also help to develop the musky flavours

enhance fresh notes with more citral:

⊕ **cardamom** also adds penetrating camphorous accents

⊕ **coriander** brings zesty fruit and floral aromas, and can be added generously

boost the heat with more zingiberene or spices with different pungency:

⊕ **ginger** also adds complexity due to shared zingiberene

⊕ **black pepper** adds pungency due to piperine, which complements the pungency of turmeric's zingiberene

FOOD PARTNERS

⊕ **White fish** Stir together turmeric, yoghurt, and crushed garlic, and then spoon over fish fillets before grilling.

⊕ **Lamb and pork** Combine with paprika, lightly crushed cumin, and oil for a meat rub, and massage into the skin before roasting.

⊕ **Squash and cauliflower** Mix a teaspoonful with oil and honey, and toss with the vegetables before roasting.

⊕ **White chocolate** Add a good pinch to cupcake batter along with chunks of white chocolate.

⊕ **Pickles** Include thin slices of fresh rhizome in fish and vegetable pickles.

RELEASE THE FLAVOUR

Frying in fat causes flavour compound molecules to disperse and form new compounds. This only happens above 130°C (266°F), so does not occur in boiling water.

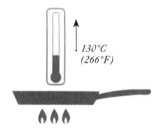

130°C (266°F)

Cooking with curcumin

The incredible staining power of ground turmeric is due to a pigment called curcumin, but you may be surprised to discover that its hue can vary according to how it is used and stored.

Acid effect
Acids, such as lemon juice, help to retain the yellow colour.

Alkaline effect
Alkaline substances, such as baking soda, turn it orangey-red.

Iron reaction
Toasting or frying in an iron skillet will darken the spice.

Photosensitivity
Exposure to light destroys the pigment, so store it in the dark.

BLENDS TO TRY

Use and adapt these recipes for classic blends featuring turmeric:

Hawaij p29
Niter kibbeh p32
Malaysian fish curry paste p51
Bumbu p52

FENUGREEK

Bittersweet | Warm | Musty

BOTANICAL NAME
Trigonella foenum-graecum,
T. caerulea (blue fenugreek)

ALSO KNOWN AS
Goat's horn, Greek hayseed,
Greek clover.

MAJOR FLAVOUR COMPOUND
Sotolon.

PARTS USED
Seeds; young leaves.

METHOD OF CULTIVATION
When the seed pods are ripe, plants are
pulled up, bundled together, and dried for
about a week.

COMMERCIAL PREPARATION
The stems are threshed to release the
seeds, which are then dried and graded.

NON-CULINARY USES
As a dye; in herbal medicine as a digestive
aid and stimulant; in Ayurvedic medicine
for hair loss and skin complaints.

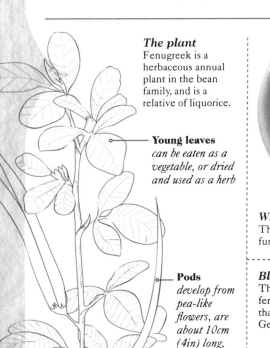

The plant
Fenugreek is a
herbaceous annual
plant in the bean
family, and is a
relative of liquorice.

Young leaves
*can be eaten as a
vegetable, or dried
and used as a herb*

Pods
*develop from
pea-like
flowers, are
about 10cm
(4in) long,
and contain
10–20 seeds*

Whole
The angular, brownish-yellow seeds have a
furrow running across one side.

Blue fenugreek powder
The ground leaves and seeds of blue
fenugreek have a milder, less bitter flavour
than ordinary fenugreek and are used in
Georgian cuisine (see p77).

Spice story

The oldest fenugreek seeds were
found at an archeological site in Iraq,
and date back to 4000 BCE. Seeds were
also found in the 3,000-year-old tomb
of the Egyptian pharaoh Tutankhamen:
the Egyptians regarded fenugreek as
a panacea. By Roman times, the plant
was such a common crop that it was
used as fodder for cattle – its name
comes from the Latin for "Greek hay".
Its use as a spice crop was mentioned
in the 1st century CE by the Greek
physician Dioscorides in *De Materia
Medica*. At an athletics games held by
the Syrians a century later, it was a
component of a ritual perfume with
which participants were anointed. By
the Middle Ages, fenugreek was being
cultivated as a medicinal herb in
Europe. Today it is frequently used as
in Iranian, West Asian, Indian, and Sri
Lankan cuisine, and has spread round
the world via commercial curry powder,
of which it is a key ingredient.

Region of cultivation
Fenugreek is native to the eastern
Mediterranean region and southwest Asia.
It is cultivated mainly in India, but also in
Mediterranean countries and North Africa.

Kitchen creativity }

Fenugreek seeds have a sweet, strong taste, with hints of caramel, maple syrup, burnt sugar, and coffee. While its musty aroma is not to everyone's liking, the spice provides a savoury, bittersweet background for many dishes.

BLENDING SCIENCE

Fenugreek's flavour is dominated by sotolon, a sweet lactone compound with a taste like brown sugar with hints of candy floss. This spice also has woody caryophyllene, with some buttery diacetyl, and mushroom-like vinyl amyl ketone. Pyrazines give toasted seeds roasted, smoky flavours. The sweaty, rancid, musty aromas are produced by a trio of fragrant acids, which some people dislike.

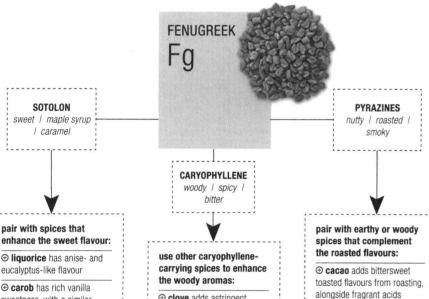

FENUGREEK
Fg

SOTOLON
sweet | maple syrup | caramel

CARYOPHYLLENE
woody | spicy | bitter

PYRAZINES
nutty | roasted | smoky

pair with spices that enhance the sweet flavour:

⊕ **liquorice** has anise- and eucalyptus-like flavour

⊕ **carob** has rich vanilla sweetness, with a similar sweaty aroma from acids

⊕ **allspice** brings peppery sweetness and also shares caryophyllene

⊕ **cinnamon** has penetrating sweetness and warmth, as well as shared caryophyllene

use other caryophyllene-carrying spices to enhance the woody aromas:

⊕ **clove** adds astringent, distinctive floral woodiness

⊕ **annatto** contributes gentle earthiness and a mild flavour

⊕ **curry leaf** adds warming, meaty, sulphurous complexity

⊕ **black pepper** has mild pungent heat as well as woody qualities and citrus notes

pair with earthy or woody spices that complement the roasted flavours:

⊕ **cacao** adds bittersweet toasted flavours from roasting, alongside fragrant acids

⊕ **cumin** when toasted has warm, earthy, bitter flavours

⊕ **turmeric** adds harmonizing muskiness with hints of ginger

⊕ **paprika** shares smokiness and adds sweet warmth

FOOD PARTNERS

⊕ **Pumpkin, sweet potato** Soak fenugreek seeds and add to the base of a pumpkin or sweet potato stew.

⊕ **Walnuts** Use blue fenugreek to make the Georgian spiced walnut paste *satsivi*, which can be enjoyed as a dip or used for flavouring meat stews.

⊕ **Beef, lamb** Add toasted and soaked fenugreek seeds to add depth to a rich beef or lamb curry.

⊕ **Fish** Fry toasted, ground fenugreek seeds in ghee or coconut oil before mixing in fish chunks and coconut milk for a Keralan-style curry.

⊕ **Baking** Add soaked and pounded seeds to savoury yeasted breads.

⊕ **Preserves** Add the ground seeds to fruit chutneys and relishes.

BLENDS TO TRY

Use and adapt these classic blends featuring fenugreek:

Niter kibbeh p32

Durban curry masala p37

Panch phoran p43

Vindaloo paste p44

Khmeli-suneli p77

RELEASE THE FLAVOUR

Fenugreek seeds can help diffuse flavours throughout a dish and thicken sauces by the action of a special emulsifier called galactomannan.

Oil droplets suspended in water

Galactomannan in seeds forms a gel in a liquidy dish, allowing oil and water to mix.

Extract galactomannan by soaking seeds in water overnight or by simmering.

Grind the seeds so galactomannan releases faster. Ground fenugreek can be added directly to a dish.

Lightly toast seeds to create nutty, coffee-and-chocolate roasted pyrazine flavours.

SPICED FILIPINO ADOBO WITH CHICKEN AND PORK

This spicy take on the usually mild Filipino dish imagines what it might taste like had the nation embraced more influences from the spice trade. A classic adobo is made with pork and chicken, but you could use just one or the other – or make a meat-free version with sturdy vegetable chunks, such as butternut squash.

SPICE IDEAS

Replace the first three sweetly fragranced spices with a **more earthy mix** of cumin, paprika, and turmeric.

Use sulphurous spices, such as mustard, curry leaves, and asafoetida, to **emphasize the meatiness** of the dish.

Alter the citrus-sour profile by replacing the vinegar with tamarind water and adding lemongrass to the paste mix.

Serves 4–6

Prep time 25 mins

Cooking time 1 hour

seeds of 5 cardamom pods

1 star anise

2.5cm (1in) piece of cinnamon

½ tsp roasted chilli flakes or chilli powder

1 tsp black peppercorns

6 garlic cloves, peeled

5cm (2in) piece of fresh root ginger, roughly chopped

2 tbsp coconut oil or vegetable oil

6 spring onions, chopped

2 tbsp palm sugar or muscovado sugar

1 kg (2¼lb) chicken thighs and drumsticks

300g (10oz) pork tenderloin, cut into chunks

100ml (3½fl oz) coconut vinegar or white wine vinegar

100ml (3½fl oz) dark soy sauce

250ml (9fl oz) chicken stock

3 bay leaves

1 Place the cardamom seeds, star anise, cinnamon, chilli flakes, and peppercorns in a pestle and mortar, and grind vigorously until the spices have been pulverized. Add the garlic and ginger, and pound to a rough paste.

2 Put a heavy-based pan or wok on a medium heat, add the oil and spice paste, and stir-fry for 2–3 minutes, until the garlic and ginger become fragrant and begin to colour.

3 Stir in the spring onions and sugar, then add the chicken and pork. Stir to coat them with the spice mix.

4 Pour in the vinegar, soy sauce, and chicken stock. Add the bay leaves and bring the pan to the boil.

5 Reduce the heat and cover the pan – use foil if your pan does not have a lid. Simmer gently for 1 hour, until the meat is tender and the liquid has reduced. Serve with steamed rice and stir-fried greens.

WORLD OF SPICE FURTHER RECIPES

The following recipes for classic dishes from around the world are as delicious as they are authentic; each features one of the traditional spice blends or sauces from the World of Spice chapter (pp18–77).

LAMB KOFTE

Makes 12

Prep time 20 mins, plus 20–30 mins soaking

Cooking time 8–10 mins

50g (1¾oz) bulgur wheat
50g (1¾oz) apricots, roughly chopped
500g (1lb 2oz) lamb mince
1 small onion, finely chopped
1 tbsp pine nuts
2 cloves garlic, peeled and crushed
1 tbsp chopped fresh mint, plus extra leaves to serve
3 tbsp *baharat* spice (see p23)
salt, to taste
flatbreads, red onion, tomatoes, and plain yogurt, to serve

1 Put the bulgur and apricots into a small pan. Pour over 100ml (3½fl oz) boiling water, cover, and set aside for 20–30 minutes, until all the liquid is absorbed.

2 Put all the remaining ingredients together in a bowl with 1 tbsp of *baharat* spice and a pinch of salt, and mix together with a fork. Add the bulgur and apricots, and knead the mixture until it forms a paste and holds together well.

3 Divide the lamb mixture into 12 portions and roll each portion into a ball.

4 Sprinkle the remaining 2 tbsp of *baharat* spice onto a plate, then roll each ball to coat it evenly with the spice.

5 Thread a skewer through the centre of each ball, and squeeze the ball into a sausage shape about 8–10cm (3–4in) long around the skewer.

6 Preheat a grill or a griddle pan to a medium–high heat. Cook for 8–10 minutes, turning until crisp and evenly browned on the outside and cooked through in the centre. Cook in batches if necessary.

7 Serve with flatbreads, topped with sliced red onion, diced tomatoes, fresh mint leaves, and a dollop of yoghurt.

PERSIAN RICE PUDDINGS

Serves 6

Prep time 15 mins, plus up to 1 hour infusing

Cooking time 45–50 mins

150g (5½oz) short-grain pudding rice, washed
600ml (1 pint) full-fat milk
300ml (10fl oz) double cream
2 tbsp runny honey
strip of zest from 1 orange
2 tsp orange flower water
1 vanilla pod, split and seeds scraped out
pinch of saffron strands, ground to a powder
1 tbsp *advieh* spice mix, plus extra to serve (see p27)
6 Medjool dates, pitted and roughly chopped
1 tbsp pistachio kernels, cut into slivers
1 tbsp dried rose petals

1 Preheat the oven to 160°C (325°F/Gas 3).

2 Divide the rice between six 200ml (7fl oz) ramekins.

3 Combine the milk, cream, honey, orange zest, orange flower water, vanilla pod and seeds, and ground saffron in a large, heavy-based saucepan. Set over a medium heat, stirring until the honey dissolves and the saffron turns the milk pale yellow.

4 Heat to just below boiling point, then turn off the heat and allow to infuse for at least 10 minutes, or up to 1 hour.

5 Strain the milk, discarding the zest and vanilla pod, and divide between the six ramekins, pouring it over the rice. Sprinkle the *advieh* spice mix over the surface of each pot.

6 Cook for 45–50 minutes or until the rice is completely soft and the spice has formed a thin brown skin on top.

7 Remove the pots from the oven and allow to cool a little.

8 Top each pudding with chopped dates, pistachios, and a scatter of dried rose petals. Sprinkle over a little more of the *advieh* and serve warm or cold.

DURBAN BEEF BUNNY CHOW

Serves 4

Prep time 30 mins

Cooking time 40–50 mins

2 tbsp olive oil
2 black cardamom pods
2 small cinnamon sticks
1 tsp fennel seeds
1 large onion, chopped
2 tbsp Durban curry masala (see p37)
2 tsp fresh root ginger, grated
4 garlic cloves, peeled and crushed
2 tbsp tomato purée
2 ripe tomatoes, roughly chopped
500g (1lb 2oz) lean stewing beef, cut into 1–2cm (½–¾in) pieces
1 large potato, cut into 1–2cm (½–¾in) pieces
12 fresh curry leaves, or 6 dried curry leaves
handful of fresh coriander, chopped, plus extra to garnish
½ lime
2 small white crusty bread loaves (a 400g/14oz tin loaf is perfect), halved and hollowed out

1 Heat the oil in a large pan, then fry the cardamom, cinnamon, and fennel seeds for a minute or so, until aromatic.

2 Add the onion, and soften for 5–8 minutes over a medium heat.

3 Sprinkle the masala and stir to coat the onions, then add the ginger, garlic, and tomato purée, and cook for 1 minute.

4 Add the tomatoes, stir, and cook for 4–5 minutes, until the mixture becomes sauce-like.

5 Stir in the beef and the potatoes, the curry leaves, and 300ml (10fl oz) of water. Season with salt and pepper.

6 Bring to a simmer, cover, and cook for 40–50 minutes, stirring occasionally, until the meat is tender and the potatoes are soft.

7 Stir in the coriander plus a squeeze of lime to taste. Remove and discard the cinnamon, cardamom, and curry leaves before serving.

8 Divide the curry between the four half loaves of bread, spooning it into each hollowed-out half. Garnish with the extra coriander and serve immediately.

CHANA MASALA WITH SWEET POTATO AND SPINACH

Serves 4

Prep time 20 mins

Cooking time 30–35 mins

1 tbsp vegetable or coconut oil
1 tsp cumin seeds
1 large onion, roughly chopped
2 garlic cloves, crushed
2cm (¾in) fresh root ginger, peeled and grated
2 tsp ground coriander
1 tsp paprika
1 tsp ground turmeric
1 medium sweet potato, peeled and cut into 2cm (¾in) chunks
400g can chopped tomatoes
2 x 400g (14oz) cans chickpeas in water, or 200g (7oz) dried chickpeas or chana dhal, soaked overnight then cooked
in fresh water until tender, with cooking water reserved
salt, to taste
1 or 2 green chillies, cut into chunky pieces
75g (2½oz) baby spinach, washed
1–2 tsp garam masala, to taste (see p40)
½ lemon
naan breads, to serve

1 Heat the oil in a large, heavy-based pan over a medium–high heat. When the oil is hot, add the cumin seeds. Fry for 1 minute or so until aromatic, add the onion, and then reduce the heat. Cook for 5–8 minutes until softened.

2 Add the garlic and ginger and stir for 1 minute or so, then add the ground coriander, paprika, and turmeric, stirring for a further 2 minutes.

3 Add the sweet potato, turning it to coat it well with the spices.

4 Stir in the tomatoes and chickpeas with their liquid. Alternatively, if using dried chickpeas or chana dhal, add about 300ml (10fl oz) of the reserved cooking water. Stir in the chilli pieces (include the seeds for extra heat), bring to a simmer, then turn the heat to low, cover, and cook for 25–30 minutes, until the potatoes are tender and the sauce has thickened. Season with salt.

5 Add the spinach, and stir for 3–4 minutes until it wilts.

6 Stir in the garam masala, and squeeze in some lemon juice to taste. Adjust the seasoning, then serve immediately with warmed naan breads.

MASOR TENGA FISH CURRY

Serves 4

Prep time 10 mins, plus 10–15 mins marinating

Cooking time 30 mins

4 sea bream or grey mullet fillets, de-scaled, with skin on
½ tsp salt
1 tsp ground turmeric powder
2 tbsp oil, such as coconut or rapeseed
1 tsp yellow mustard seeds, coarsely ground
1 tbsp *panch phoran* (see p43)
1 onion, sliced
2 green chillies, deseeded and halved lengthways
2 ripe tomatoes, roughly chopped
1–2 tsp red chilli flakes
1 tbsp yellow mustard paste
juice of 1 lime
handful of fresh coriander leaves, to garnish

1 Place the fish on a plate and rub with the salt and turmeric. Cover, and set aside for 10–15 minutes.

2 Melt half the oil in a frying pan over a medium–high heat and add the mustard seeds. Stir for a few minutes until they become fragrant. Lay the fish in the pan, skin side down, and leave to cook for 3–4 mins. Once the skin is crisp and golden, turn and cook for another 2–3 minutes until the fish is just cooked through. Transfer the fried fish to a plate, cover, and set aside.

3 Heat the remaining oil in the pan over a high heat, and add the *panch phoran*. Let the seeds splutter and pop for 1 minute.

4 Turn the heat down to medium and stir in the onion and chillies. Fry gently for 3–4 minutes, until they are just softened and golden.

5 Now stir in the chopped tomatoes and cook for 4–5 minutes until they soften.

6 Add the mustard paste with the chilli flakes and cook for another 4–5 minutes, stirring.

7 Pour in 150–200ml (5–7fl oz) water, then add lime juice to taste. Bring to a gentle simmer.

8 Carefully add the fried fish pieces back into the sauce, skin side up, and heat through for 2–3 minutes.

9 Garnish with chopped coriander leaves and serve with rice.

GOAN VINDALOO

Serves 4

Prep time 30 mins, plus 1 hour or overnight marinating

Cooking time 30–40 mins

2 tbsp olive oil
500g (1lb 2oz) skinless, boneless chicken thighs or pork shoulder, cut into 3cm (1in) chunks
1 medium aubergine, cut into 2cm (¾in) chunks
1 batch vindaloo paste (see p44)
2 large garlic cloves, peeled and crushed
5cm (2in) fresh root ginger, peeled and grated
2 tbsp coconut oil
1 large onion, roughly chopped
2 ripe tomatoes, cut into chunks
1 or 2 green chillies, thickly sliced
250ml (9fl oz) chicken stock
1 tbsp jaggery or soft brown sugar, plus extra if needed
1 tbsp coconut or cider vinegar
1 tsp salt
handful of coriander leaves, to garnish
rice, yoghurt, and lime pickle, to serve

1 Put the chicken or pork and aubergine in a bowl, and stir in the vindaloo paste along with the garlic and ginger. Mix well, cover, and marinate for at least 1 hour, or refrigerate and leave overnight if preferred.

2 Preheat the oven to 190°C (375°F/Gas 5).

3 Heat the oil in an ovenproof pan and fry the onion over a low heat for 10–15 minutes, until soft and golden.

4 Add the meat and aubergine, along with the marinade, and cook, stirring, for 4–5 minutes to brown all over.

5 Now add the tomatoes, chillies, and stock, and bring to a simmer. Stir in the jaggery and vinegar until the sugar has dissolved.

6 Cover and transfer to the oven. Cook for 30–40 minutes, until the chicken is tender, the aubergine is soft and melting, and the sauce has thickened. Taste and adjust the seasoning.

7 Sprinkle with coriander and serve immediately with rice, yoghurt, and lime pickle.

PRAWN SUMMER ROLLS

Makes 12

Prep time 45 mins

100g (3½oz) dried vermicelli rice noodles or bean thread noodles, or use a 300g (10oz) pack of cooked rice noodles
12 round rice paper wrappers, 20cm (8in) in diameter
handful of Thai basil
24 cooked prawns, cut in half lengthways
2 or 3 large iceberg lettuce leaves, torn into 12 pieces
1 carrot, grated
½ cucumber, cut into 5cm (2in) long matchsticks
2 spring onions, cut lengthways into strips
handful of coriander leaves
handful of mint leaves
4 tbsp salted peanuts, roughly chopped
1 lime, halved
nuoc cham dipping sauce, to serve (see p50)

1 Soak the dried rice noodles, if using, in a bowl of hot water for 3 minutes, and then drain and rinse with cold water. They should be just tender, but not too soft.

2 Lay out all the ingredients ready to make the rolls. Dip one of the rice papers in a bowl of hot water, moving it around for 10–15 seconds until the whole wrapper is pliable but not completely soft. Lay it on a board and pat dry with a tea towel.

3 At the bottom edge of the wrapper, place three Thai basil leaves face down, side by side, then lay four prawn halves on top in a horizontal row.

4 Place a piece of lettuce on top of the prawns, followed by some noodles, a few strips of carrot, cucumber, and spring onions, then some coriander and mint leaves, and finally the nuts. Squeeze a little lime juice over the vegetables. Do not overfill the rolls or they will be hard to shape.

5 Lift the edge of the rice paper wrapper nearest to you over the filling and, holding the filling in position with your fingers, tuck it under and start rolling tightly.

6 When you are about halfway, fold the ends of the rice paper in and over the filling. Continue rolling the filling as tightly as possible so that it is completely enclosed, and press lightly to ensure that it has stuck.

7 Repeat with the other wrappers and the remainder of the fillings. To serve, cut the rolls in half on the diagonal, and serve at room temperature with the *nuoc cham* dipping sauce.

8 If you are making the rolls in advance, cover them with cling film or a damp tea towel to prevent them from drying out.

NANJING SALTED DUCK

Serves 4

Prep time 20 mins, plus overnight marinating

Cooking time 15 mins, plus 2 hours cooling

2 tbsp salt
2 tbsp whole Sichuan peppercorns, lightly crushed with a pestle and mortar
2 whole duck legs, about 200g (7oz) each
2 duck breasts, about 175g (6oz) each
1 Nanjing spice bag (see p59)
5cm (2in) fresh root ginger, sliced, and then pulverized using a pestle and mortar
3 spring onions, trimmed and cut into large segments
125ml (4fl oz) Shaoxing wine
2 tsp sesame oil

1 Heat a frying pan over a medium heat. Add the salt and Sichuan peppercorns and dry roast them, stirring for 5–8 minutes until the salt turns yellow/brown. Let the pan cool.

2 Lightly score the skin of the duck pieces with a sharp knife. Rub the salt and peppercorns into the skin and flesh, cover loosely with foil, and then marinate overnight in the fridge.

3 When you are ready to cook the duck, lay all the pieces in the bottom of a large pan with the salt and peppercorns. Cover with 1.5–2 litres (2¾–3½pints) of water. Add the spice pouch, ginger, and spring onion. Bring to the boil, then add the Shaoxing wine. Reduce the heat, and simmer gently for 15 minutes.

4 Turn off the heat and allow the duck to cool in the liquid, with the pan covered.

5 Transfer the duck to a cutting board and discard the cooking liquid, or strain and reserve it for use as stock.

6 Drizzle the sesame oil over each piece of duck. Cut the breast into thick slices, and divide the legs in half between the joint to separate the leg and thigh. Eat warm, or leave to cool. Serve one piece of leg and some sliced breast per person.

PRAWN AND VEGETABLE STIR-FRY

Serves 4

Prep time 10 mins

Cooking time 10 mins

250g (9oz) fine egg thread noodles
2 tbsp groundnut oil
1 onion, peeled and cut into chunks
1 red pepper, deseeded and cut into chunks
2cm (1in) fresh root ginger, peeled and cut into matchsticks
2 large garlic cloves, peeled and sliced
250g (9oz) large, raw prawns, peeled and de-veined
100g (3½oz) baby corn, sliced in half on the diagonal
2 tbsp light soy sauce
2 tbsp Shaoxing wine, or similar rice wine
juice of half a lime
100g (3½oz) mangetout
1 tbsp five-spice powder (see p60)
2 tbsp black sesame seeds
2 tbsp toasted sesame oil

1 Put the noodles into a saucepan and pour boiling water over them. Cover and leave to stand while you make the stir-fry.

2 Heat the oil in a large frying pan or wok, and stir-fry the onion and pepper over a high heat for 2 minutes, until softened and slightly charred.

3 Add the ginger, garlic, and prawns, stirring constantly for 2 minutes until the prawns are just pink.

4 Add the baby corn to the pan with the soy sauce and wine. Simmer for 1 minute.

5 Stir in the mangetout and five-spice powder, then remove from the heat.

6 Drain the noodles, and stir in the sesame seeds and oil. Serve immediately with the hot stir-fry.

PIPARKAKUT

Makes about 40

Prep time 20 mins, plus cooling, chilling, and resting

Cooking time 10–12 mins

60g (2oz) pure runny honey
60g (2oz) black treacle
125g (4½oz) unsalted butter
100g (3½oz) soft dark brown sugar
350g (12oz) plain flour, plus extra for dusting
1 tsp bicarbonate of soda
1 tbsp Finnish gingerbread spice (see p72)
¼ tsp ground white pepper
1 egg
2 tbsp chopped glacé ginger, to decorate (optional)

1 Put the honey, black treacle, butter, and sugar into a saucepan, then place on a low heat, and melt all the ingredients together.

2 Once melted, set aside to cool for at least 10 minutes.

3 Sift the flour, bicarbonate of soda, spice mix, and pepper into a large mixing bowl, and stir them together.

4 Pour the treacle mix into the flour mix.

5 Crack in the egg, then stir the ingredients together to form a smooth, dark paste.

6 Cover and place in the fridge for at least 1 hour to rest. It can be left overnight if preferred.

7 Take the dough out of the fridge and allow it to reach room temperature. Then gently knead it into a ball.

8 Preheat the oven to 190°C (375°F/Gas 5), and line a baking tray with baking paper.

9 On a lightly floured surface, roll out the dough to 2–3mm (⅛in) thick.

10 Cut the biscuits out to any shape you like, re-rolling any trimmings. Then space them slightly apart on a lined baking tray. If decorating with glacé ginger, push a few pieces into each biscuit. Bake for 10–12 minutes.

11 Cool on the tray for 10 minutes, then transfer the firm biscuits to a cooling rack. They can be stored in an airtight container for up to 1 week.

PAELLA

Serves 6

Prep time 30 mins

Cooking time 50 mins

4 tbsp olive oil
300g (10oz) chicken thighs, cut into chunks
150g (5½oz) diced pancetta
150g (5½oz) cooking chorizo, cut into thick slices
1 large Spanish onion, roughly chopped
1 red pepper, deseeded and cut into chunks
1 green pepper, deseeded and cut into chunks
1 tbsp paella mix (see p74)
250g (9oz) Calasparra (Spanish short-grain) rice, or other paella or risotto rice
150ml (5fl oz) Fino sherry, or dry white wine
750ml (1¼ pints) hot fish or chicken stock
200ml (7fl oz) tomato passata
150g (5½oz) prepared squid, sliced into rings
juice and zest of 1 lemon, plus extra wedges to serve
salt and freshly ground black pepper
12 clams, cleaned
6 mussels, scrubbed and with beards removed
6 cooked crevettes or whole, large, shell-on prawns
handful of fresh flatleaf parsley, roughly chopped

1 Heat 2 tbsp of the olive oil in a paella dish or heavy-based saucepan. Add the chicken, pancetta, and chorizo, and stir over a medium–high heat for 8–10 minutes, until browned all over. Remove with a slotted spoon and transfer to a plate.

2 Add the remaining oil to the chorizo oil in the pan, then cook the onion and peppers over a medium heat for 5–8 minutes, until softened.

3 Stir in the paella spice mix along with the rice, and stir for a minute or so, until all the grains of rice are well coated and glossy.

4 Now add the sherry and turn up the heat, allowing the liquid to bubble and the rice to absorb it. Pour in the hot stock and the passata, and reduce to a simmer for 10 minutes, stirring occasionally.

5 Return the meat to the pan, stir, and cook gently for another 10 minutes.

6 Now stir the squid rings into the rice, along with the lemon zest plus juice, and add seasoning to taste. Ensure that all the clams and mussels are tightly closed, then push them into the rice and cover with a lid or foil. Steam for 4–5 minutes until all the mussels and clams have opened (discard any that have not).

7 Now sit the crevettes on top, cover, and steam for a further 5 minutes, until everything is cooked through, the rice is tender, and most of the liquid has been absorbed. Do not stir at this point – this will help a crust to form – but keep the heat low so that it does not burn.

8 Scatter the chopped parsley over the paella and serve immediately with the extra lemon wedges on the side.

TABLE OF SPICES AND THEIR FLAVOUR COMPOUNDS

This table provides an at-a-glance visual reference for identifying the principal flavour compounds of all the profiled spices, and will help you to make connections between spices through their compounds. Spices are colour-coded in their flavour groups (see pp12–15), and major and secondary compounds are highlighted by the shading of the tiles.

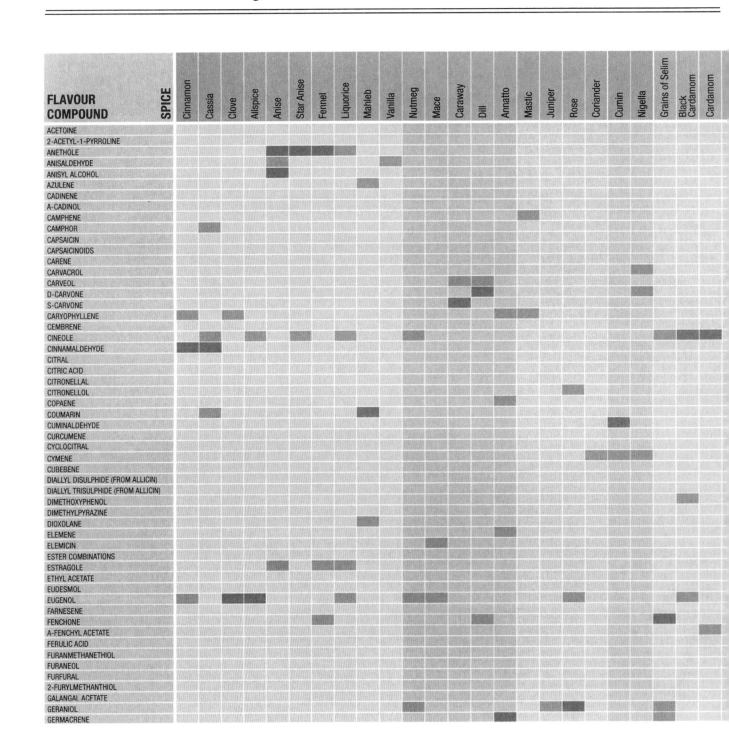

FLAVOUR GROUPS

- Sweet Warming Phenols
- Warming Terpenes
- Fragrant Terpenes
- Earthy Terpenes
- Penetrating Terpenes
- Citrus Terpenes
- Sweet-Sour Acids
- Fruity Aldehydes
- Toasty Pyrazines
- Sulphurous Compounds
- Pungent Compounds
- Unique Compounds

TYPE OF COMPOUND

- Major compound
- Secondary compound

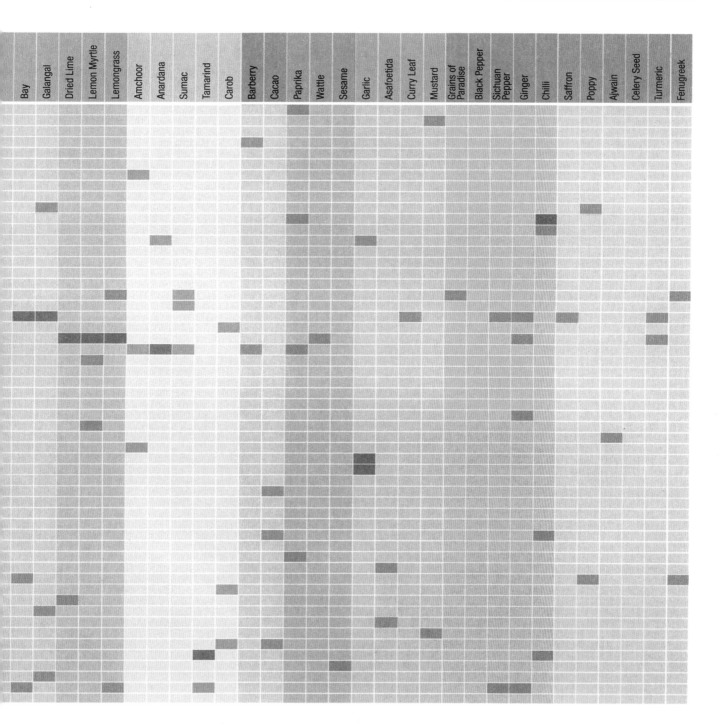

FLAVOUR COMPOUND \ SPICE	Cinnamon	Cassia	Clove	Allspice	Anise	Star Anise	Fennel	Liquorice	Mahleb	Vanilla	Nutmeg	Mace	Caraway	Dill	Annatto	Mastic	Juniper	Rose	Coriander	Cumin	Nigella	Grains of Selim	Black Cardamom	Cardamom
GINGEROL																								
GLYCOSIDE COMBINATIONS																								
GLYCYRRHIZIN								X																
HEPTANONE		X																						
HEXANAL																								
HEXANOIC ACID																								
HUMULENE																								
HUMULONE																								
4-HYDROXYBENZALDEHYDE										X														
ISOTHIOCYANATES																								
ISOVALERALDEHYDE																								
LANIERONE																								
LIMONENE					X	X	X	X				X	X	X			X		X			X	X	X
LINALOOL	X			X	X	X	X	X					X					X	X	X		X	X	
MALIC ACID																								
METHOXYCOUMARIN																								
METHOXYETHYL-CINNAMATE									X															
3-METHYL BUTANAL																								
METHYL CINNAMATE																								
METHYL HEPTENONE																								
METHYL SALICYLATE			X																					
MYRCENE	X			X												X	X			X				
MYRISTICIN											X	X												
NEROL																		X						
NONANAL																								
OCIMENE																								
PARADOL																								
PENTANOIC ACID																								
PENTANOL									X															
2-PENTYLFURAN																								
PHELLANDRENE					X									X										
PHENOL COMBINATIONS								X															X	
PHENYL ACETALDEHYDE																								
2-PHENYLACETALDEHYDE																								
1-PHENYLETHANETHIOL																								
PICOCROCIN																								
PINENE					X	X	X	X			X	X				X	X		X	X	X	X	X	
PIPERINE																								
PIPERONAL								X																
PYRAZINE COMBINATIONS																								
ROSE KETONES																		X						
ROTUNDONE																								
SABINENE											X	X											X	
SAFRANAL																								
SAFROLE						X						X												
SANSHOOLS																								
SEDANOLIDE (PHTHALIDE)																								
SELINENE																								
SESAMOL																								
SHOGAOL																								
SOTOLON																								
SULCATONE																								
SULPHIDE COMBINATIONS																								
TANNIN COMBINATIONS		X																						
TARTARIC ACID																								
TERPINENE												X		X					X	X				
TERPINEOL			X														X							
TERPINYL ACETATE																							X	
THYMOL																								
THYMOQUINONE																					X			
AR-TURMERONE																								
VANILLIN										X													X	
VINYL AMYL KETONE																								
ZINGIBERENE																								

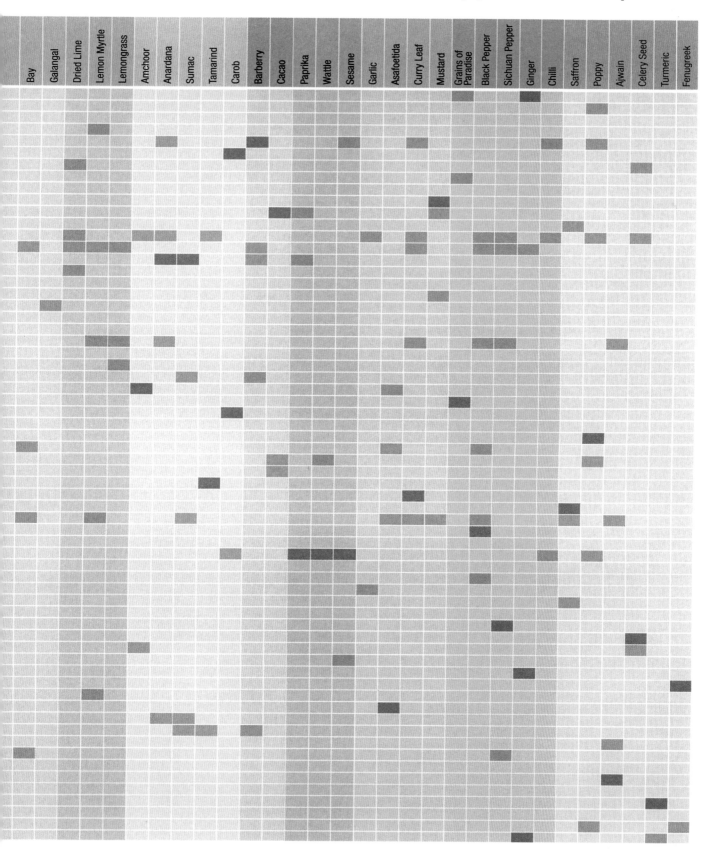

Index

About the Authors

DR STUART FARRIMOND

Specializing in food science, Dr Stuart Farrimond is a science and health writer, presenter, and communicator. He makes regular appearances on TV, radio, and at public events. He is a trained medical doctor and teacher, and his writing appears in the national and international press, including *New Scientist*, *The Independent*, the *Daily Mail*, and *The Washington Post*.
Dr Stuart presents a weekly radio science show, and his widely publicized food research has addressed a broad range of topics. He is the author of DK's *The Science of Cooking*.

Stuart oversaw all scientific aspects of the project, and wrote the Spice Science chapter and all science-based content in the Spice Profiles chapter, including information on blending science and getting the most flavour from spices.

Laura Nickoll is a writer and cookery editor based in Kent. She is a member of the Guild of Food Writers and specializes in food and eating out for online and print restaurant guides. She also edits cookbooks and has worked with many influential food writers and chefs, including Mary Berry, Rachel Allen, Ed Smith, Marcus Wareing, Signe Johansen, and Rosie Birkett.

Laura wrote all the non-science content of the Spice Profiles chapter.

Jan Fullwood is a home economist who believes she has the perfect job. Her varied career involves working for major food brands, magazines including *Good Housekeeping* and *delicious*, and books, notably for Mary Berry. Jan is constantly creating, evaluating, and eating food, and always learning something new; she lives with an overstuffed larder and her well-fed family in Hertfordshire.

Jan wrote the World of Spice Further Recipes.

Roopa Gulati is a chef, food writer, and broadcaster, who worked in India for two decades before returning to London in 2001. As a Consultant Chef to the Taj hotel group, she honed her expertise in regional cooking styles across South Asia. Back in the UK, she was deputy editor for UKTV's Good Food Channel, and is now a freelancer, writing editorial features, recipes, and restaurant reviews for leading food brands and magazines such as *BBC Good Food*, *Time Out*, and *delicious*. Assignments include cookery demonstrations at London's Borough Market, scoping Rick Stein's BBC series in India, and joining the judge's panel for BBC Radio 4's Food and Farming Awards.

Roopa wrote on South Asia in the World of Spice chapter, as well as the recipes for Date and Tamarind Granita with Caramelized Pineapple and Spiced Scallops with Saffron Beurre Blanc.

Thomas Howells is a London-based journalist. He works as a freelance food editor and writer for *Time Out London*, and has written for *The Guardian*, the *Financial Times*, and *Wallpaper**.

Tom wrote on Europe in the World of Spice chapter.

Anna Kibbey is a food and drink writer and co-founder of food copywriting agency 2Forks.co.uk. As a journalist and editor at Square Meal, she reviewed restaurants for many years, and writes food features, recipes, and reviews for *Time Out, Food & Travel, Men's Health*, and *Mr & Mrs Smith*. Anna is a keen cook, consumer, and student of Middle Eastern food, particularly Lebanese and Persian cuisine, and the owner of an encyclopaedic – and ever-expanding – collection of spices. She most often reaches for cumin, coriander seeds, cinnamon, and (always) chilli flakes.

Anna wrote on the Middle East in the World of Spice chapter, as well as the recipes for Chicken and Aubergine Biryani with Seven-spice and Ejjeh with Courgette, Feta, and Dill and Black Lime Harissa.

Sorrel Moseley-Williams is a British freelance journalist and sommelier who has been based in Argentina since 2006. She focuses on Latin American food, travel, and wine, and can be found on the pages of *Wine Enthusiast, Monocle, Condé Nast Traveller, Travel + Leisure, Decanter*, and *Lugares* in Spanish, among other publications; she translated the Mirazur, Tegui and La Cabrera books. She co-runs the pop-up wine bar "Come Wine With Us" in Buenos Aires and can be found on Instagram as @sorrelita.

Sorrel wrote on the Americas in the World of Spice chapter.

Freda Muyambo is a food writer with expertise in African cuisine and a passion for sharing African culture through food. She often describes herself as having a pan-African palate; born and raised in Botswana to Ghanaian parents, she currently lives in Nigeria, and has travelled extensively across the continent. Freda resides in the Nigerian city of Lagos where she is acquiring primary knowledge in the use of local spices, from fermented locust beans to a vast array of chillies, pipers, and cubebs.

Freda wrote on Africa in the World of Spice chapter, as well as the recipes for West African Peanut Curry with Durban Masala and Sweet and Spicy Apple Pastry Rosettes.

Annica Wainwright is a food and drink writer and co-founder of food copywriting agency 2Forks.co.uk. She has travelled extensively in Southeast Asia and is a self-confessed Thai food geek. Her favourite spices are garlic, ginger, star anise, and the highly addictive endorphin-producer also known as the red hot chilli pepper. Annica never leaves home without sriracha sauce (she's got a mini bottle attached to her keychain) and will forever be grateful to the Portuguese traders who brought us the hot stuff.

Annica wrote on Southeast Asia in the World of Spice chapter, as well as the recipes for Asian Larb Salad with Curried Duck and Khao Kua, and Spiced Filipino Adobo with Chicken and Pork.

Yolanda Zappaterra is a food, travel, and design writer. Born to Italian parents in South Wales, Yolanda's early introduction to "spicy" cooking was Vesta curries, her mother's misguided attempts to anglicize the repertoire of Neapolitan cuisine that she had brought with her, as a way of fitting in. None of this deterred Yolanda's palate or food-writing ambitions, and she has since worked as a food writer and editor for *Time Out, Lonely Planet*, and *The Independent*, amongst many others. Her home cooking has broadened out from the regional Italian dishes she learnt in her mother's kitchen to include her in-laws' Chinese and Caribbean dishes, so dinner at hers could be a multi-layered *parmigiana*, a spicy *mapo tofu*, or Trinidad doubles.

Yolanda wrote on East Asia in the World of Spice chapter, as well as the recipes for Chinese Steamed Salmon with Chilli and Star Anise and Black Sesame, Liquorice, and Cardamom Ice Cream.

Acknowledgements

FROM THE AUTHORS

Dr Stuart Farrimond

Cataloguing the flavourful science behind our diverse world of spices is quite an undertaking. I am indebted to family and friends for their understanding and tolerance of the many days I have spent in the writer's "cave", surrounded by boxes, bags, and tubs of spices. My wife, Grace, been steadfastly supportive throughout this ambitious project; even enduring the (mis)fortune of being subject to a barrage of spice blending experiments. As she was to discover, culinary scientific endeavours are fraught with taste bud peril!

As with last year's publication, *The Science of Cooking*, I am once again awed by the talents of DK's designers, artists, and photographers, who have woven their magic to help bring the science of spices to life so beautifully. Thanks go to Dawn Henderson and Mary-Clare Jerram for inviting me back to crack open this truly tasty topic, and to editor Alastair Laing who slaved over a hot computer to bring all the ingredients of this book together harmoniously. My literary agent Jonathan Pegg has also been a dependable support, for which I am hugely grateful. A final word of thanks goes to Winston, our Patterdale terrier, whose insatiable appetite for long walks has helped keep body and mind healthy throughout.

Sorrel Moseley-Williams would like to thank Anthony Vásquez of La Mar Buenos Aires, Leonor Espinosa of LEO in Bogotá, Virgilio Martínez of Central in Lima and Mil in Moray, Jaime Rodríguez Camacho of Proyecto Caribe in Cartagena de Indias, Pedro Miguel Schiaffino of ámaZ in Lima, and Tom Le Mesurier of Eat Rio in Rio de Janeiro.

FROM THE PUBLISHER

We would like to acknowledge the help of the following in the production of this book: special thanks to Rona Skene and Megan Lea for stepping in and working well beyond the call of duty; thanks to Jo Hargreaves and Jane Simmonds for copy editing, Jan Fullwood for recipe testing, and Vanessa Bird for indexing. We would also like to thank Sean @ kja-artists for artworks on pages 12, 13, 20, 21, 30, 31, 38, 39, 46, 47, 54, 55, 62, 63, 70, 71, 82, 102, 110, 116, 142, 144, 164, 174, 184, and 206.
DK Delhi would like to thank Anukriti Arora for design assistance.

Senior Editor Alastair Laing
Senior Designers Saffron Stocker, Alison Gardner
Project Art Editor Louise Brigenshaw
Designers Simon Murrell, Mandy Earey
Producer (Pre-Production) Robert Dunn
Senior Producer Ché Creasey
Managing Editor Dawn Henderson
Managing Art Editor Marianne Markham
Art Director Maxine Pedliham
Publishing Director Mary-Clare Jerram

Recipe Photographer Mowie Kay
Food Styling Tamara Vos
Prop Styling Linda Berlin
Spice Photographer Gary Ombler
Jacket Photographer Ruth Jenkinson
Jacket Prop Styling Isabel de Cordova

DK Delhi
Senior Editor Janashree Singha
Assistant Editors Devangana Ojha, Tanya Singhal
Project Art Editor Vikas Sachdeva
Art Editor Roshni Kapur
Asst Art Editors Amrai Dua, Monam Nishat, Simran Saini
Managing Editor Soma B. Chowdhury
Senior Managing Art Editor Arunesh Talapatra
Production Manager Pankaj Sharma
Pre-production Manager Sunil Sharma
DTP Designers Nandkishor Acharya, Umesh Rawat, Vikram Singh

First published in Great Britain in 2018 by
Dorling Kindersley Limited
One Embassy Gardens, 8 Viaduct Gardens,
London, SW11 7BW

The authorised representative in the EEA is
Dorling Kindersley Verlag GmbH. Arnulfstr. 124,
80636 Munich, Germany

A CIP catalogue record for this book
is available from the British Library.
ISBN: 978-0-2413-0214-9

Printed and bound in Slovakia

For the curious
www.dk.com